WAR, BUSINESS, AND
AMERICAN SOCIETY

Kennikat Press
National University Publications
Series in American Studies

WAR, BUSINESS, AND AMERICAN SOCIETY

HISTORICAL PERSPECTIVES ON THE MILITARY-INDUSTRIAL COMPLEX

Edited by

BENJAMIN FRANKLIN COOLING

National University Publications
KENNIKAT PRESS // 1977
Port Washington, N. Y. // London

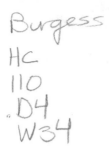
Manufactured in the United States of America

Published by
Kennikat Press Corp.
Port Washington, N. Y./London

Library of Congress Cataloging in Publication Data
Main entry under title:

War, business, and American society.

(Series in American studies) (National university publications)
    Bibliography: p.
    Includes index.
    1. Disarmament—Economic aspects—United States —Addresses, essays, lectures. 2. Industry and state—United States—Addresses, essays, lectures. 3. Disarmament—Economic aspects—Addresses, essays, lectures. I. Cooling, B. Franklin. II. Title: Military-industrial complex.
HC110.D4W34   338.4'7'62340973   76-18163
ISBN 0-8046-9156-8

CONTENTS

WAR, BUSINESS, AND AMERICAN SOCIETY

INTRODUCTION

Writing in 1969, Samuel P. Huntington quite appropriately observed that he had never read any essay or speech dealing with the so-called military-industrial complex (MIC) that did not commence with the famous warning of President Dwight D. Eisenhower concerning the acquisition of unwarranted influence by the complex. Indeed, Eisenhower's 1961 comment has been the starting point for most contemporary investigations of a question which continues to confuse and challenge students of military affairs in the post-Vietnam era.

Nevertheless, the relationship between national economic power, national and foreign-policy aspirations, and the national military establishment has been of concern to some academicians, theologians, businessmen, and statesmen (not to mention the professional military) for at least eight decades. From the isolationist cries of senators and newsmen in the 1890s ("Pitchfork Ben" Tillman sounded much like George McGovern) to the recent shrill notes of spokesmen like Sidney Lens, Daniel Ellsberg, Gabriel Kolko, and others, linkage between the military and business communities has been of substantial significance to this nation. Unfortunately, the historical craft has lagged behind its professional colleagues in political science, sociology, and economics, as they quantify and qualify the phenomenon we call MIC.

If relatively few analysts of MIC have taken the trouble to search for historical antecedents, they have often unwittingly provided the social-science tools, jargon, and models with which historians may now probe backwards in time. Whether couched in terms of war profiteering (as done by Richard F. Kaufman),[1] testing the theory of the military-industrial complex like Steven Rosen and colleagues,[2] or setting up the model of a hypothetical military-industrial firm like John Francis Gorgol,[3] hard work remains to be accomplished by application of modern models to the historical scene. Even Stanley Lieberson's empirical study of military-industrial linkages,[4] with its focus on the elitist and pluralist perspectives of power to explain MIC, yields useful guidelines for historians.

Yet one may expect that among the methodological problems in research on the military-industrial complex only dimly perceived by Edward P. Levine[5] lies in the real issue—semantic differences—and the need to establish a working definition that will satisfy all social scientists of the past and present. Is the military-industrial complex merely a subsystem of the postindustrial society, or is it, rather that very society itself in toto? Unfortunately, historical subjectivity of the democratic mind tends to reject the latter definition as the citizen wraps himself in the hypocritical cloak of separation of civilian and military to explain the American experience.

The dangers and frustrations of defining MIC are reflected in four of the myriad of definitions contributed by recent social-science analysis. Huntington terms it ". . .a large permanent military establishment supported by and linked to a variety of related industrial, labor, and geographical interests." David Mooney, a professional Army officer, called it ". . .a group of national resources—public and private; military and civilian; political and academic—combined together for the provision of the common defense in support of a national strategy of deterrence through preparedness." Marc Pilisuk and Thomas Hayden saw it as ". . .an informal and changing coalition of groups with vested psychological, moral, and material interests in the continuous development and maintenance of high levels of weaponry, in preservation of colonial markets and in military-strategic conceptions of internal affairs." Finally, Carroll Pursell, one of the handful of historians concerned with MIC thus far, concluded that the ingredients comprised "such diverse persons as congressmen, labor leaders, corporation executives, church spokesmen, university professors, and professional soldiers along with the host of followers and families dependent upon them." He pinpointed a focal point of the unique relationship between the defense establishment as buyer and defense industries as seller.[6]

Pursell, and the authors in this volume, probably tend toward the broader school of semantics, which sees the need to study economic, business, technological, social, and political dimensions of the human activity of preparing for war. It may even be a fact that historians have really studied MIC all along, couching their work in terms which have escaped the gaze of ardent enthusiasts from other social sciences. Werner Sombart, John U. Nef, Quincy Wright, and S. Andreski have sought for years to explain the economic and social history of war. Of course, the term "war" is deceptive, since we tend to live in a world of continuous conflict, but seek to define the term only by those periodic eruptions with clear-cut beginnings and endings. Perhaps more readers should refer to *War and Economic Development,* edited by J. M. Winter,[7] for additional clues as to approaching MIC from a long-standing, but different, semantic perspective.

THE PAPERS

The present volume of essays, by a cross-section of historians involved with various facets of the problem, seeks to illustrate the intricacies and nuances implied in the term "military-industrial complex" or interlock. Their perspective is historical. Not all of them agree either on the makeup of the complex or its impact. Several of the papers disconfirm seemingly apparent ingredients of MIC; others support the notion that the phenomenon has roots deep in the nation's history. Still others are equivocal in their findings. Yet their work suggests that we have just begun to comprehend the fuller dimensions of the problem and its persuasive and pervasive influence in the fabric of American society. It may be useful to review briefly the twelve essays and their highlights.

Theodore Ropp provides a catholic opening by portraying the broader international complexion of origins of military-industrial linkages in the nineteenth century. He shows the difficulties of semantics interpretation as well as generational focus. If key elements were present for MICs after the industrial revolution, neither contemporaries of Napoleon, Bismarck, nor Alfred Thayer Mahan necessarily perceived the dangers of combines which President Eisenhower frowned upon a century later. Ropp's thesis holds that studies of earlier MICs may be more useful in detail than in history's totality. Still, the "totality" of the period stretching from the industrial revolution into our own time may escape those scholars and laymen seeking to interpret MIC as a transitory happening rather than as part of a continuum.

Merritt Roe Smith keys upon American military-industrial relations in the earlier days of the republic. It seems too simplistic to us today—small army and navy; almost cottage-like industries; and ordnance, subsistence, and personnel procurement which rose and fell in direct proportion to the young nation's proclivity for war. Still, Smith illustrates the deceptive insinuation of armed forces' participation in domestic economic affairs. This included more than turning ploughshares into swords, and ran the gamut of contribution to both transportation and industrial revolutions. Of course MIC was small—so too were population, industrial output, and the measuring devices of national greatness. But his essay illustrates the gradually escalating effect of MIC from the founding of the nation to the era of World War I.

Johannes R. Lischka traces evidence of historical antecedents of the modern MIC to the period of naval armaments races in the late nineteenth century. He shows how an unsung element such as the nickel industry was an important member of the American naval-industrial team. Furthermore, he observes that the so-called merchants of death served an important function in the economic maturing process of the United States. His approach to the navy's need for nickel and steel should challenge other historians to reexamine numerous smaller industries like plastics, fuels, explosives, et cetera for their dimly seen centricity in the spectrum of MIC.

Henry C. Ferrell, Jr. carries Lischka's approach a step further. He introduces the vital element of politics in MIC. But his focus comes at the local, not the national, level. The historical spectrum of MIC can only be fully appreciated by relating local with national needs, maneuvers, and contributions which combine political oratory, horse trading, and accommodation to the needs of workers, managers, and communities in congressional voting districts. This phenomenon is not contemporary with us today. This essay sets the discussion in the era of southern regional rivalries for naval shore facilities just before World War I.

Daniel R. Beaver returns to the national scene with a look at the war effort in World War I from the perspective of bureaucratic infighting and MIC. Wartime production, mobilization, procurement, and man's attempt to control the complex mechanism which he creates to bring order from chaos—the bureaucracy—provide the story. Beaver's theme is the drama of institutional modification, internal tinkering, power struggles, and human frailties. This dimension of MIC may remain as unclear to modern analysts as it is vital to the historical discussion. This essay illustrates the continuum of tradition, misconception, and growth pains as MIC becomes involved with total war.

Anne Trotter introduces us to the post-World War I criticism of the so-called merchants of death. This criticism continues to confuse and baffle, as well as symbolize, military-industrial relations for a generation. Clarification of misconceptions, delineation of the main tenets of the theory, and general perspective on the era of its emergence, all appear in this essay. Again another element of MIC's continuum is introduced—criticism and public outcry, followed by eventual apathy as time overtakes events.

Allison W. Saville examines the naval-industrial complex of the interwar years—the period when merchants of death were public villains in many American eyes. But he introduces the realities of detail which often escape in syntheses of MIC. Specific dimensions, classifications, and purposes of naval vessels are vital ingredients of technological economic planning for industry as well as for naval policy makers. Comprehension of MIC transcends management theory, economic quantification, and political maneuvers on Capitol Hill. Contractual bidding, budgetary strictures, problems of research and development as well as the pedantry of naval ship lists are also important. Saville concludes that a naval-military-industrial complex may have been eclipsed after World War I, reemerging only under the threat of a second such cataclysm.

Roger A. Beaumont concentrates on that second cataclysm with his probing of the thesis that World War II was the great progenitor of MIC. His essay implies the quantitative increase to already-present linkages and associations between institutions. It goes even further by suggesting qualitative escalation due to developments in military technology and methods of war. But he also makes the subtle, subjective hypothesis that spectacular success with the military-industrial partnership in World War II created a false euphoria. America's military-industrial power could solve any international problem. In a way, Beaumont suggests an inherent contradiction represented by the very slogan of American victory in World War II—"Arsenal of Democracy."

Thomas E. Kelly moves into the Cold War period for MIC by departing from the general concept that MIC may be all-pervasive in a period of continuing international stress. While National Defense Highways were constructed in the 1950s, at least partially with military need in mind, he notes that military influence in American land transportation (by tradition) began to wane following creation of the Highway Trust Fund in 1956. Other combinations and complexes—in this case auto-truck, oil and rubber, and construction industries—have ousted colonels and generals and their pressures. Kelly's thesis bears further scrutiny if only to cause us to refrain from jumping too quickly to find the omnipresence of MIC in the contemporary setting.

Edward C. Ezell reinforces Saville's marriage of technological with economic history in his discussion of small-arms procurement since World War II. He shows the difficulties of contemporary historical research as well as the fine opportunities for major interpretive breakthroughs. Neither the contemporary military-industrial scene nor its interpreters have yet clarified practical solutions to problems faced by MIC. Many commentaries seem more concerned with exposé than with offering positive aid through the discovery of evidence. Ezell's message points to a reorientation of priorities among scholars and publicists which will provide useful lessons for practicioners rather than mere grist for the muckrakers.

Alvin R. Sunseri may point the direction for future studies of military-industrial linkages through his microcosmic rather than macrocosmic focus. His investigation, like Ferrell's, concentrates at the local or state level. He singles out the unlikely state of Iowa for evaluation of the intrusion and influence of MIC. His observations are somewhat fluid, yet perceptive. They will challenge historians to search all fifty states for the tentacles of MIC in modern America.

Finally, Earl A. Molander offers a capstone essay in which he builds upon Anne Trotter's discussion of military-industrial criticism. He shows that popular outcry against the real or imagined evils of the merchants of death was not limited to either the 1930s or 1960s. Opposition to war profiteering forms another element of the MIC continuum. He subtly suggests that such criticism can be viewed either as a positive evil or a positive good, as it provides an ideological base for change both within and without the parameters of MIC.

These essays are offered as stimulants to further consideration. They hopefully portray the colorful fabric of MIC. Obviously, no consensus exists on the diversity, intricacy, or immensity of MIC in its historical setting. No longer can we rely on the polemics which have characterized recent analyses of military-industrial interlock. We must conclude that MIC has a historical past, stretching beyond that perceived by C. Wright Mills and Dwight D. Eisenhower in our time. But further study must be done, in breadth, depth, and in candor. This volume will possibly suggest new directions for determining the meaning of the military-industrial complex for America—past, present, and future.

Carlisle, Pennsylvania　　　　　　　　　　　　　　B. Franklin Cooling

NOTES

1. Richard F. Kaufman, *The War Profiteers,* (Indianapolis, Bobbs Merrill, 1970), especially Introduction and Chapter 1.
2. Steven Rosen, ed., *Testing the Theory of the Military-Industrial Complex* (Lexington, Mass., Lexington Books, 1973), especially Chapters 1 and 2.
3. John Francis Gorgol, with Ira Kleinfeld, ed., *The Military-Industrial Firm; A Practical Theory and Model* (New York, Praeger, 1972).
4. Stanley Lieberson, "An Empirical Study of Military-Industrial Linkages," *The American Journal of Sociology,* vol. 76 (January, 1971), pp. 562-84.
5. Edward P. Levine, "Methodological Problems in Research on the Military-Industrial Complex," Chapter 12 in Rosen, op. cit. pp. 291-308.
6. Samuel P. Huntington, "The Defense Establishment: Vested Interests and the Public Interest," in Omer L. Carey, ed., *The Military Industrial Complex and U. S. Foreign Policy,* (Pullman, Wash., Washington State University Press, 1969) p. 3; David Mooney, "The Roles of the Military Industrial Complex," unpublished Master's Thesis, The George Washington University (Naval War College Center, 1973), p.8; Marc Pilisuk and Thomas Hayden, "Is There a Military Industrial

Complex Which Prevents Peace?", *Journal of Social Issues* (July, 1965), p. 103;
Carroll Pursell, ed., *The Military-Industrial Complex,* (New York, Harper & Row,
1972), p. ix.
7. J. M. Winter, ed., *War and Economic Development* (Cambridge and London,
Cambridge University Press, 1975), especially the Introduction.

NINETEENTH CENTURY EUROPEAN MILITARY-INDUSTRIAL COMPLEXES

Is "military-industrial complex" a scientific or a rhetorical term? How is it related to nineteenth-century European militarism, now that Bismarckian Germany is as distant from ourselves as it was from the mercantilistic "garrison state" of Frederick II. Our own military-industrial complex was officially discovered in 1961. "It took five years and a festering war," Carroll W. Pursell, Jr. remarks, to see "Eisenhower's farewell warning" as "anything more than the swan song of an old and naive man. . .in a situation he neither understood nor controlled." Until World War II, Eisenhower had claimed, "the United States had no armaments industry. . . . We have [now] been compelled to create a permanent arms industry of vast proportions. . . . This conjunction of an immense military establishment and a large arms industry is new in the American experience. . . . Akin to, and largely responsible for [these] sweeping changes in our industrial-military posture, has been the technological revolution."[1] The question for this survey of nineteenth-century European militarism is whether the American military-industrial complex is so much larger in scale that only a few details of "unwarranted" political or social "influence" are in any way analagous.

When modern economic, political, and military history is fully quantified, this question may be answered statistically. Until then we can note that Eisenhower's warning represented the real concern of a President who had spent much of his early military career dealing with national mobilization problems, but who—with Charles E. Wilson of General Motors—had been quite unable to control the manufacturers of the most advanced, costly, and abuse-prone weapons, and their military and political allies. That the "weight of this combination" might "endanger our liberties or democratic processes" had been possible in nineteenth-century Europe. But the late nineteenth-century British, French, and German cases of "unwarranted influence, whether sought or unsought, by the military-industrial complex" were ones of smaller industrial interests in differing political and military contexts.

Adam Smith had never recommended the nineteenth-century industrial state's liberal "division of labour" with private arms makers. "The great expense of firearms, an invention which at first sight appears to be so pernicious," had, however, been so "favourable both to the permanency and to the extension of civilisation," that the state had to bear without creating "particular tribes" of arms makers to support those other protected manufacturers who, "like an overgrown standing army, . . . have become formidable to the government, and upon many occasions intimidate the legislature." More important, the military overgrowth standards of eighteenth-century mercantilistic states were low. "In the little agrarian states of ancient Greece," Smith remarked, "a fourth or fifth part of the . . . people would sometimes, it is said, take the field." In "modern Europe, it is commonly computed that not more than one-hundredth part of the inhabitants. . .can be employed as soldiers without ruin to the country which pays the expenses of their services."[7] Lord North's remark about its being "all over" after Yorktown was in reference to the fact that there were no more trained Germans to be hired, not to the money needed to hire them. A Prussian army equal to 2.5 percent of the population was that of a permanently mobilized garrison state, and Frederick the Great felt that 3 percent of the male population was the upper limit for his system of cantonal conscription.

The military-industrial problems of the French Revolutionary era were to be seen by interpreters of that era as problems of men rather than materiel. Traditional mercantilistic ideas changed very little, perhaps because each power's efforts peaked independently and private manufacturers and traders could take up the slack during a series of wars which were nearly as long as the total wars of the twentieth century. If only to prevent gold drain, mercantilistic states did their military work in their own arsenals and kept their labor employed by stockpiling. When Prussia had set up the Spandau Royal Arms Factory in 1721, two arms sellers had imported the tools and workers—a musket and a stock maker for each regiment—from the Austrian Netherlands, and tied the workers to their jobs with free houses, wood, fuel, medical care, and pensions for themselves and their widows. Ships, to take another example, were commissioned from dockyard stocks. Repairs were less likely to require docking and new construction space than materials and work—some of which could be done by the crews—on side and top hamper. Only the state could afford stocks of guns, masts, and seasoned timber. Wartime green timber or pine ships did not convince naval officers of the technological advantages of private enterprise. Well into the nineteenth century the concentration of military-industrial interests in a few areas limited the political influence of this part of Europe's military-industrial complexes.

France's revolutionary armies had been armed with some 730,000 muskets from the royal arsenals. Emergency shops had eventually produced some 750 pieces a day, but conquered stores and production facilities had then eased France's armament problems. Naval stores had always been short—Britain's control of the sea had interfered with coastal traffic—but weapons shortages had not been a major factor in Napoleon's defeat. The private arms makers who had maximized British sales to slave traders could not cope with the extra demands of a major war, though coal and iron production were booming. But after the government had established an effective buying monopoly, Britain had helped to arm much of Europe against Napoleon. Prussia had adopted a new musket in 1801, but only 43,000 of them had been produced before the disaster of 1806, and foreign suppliers had equipped the armies of Germany's War of Liberation. But the technological and production problems of a musket which had been made so easy to load that it was the least accurate in Europe had seemed so much less critical than those of manpower, training, and national morale that Carl von Clausewitz's famous chapter on "Arming the Nation" hardly mentioned armaments at all.

So nineteenth-century economic and military theorists were not particularly concerned with war production, or with the detailed military-economic problems posed by the industrial revolution. No general war was fought for nearly a century (i.e. 1815–1914). International traders could help to arm American recruits in 1861 and French recruits in 1870. The American Civil War had lasted long enough to consume large quantities of munitions; but its slow peaking had again enabled private firms to supplement the arsenals. No mid-century war had been as clearly won by superior weapons as by superior numbers, mobilization, and staff work. Since the next war would also be decided by the forces mobilized for the first campaigns, late nineteenth-century military theorists were little more concerned with weapons technology, as distinct from procurement, than the Marquis de Vauban had been nearly two centuries before. Since such mind-sets help to determine statistical and other documentation; their resulting lack of interest makes many of Eisenhower's later questions hard to answer. How large— in population or Gross National Product (GNP) percentages—were Europe's "immense" peacetime "military establishments" and "permanent arms industries" when Eisenhower was born in 1890? How were the civilian and military bureaucrats and parliamentarians who increasingly influenced some military policies "unduly" influenced by jobs and profits?

Nineteenth-century peacetime armies were smaller in proportion to

population than the professional army of Frederick the Great, while France's
million men under arms in 1794-95—3.5 percent of the population and

Table 1.

AVERAGE ANNUAL PEACETIME MILITARY PERSONNEL PER
MILLION POPULATION

	Britain	France	Ger-many	Russia	Italy	United States
1816-25		8,706	11,247	15,169		
1826-35		8,060	9,982	11,020		
1836-45		8,399	8,860	9,721		
1846-55		11,111	8,178	12,456	10,922	
1856-65	7,243	11,240	9,405	5,964	14,842	
1866-75	6,272	11,567	10,710	8,824	9,520	
1876-85	5,630	11,100	9,787	8,565	8,354	
1886-95	5,773	15,888	10,404	7,455	9,285	
1896-1905	6,245	18,200	11,105	8,157	9,262	
1906-15	6,840	19,735	10,957	7,450	8,709	
1916-25	7,898	19,193	2,499	4,715	9,028	
1926-35	6,006	16,591	2,896	4,388	13,860	
1936-45	7,124	19,905	14,550	15,612	15,416	
1946-55	21,014	15,441		34,527	6,442	
1956-65	12,085	14,796	5,030	18,061	8,777	
1971-72	6,600	10,000	8,000	13,600	7,800	11,400
% GNP	4.7	3.1	2.8	11.0	2.6	7.3

the peak for that era—was under Frederick's theoretical wartime peak of
3 percent of the male population. The 1816 Prussian peacetime legal standard of 1 percent of the population was Adam Smith's wartime peak. The
new conscript armies had to sacrifice training for numbers. They were
militarily harder to train and mobilize and politically less reliable than their
predecessors. So one reason why comparatively little thought was given to
technological and industrial problems was that so much was expended on
training, indoctrination, and mobilization. In a study for the United States
President's Commission on an All-Volunteer Armed Force, James M.
McConnell used the percentage of the population in the peacetime armed

forces, or "the manpower burden of defense" as a "proxy for the total
burden of defense" and possible indicator of "the degree of military influence within society." Whether Prussia and Germany are synonymous is
unclear, but McConnell's table does suggest the relative stability of the
1 percent standard (10,000 men per million people) for most of the peaceful nineteenth century, the burdens of the arms races of the twentieth
century, and a gradual return to the 1 percent norm since about 1955.[3]

What table 1 does not indicate is the number of men supporting each
man in the armed forces, or the size of the industrial interest in the military-industrial complex. McConnell notes that "GNP data is simply not available in any lengthy series for many European countries." He does not add
that the GNP is only the part of the social product which enters the money
economy, or that such estimates could not measure military influence even
in developed countries until the twentieth century, when econometrists—
with rather different assumptions—took over the mercantilists' job of measuring military-industrial capabilities. Some concepts which now seem very
simple—e. g., the Belgian Adolphe Quetelet's "average man"—are nineteenth century, but that of a Gross National Product is twentieth century
and not very helpful in estimating social costs or the degree of military influence in earlier societies.

Eighteenth-century monarchs had kept mining, agricultural, and manufacturing statistics for taxing and military purposes. Prussia had collected
figures on fifty-eight industries, but had abandoned much of this effort
when such figures no longer seemed to concern the state. Vauban had tried
to estimate French income in 1707 to support his income-tax proposals,
and two other estimates had been made before the Revolution. But many
of the more than fifty nineteenth-century French estimates, Rondo E.
Cameron notes, are "little more than isolated informed guesses—sometimes
not even well-informed." Even the best ones vary greatly "in the absolute
figures," though they suggest the same "general pattern and rate of growth."[4]
Though the United States had taken the first national production census
in 1850 to inform the voters of the successes of governmental policies, only
one of Pursell's twenty-three statistical tables on the military-industrial
complex goes back to 1939, when military outlays took 1.3 percent of the
American GNP. This rose to 8.7 percent in 1960-61, the year of Eisenhower's
warning, and fell to 8.3 percent in 1970-71.[5] By 1939 European standards
1.3 percent was abnormally low. What we do not know—because of the
hidden tax of conscription, the relatively low level to mechanization of
nineteenth-century armies, and the lack of GNP statistics—is how low this
would be by late nineteenth-century standards.

Contemporary arguments for the private manufacture of armaments
were seldom in terms of free enterprise as the best method for ensuring

technological progress or the most rational allocation of national military resources. Adam Smith's theories did not override military considerations; his followers paid little attention to military economics. German liberal nationalists accepted the neo-mercantilistic ideas of Friedrich List. But, except for such familiar mercantilistic measures as tariffs to protect the national grain supply, they developed few new military-economic controls before the wars of the twentieth century. And Adam Smith's ideas about navies had not been unlike those of Alfred Thayer Mahan. The state, Smith felt, should protect trade, with "extraordinary protection" to that "with barbarous and uncivilised nations." While the British Navigation Acts had overridden "the obvious and simple system of natural liberty" by giving special advantages to the "ships and sailors" of a country which was especially dependent "upon the numbers of its sailors and shipping," the Acts had also aimed "at the very same object which the most deliberate wisdom would have recommended, the diminution of the naval power of Holland, the only naval power which could [then] endanger the security of England."[6]

The problem in evaluating military-industrial complexes is, to use Eisenhower's terms, to determine how far political military decisions are "unduly" influenced by jobs and profits. Since the ways in which these are protected changed considerably between the eighteenth and twentieth centuries—the generalized scientific concern for technological military superiority is a twentieth-century factor—it is hard to say how many major political-military decisions were influenced by the pressures which Eisenhower came to associate with "an immense military establishment and a large arms industry." We can say, in this quarter of the twentieth century, that nobody wants to turn the CIA back to the Pinkertons, or that the simplistic arguments against food rationing during the 1870-71 siege of Paris would not have been heard in the Paris of Vauban, Lazare Carnot, or Georgès Clemenceau. Beyond that it is hard to go. That a peacetime dockyard worker was being paid for his wartime availability was as obvious to Adam Smith as a soldier's being paid for drilling. Two generations later, when war was becoming abnormal and technological obsolescence normal, it was easier to attack make-work stockpiling. One British investigating committee rated seven anchors by their percentage superiorities over an obsolete Admiralty pattern. Another figured excess profits by simply subtracting other foundries' posted prices from those paid by the Admiralty. But it is hard to know how seriously policy makers took such simple statistics, particularly since no one tried to calculate the costs of an armaments industry, even in such technological and capital-intensive sectors as heavy ordnance and warships.

National styles and presumed military needs seem to have been more important than those of particular military-industrial interest groups in determining late nineteenth-century British, French, and German military policies. Such groups used prevailing economic theories to advance their interests, but military-economic theories were not the main determinants of policy. Mercantilistic practices remained entrenched in the navy of Jean Baptiste Colbert, perhaps because the German victories of 1870-71 had made that navy a very secondary national concern, while the French and German armies and the Royal Navy were their countries' paramount armed services. So the German navy provided the best late nineteenth-century example of a secondary military-industrial interest group seizing a politically opportune moment to get a national military decision which proved to be politically irreversible.

The French navy had five major and three secondary (for guns, anchors and cables, and engines) arsenals. Each, when France had a parliament, had its parliamentary supporters. To check post-Napoleonic rot, half of the warships had been kept in dry-land reserve, ready for launching, with their stores in adjacent warehouses. This old Venetian practice had left the fleet unready for action during the Near Eastern crisis of 1840. Iron ships did not store labor on the stocks, but the warehouse system was full of bureaucratic horrors. A commissioner for materials kept the warehouses full. One for construction kept the workers busy and drew stores from a partly fictitious general warehouse. By 1883 the navy had six times as many anchors and chains, three times as many cables, and twice as many sails and capstans as it needed. The Toulon Arsenal generated 14,332 records in one year's interwarehouse transactions. One constructor found uses for a dozen obsolete steam valves and their replacements on the same shelves a few months later. And occasional special parliamentary committees investigated, made recommendations, and got masterly inactivity.

Guild habits survived longer in France than in Britain. The Le Creusot worker who said that people were mostly concerned with "keeping their jobs and working as long as possible"[7] before drawing their pensions was more like an arsenal *fonctionnaire* than an English factory worker. The former worked longer hours for lower pay and a chance to send his son into his job; the latter had more competitors for a job at higher pay, with shorter hours, piecework rates, and less modern machinery. As late as the 1880s, however, there were few significant cost or design differences between French and British warships. High British repair bills—£5,244,000 for repairing to £6,672,000 for building unarmored ships in 1869-78—reflect efforts to keep more old ships operational, rather than shoddy construction. Outsiders had to industrialize merchant shipbuilding to meet the demands of the two World Wars. A "class" of eight battleships—a practice which became general in the naval boom of the 1890s—was hardly mass-produced. There were design and training savings, but the main reasons for this new practice were tactical, not industrial, efficiency. And the overdesign of the battleship *Magenta,* commissioned in 1893 in her thirteenth year—300 tons overweight and a third less stable from add-on guns, searchlights, military masts, and an armored conning tower—came less from a French search for technological superiority than from everyone playing ship designer.

In *A Generation of Materialism, 1871–1900,* published in 1941, Carlton J. H. Hayes showed that "navalism was extraordinarily popular toward the close of the 1890s" by "two facts. First, naval expediture steadily increased" to $230 million for Britain, France, and Germany in 1900, a bit less than a ninth of Lockheed Aircraft's 1969 take on Pursell's list of American defense contractors. "Second, practically all political parties, except the Marxist, now voted unquestioningly for naval bills: . . . a natural product of the combination of economic nationalism with economic imperialism."[8] In *Sea Power in the Machine Age,* also published in 1941, Bernard Brodie noted that between 1858 and 1893, "the proportion of wealth expended by Great Britain on her navy decreased most sharply. . .when the cost of the individual ship expanded most rapidly." Navalism was the result of many "imponderables: intensification of nationalism and of international rivalries, the rise of new and powerful maritime nations, . . .and the long concatenation of international crises." And it was "impossible to isolate the factor of technological development" in increasing warship costs "until the entire annual British navy estimates a century ago would not suffice to build a single battleship today."[9]

Such figures chiefly show our increasing historical distance from the late nineteenth century. A 1968 United States Arms Control and Disarmament Agency statement that "since 1900 more than $4,000 billion have been spent on wars and military preparedness," and that if the recent rate of *increase* should continue, "the arms race will consume another $4,000 billion in only ten years" is as meaningless as Arthur Guy Enock's *This War Business* figure of £321 billions spent by governments on war and armaments from 1900 to 1946, against other expenditures of £314 billions, except to support Enock's conclusion, "And so it continues—up and up and up."[10]

Detailed bits may be more suggestive than gross ones, but again mainly to suggest that there are as many differences from as similarities between the world of Eisenhower's birth and that of his presidency. One bit is Alfred Vagts's note in his study of militarism that in 1866—a date closer to 1776 than to 1974—"when Bismarck established manhood suffrage for the [North German] Reichstag, the rural workers still numbered 3,430,000 as against 770,000 in industries and 1,000,000 in the handicrafts."[11] That *Mittelstand* of small businessmen who were to support National Socialism employed twice as many workers as large-scale industry in the 1920s; their numbers in France were proportionately larger.

Arthur J. Marder found 1,000,000 Britishers allegedly "interested" in the building of "men-of-war" in 1897,[12] but it is impossible to tell how dependent they were on such building, or which power employed the highest percentage of its labor force in arms making. Armstrong-Whitworth had 20,000 employees, as many as Le Creusot or Krupp, in 1898; some details of capitalization, profits, and political clout are available for these giants. But small subcontractors—the relative power of present truck and rail, air and naval lobbies suggests—might even then have swung more votes in more districts.

Parliament had forced the Admiralty to buy H. M. S. *Captain*, built privately after the Board would not approve her design. Her loss on her first commission in 1870 led to more stable warships and stiffened the Admiralty against the private designers who, working for Italian and other foreign buyers, produced the most technologically advanced triumphs and disasters of the 1880s. By 1900, Marder feels, the Germans were building better ships than the British, because they paid more attention to detail. Marder's examples of boom and bust in the arms trade; of its ties with retired officers, journalists, politicians, and social leaders; of arms scares; and of quarrels between public and private yards can be duplicated elsewhere. But the main reason for the Admiralty's 1905 decision to give most new building to private firms was military—"In time of war it is essential to have all the plant in the Royal Dockyards available for repairs"—and Marder agreed with Brodie and Hayes that national "ambitions, jealousies, and fears" were the primary factors in a situation in which Britain and Germany were to continue "their competition in naval armaments, . . . because no policy-maker in either country . . . [could] break the vicious circle."[13]

The German military-industrial complex has attracted whole schools of historians. The reasons are obvious: the bitterness of civil-military relations, the rise of the Social Democrats and of Marxist scholarship, the opening of the archives after two lost wars, the links between nineteenth-century militarism and twentieth-century totalitarianism, and even the Krupp's notoriety among arms makers. Even Prussia's War Minister admitted the army's "total dependence on them in the matter of prices," after giving them "many millions" in orders and "interest-free loans" to "let the firm prosper and to keep it at the height of its effectiveness."[14] But other studies stress the German military-industrial complex's internal strains. A costly navy threatened army, economic, and tax interests, which the Junkers had to defend. The army sided with labor against big business to increase production during World War I. So Gerhard Ritter noted "how well the British government, so ill suited to the centrallized running of a great war, stood the test, . . .while the German military monarchy failed" and lost contact with "the masses. . .in a struggle in which the whole life of the people was involved. . . . The practical successes of the French system were no less surprising." But such comparisons may also show how unimportant "political forms of organization are in the face of the fearful power of military success or failure, with its strong impress on public opinion, and . . . the achievements and shortcomings of the leading personalities."[15]

Ritter's remarks and McConnell's percentages of the population in the peacetime armed forces may also suggest that France was the most "militarized" power in late-nineteenth-century Europe. Having only one national enemy made France, in Hayes' view, the preeminent *Nation of Patriots*. And as many French and German intellectuals were precursors of totalitarian nationalism. It was Émile Durkheim, not Max Weber, among the gurus of modern sociology, who "taught that the nation state, the *patrie*, is a 'psychic being,' that of all 'societies'—family, class, church, etc.—it is the most basic, . . .and that as its function is the supreme one of directing and giving harmony to the ideal 'corporative society,' so its members owe it supreme allegiance and the highest public worship."[16]

French arms firms and arsenal towns got their shares of money and jobs, but French military policy was never their exclusive political preserve. Though the British were equally united on their need for sea power, France may have been late-nineteenth-century Europe's best example of that popular militarization under which, in the words of Charles de Gaulle, "a quarter of the active population left their farms, their factories, or their offices, . . . half the national wealth . . . was swallowed up, . . . [and] all men's thoughts, desires, and interests became focused upon the same grim, haunting drama."[17]

Our argument may be circular, but enough is known about the three most-developed late-nineteenth-century European military-industrial complexes to suggest that analogies to the late twentieth-century United States may be rather limited. Edwardian Britain's navalists, Wilhelmine Germany's militarists, and France's integral nationalists never let military-industrial considerations become as dominant as Eisenhower feared they would become in the United States. While none of their military-industrial complexes had the aid of a legislative seniority system, the main reason for the American military-industrial complex's greater influence was surely that technological revolution which affected navies more than armies until World War I. And legislators' concern with jobs, arms makers' with profits, and soldiers' with machines and their scientific development did not really come together until after military-industrial technology's even more spectacular triumphs in World War II.

Clausewitz's ideas of the nation in arms reflected the successes of the French revolutionary system of "universal conscription and . . . the *levée en masse* . . . . The moral element is indeed only called into existence . . . in this kind of way. Therefore, we no longer ask: How much does the resistance which the whole nation in arms is capable of offering cost that nation? Rather, we ask: What is the influence which such resistance can have? What are its conditions and how is it to be used?"[18] The more-than-Napoleonic victories of the Prussian nation in arms heightened the same concerns. Soldiers became less interested in machines just when a "second" industrial revolution dramatically increased the firepower of their basic infantry and artillery weapons. Late-nineteenth-century soldiers were not the first to leap ahead to the last war; this particular leap was away from industrial planning for machine warfare. This does not mean that parts of their industrialized economies did not profit from peacetime arms production, or that those who profited from it did not try to manipulate governmental and public opinion. It means only that the size of and balances of forces within the late-nineteenth-century's military-industrial complexes were not those which were to worry Eisenhower two generations later.

Reluctant as Europeanists may be to see novelty in America, or as Americanists may be to see evils which are not imported, the contemporary American military-industrial complex is different. The reasons may again lie in policy makers' perceptions of the future. World War II was seen as a triumph of machines, of a "technological revolution" in which, in Eisenhower's words, research was so "central . . . that public policy could itself become the captive of a scientific-technological elite."[19]

This elite is not an issue here. Nor are the ideas of a Soviet elite, which may reflect other perceptions of strength and weakness in its World War II combinations of Marxism, the nation in arms, and a less-developed industrial establishment. But still different ideas about military and industrial needs in late-nineteenth-century Britain, France, and Germany had so affected the ways in which decisions were made within their military-industrial complexes that Eisenhower correctly saw the American one of the 1950s as a new phenomenon.

Would studies of the military-industrial complexes of the interwar era suggest more fruitful analogies? We can only note that Eisenhower's generation had little detailed knowledge of the totalitarian economies, that it overrated the roles of the army and big business in National Socialism, and that the decisions which compelled it, in Eisenhower's words, "to spend on military security more than the net income of all United States corporations" were taken by the National Security Council before their costs were estimated. Supporters of NSC-68, the military blueprint for the 1950s, Dean Acheson noted, had to "bludgeon the mass mind of 'top government'" with such scary items as "half the total efforts of their rival society went into military power."[20] When American costs were estimated, Defense and State Department figures ranged from $17-18 to $35-50 billions a year.

NSC-68, like the German naval program or the German army's Schlieffen Plan, had been adopted without real debate over economic costs and consequences. Private arms makers stood to gain from the first two decisions, but only the German naval program involved overt political activity by a part of that kind of military-industrial complex which concerned Eisenhower. All three examples support Clausewitz's view of the importance of military history's intangibles. If Germany's navy was—in the words of her 1914 Chancellor—"for the general purposes of her greatness," and if the Schlieffen Plan began—in Ritter's phrase—as "a purely theoretical operational study," then NSC-68 may also have to be explained by a fortuitous combination of political, military, and economic facts, hopes, and ideas.

The dangers of generalizing from late-nineteenth-century European to late-twentieth-century American experience are very great. This volume's other essays show how much remains to be done on the problem of arming the American people from scratch, rather than from a mixture of old mercantilistic and new industrial plants and practices. European navies have been more studied than armies, which were technologically less advanced, militarily more important, and politically less controversial. Private firms have been more studied than dockyards and arsenals, and their capitalization, costs, labor practices, and technological spin-offs, which may have been spin-ins from "peaceful" industry, even in the field of explosives. And another factor in Eisenhower's analysis—the concern of popularly-elected legislators for jobs in their districts—may be even harder to trace in the mazes of nineteenth-century French or German, than in British or American parliamentary history.

By 1914, the Royal Navy and French army were parts of the most smoothly working military-industrial complexes because they met "real" national military-political needs. The differing speeds of Germany's economic and political development made the "proper" meshing of national attitudes, political institutions, military needs, and economic interests more difficult. So Gerald D. Feldman's *Army, Industry, and Labor in Germany, 1914-1918* shows the outbreak of war "catapulting . . . the army into [the] totally unanticipated . . . [job] of mastering and overcoming a dismal heritage of administrative confusion, political bitterness, and social tension,"[21] while Fritz Fischer's revisionist *Germany's Aims in the First World War* contrasts "an economy organized on the most modern lines, regularly introducing every modern innovation . . . and manned by a disciplined, industrious, and thrifty population" with an army whose "conservative leadership and methods . . . retarded not only democratisation, but even. . . technical modernisation."[22] In both cases "a community of interest . . . among some corporations, military officers, civilian bureaucrats, labor leaders, scientists and others" may have tended "to dictate the dimension and direction of both foreign and domestic policies," but problems of scale make Pursell's definition more applicable to the United States in the 1960s, while modifying his ideas that "the military-industrial complex is only a special case of the more general problem of the maldistribution of wealth," and that the Progressives' Welfare—or the Liberal Corporate—State carried "within it the institutional and ideological seeds of the military-industrial complex."[23]

World War I showed the need for more economic planning and machine weapons. Though these needs were to be as well met by capitalists as by Marxists or Fascists, interwar planners only sporadically applied the scientific method to military technology. Decisions were not made in 1961 as they had been made in 1931 or 1901. Except perhaps in Communist Russia, 1961's resulting "military organization," Eisenhower felt, bore "little relation to that known by any of my predecessors in peacetime, or indeed by the fighting men of World War II or Korea."[24] While its elements can be studied historically, this "complex" represents what French historians call a "conjuncture" of forces. Many 1961 ideas about economics, war, and arms production were old. But the "mental tool kits" (*l'outillage mental* is collective) with which soldiers, politicians, and scientists decided which machines to build were as different from those of 1931 as those of 1931 had been from those of 1901. That Theodore Roosevelt was not Franklin D. Roosevelt is a truism that can often be overlooked. And the latter might have been as lost as Eisenhower in a conjuncture which, in 1961, seemed to be historically unique.

This paper's thesis is that studies of previous European or American military-industrial complexes may be more useful in detailed than in "total" history. Desires for private profit and for military, political, and bureaucratic status, and the need for planning and machine weapons had all been present in 1901 and 1931. The new elements of 1961 were the technological revolution—with, Eisenhower felt, the Progressives' "recurring temptation to feel that some spectacular and costly action could become the miraculous solution to all current difficulties"—and, though it has been little studied in this connection, the concentration of advanced weapons research and production in two power centers. The resulting conflict he saw as one "of indefinite duration," not to be met by "the emotional and transitory sacrifices of crisis," but by those of "a prolonged and complex struggle."[25] Because so many other decision makers saw the world his way, that world was historically unique. Not surprisingly, it produced a new military-political-economic-scientific institution, that of the contemporary American military-industrial complex.

NOTES

1. Carroll W. Pursell, Jr., ed. *The Military-Industrial Complex* (New York, Harper & Row, 1972), pp. 209, 206-07. Dwight D. Eisenhower, *Mandate for Change, 1953-1956.* (Garden City, N. Y., Doubleday, 1963), p. 163.
2. Adam Smith, *An Inquiry into the Nature and Causes of the Wealth of Nations* (New York, A. M. Kelley, 1966 ed.) Book IV, Ch. 2; Book V, Ch. 1, Part 2.
3. James M. McConnell, "European Experience with Volunteer and Conscript Forces," *Studies Prepared for the President's Commission on an All-Volunteer Armed Force,* 2 vols. (Washington, D. C., Government Printing Office, 1970), vol. II, pp. iii, 2-4.
4. Rondo E. Cameron, *France and the Economic Development of Europe 1800-1914: Conquests of Peace and Seeds of War* (Princeton, N. J., Princeton University Press, 1961), pp. 513-16.
5. Pursell, op. cit., Appendix 9.
6. Smith op. cit., Book V, Ch. 1, Part 2; Book IV, Ch. 2.
7. S. Pollard and C. Holmes, eds., *Documents of European Economic History,* vol. II, *Industrial Power and National Rivalry* (New York and London, St. Martin's, 1972), pp. 326-29.
8. Carlton J. H. Hayes, *A Generation of Materialism 1871-1900* (New York, Harper, 1941), p. 241. Pursell, op. cit., p. 320.
9. Bernard Brodie, *Sea Power in the Machine Age* (Princeton, Princeton University Press, 1941), pp. 238-39.
10. Archibald S. Alexander, "The Cost of World Armaments," *Scientific American,* vol. 221, No. 4 (October. 1969), pp. 21-27. Arthur Guy Enock, *This War Business: A Book for Every Citizen of Every Country* (London, The Bodley Head, 1951), p. 87.
11. Alfred Vagts, *A History of Militarism: Romance and Reality of a Profession* (New York, W. W. Norton, 1937), p. 217.
12. Arthur J. Marder, *The Anatomy of British Sea Power: A History of British Naval Policy in the Pre-Dreadnought Era, 1880-1905* (New York, Knopf, 1940), pp. 30, 42-43.
13. Arthur J. Marder, *From the Dreadnought to Scapa Flow: The Royal Navy in the Fisher Era, 1904-1919,* 5 vols. (New York, Knopf, 1961-70), vol. V, pp 308-13, 337.
14. Verdy to William II, 20 July, 1890. Pollard and Holmes, op. cit, vol. II, p. 82.
15. Gerhard Ritter, *The Sword and the Scepter: The Problem of Militarism in Germany,* Trans. Heinz Norden, 4 vols. (Coral Gables, Fla., University of Miami Press, 1970-73), vol. II, pp. 58, 26.
16. Carlton J. H. Hayes, *France: A Nation of Patriots* (New York, Columbia University Press, 1930), *A Generation of Materialism,* p. 247.
17. Charles de Gaulle, *France and Her Army,* Trans. F. L. Dash, (London, Hutchinson, 1945), p. 90.
18. Carl von Clausewitz, *On War,* Trans. O. J. M. Jolles (New York, The Modern Library, 1943), pp. 457-58.
19. Pursell, op cit., p. 207.
20. Ibid., p. 206. Dean Acheson, *Present at the Creation: My Years in the State Department* (New York, W. W. Norton, 1969), pp. 374-79.
21. Gerald D. Feldman, *Army, Industry, and Labor in Germany 1914-1918* (Princeton, N. J., Princeton University Press, 1966), p. 38.
22. Fritz Fischer, *Germany's Aims in the First World War* (New York, W. W. Norton, 1967), p. 19.
23. Pursell, op. cit., p. 1.
24. Ibid., p. 206.
25. Ibid., p. 205.

MILITARY ARSENALS AND INDUSTRY
BEFORE WORLD WAR I

Since the early days of the republic, the armed forces of the United
States have actively participated in domestic economic affairs. The magnitude of this involvement has fluctuated in response to political and diplomatic conditions and has had both positive and negative implications. Today
the military, tainted by an unpopular involvement in Vietnam and an un-
savory association with the "Weapons Culture," stands rather low in public
esteem. Interestingly enough, many contemporary attitudes existed during
the early nineteenth century as well. Fearful of standing armies, suspicious
of undue military influence, and critical of economic waste, a large segment
of American society held grave misgivings about the necessity of maintaining a regularized war-making establishment. Such apprehensions were partly
mollified by the Jeffersonian conviction that the army and navy should
transcend narrow militaristic pursuits and devote their resources to the
nation's struggle for internal improvement. Much of the justification for
continued congressional support of both services, therefore, depended on
how effectively they could serve civilian economic endeavor.

Between 1800 and 1860 the army responded to antimilitaristic sentiment in a highly creative, even dynamic way. Much has been written about
the Corps of Engineers and, to a lesser extent, the Quartermaster Department whose extensive reports of exploration, land surveys, and planning
activities resulted in a wide variety of civil works. Together, these projects
helped provide a network of roads, canals, railroads, and inland navigation
systems which inaugurated a transportation revolution essential for the
emergence of a national market economy.

The historical record is also replete with numerous instances of West
Point graduates who, upon leaving government service, fanned out across

the country to become prominent engineers, factory masters, and business executives. In an age that afforded few professionally trained engineers and lacked the educational facilities to meet ever-growing technical needs, the army, through its systematic programs and active involvement in internal improvements, played a significant role in providing the leadership and expertise necessary for accelerating the pace of economic growth. In doing so, it dramatically demonstrated its usefulness to a society inherently skeptical of things military.

Only rarely are the tools of war mentioned in conjunction with the brilliant scientific and technical accomplishments of the Corps of Engineers. Yet problems associated with the procurement of arms during the early national period required equivalent degrees of skill and ultimately set the stage for far-reaching changes in the mechanical arts. Of special interest are the activities of civilian contractors and government-owned arsenals and how their affairs were supervised and coordinated by the Secretary of War and, after 1814, by the Ordnance Department. The performance of the latter, an army bureau, proved particularly important from an entrepreneurial viewpoint. It is no exaggeration to say that the Ordnance Department, through its astute leadership and organization, did as much to stoke the fires of industrialism in America as did the Corps of Engineers those of transportation. What follows is an attempt to place this neglected area of military enterprise in historical perspective. Because much basic research remains to be done on the subject, it is necessarily a suggestive rather than a definitive treatment.

Prior to the War of 1812, the gun trade stood in hectic disarray Although George Washington had signed bills establishing national armories at Springfield, Massachusetts, and Harpers Ferry, Virginia, in 1794, neither institution could meet the expanding demands of both the regular army and the state militias. Springfield had manufactured only 2,111 muskets by January, 1798, and Harpers Ferry, the larger of the two armories, did not produce a single weapon until 1801. Spurred on by a diplomatic crisis with France in 1798, a nervous Congress appropriated $800,000 for the purchase of cannon, small arms, and ammunition from private contractors. Of this sum, over $500,000 was earmarked for the acquisition of .69-caliber smooth-bore muskets, the standard issue to American foot soldiers since the days of the Revolution. While this legislation helped place arms making on an industrial footing, the administration of the system and the quality of weapons left much to be desired.

Twenty-seven arms makers, nineteen of whom were New Englanders, signed contracts with the Treasury Department for the delivery of 40,200 muskets during the spring and summer of 1798. The hasty manner with which Secretary Oliver Wolcott conducted these negotiations indicates the government's utter desperation in seeking new domestic sources of supply. None of the parties involved were required to produce evidence of their ability as gunmakers, nor were they asked to produce bonds guaranteeing delivery within an allotted period of time. In addition to paying $13.40 per musket, the Treasury also agreed to help ease the financial burdens of production by making outright monetary advances to certain contractors. One of the largest, $12,725, went to Thomas Bicknell, a Pennsylvania (?) gunsmith who contracted in July, 1798, for 2,000 muskets. The government stipulated only that the arms should be fashioned after the French "Charleville" pattern, finished in a "workmanlike manner," and delivered to the appropriate authorities no later than September 30, 1800. Provided with so few restrictions and such handsome inducements, scores of enterprisers flocked to the government's gate.

If federal officals had been somewhat encouraged by the number of contracts signed in 1798, their outlook turned to gloom in June, 1801. Nearly nine months had passed since all engagements were supposed to have been completed, yet on June 10 only three of the twenty-seven original contractors had fulfilled their agreements. Some like Robert McCormick, a Philadelphian who received an advance of $4,000 for an order of 3,000 muskets, failed to carry out their assignments and defaulted. Others simply fell short of the mark. Typical was the Frederick, Maryland, firm of White, Crabb, Metzger & Barnhizle, which had delivered only 548 of 1,000 stands of arms when their contract was finally canceled late in December, 1801. Of 40,200 muskets originally assigned in 1798, only 14,244 or 35.43 percent had been turned over to the Purveyor of Public Supplies by June 10, 1801.

Undoubtedly the most famous of those who failed to meet their contract deadlines was Eli Whitney of New Haven, Connecticut. Whitney, who had absolutely no prior experience as an arms maker, signed his first contract for 10,000 muskets on June 14, 1798. By the terms of the agreement he committed himself to the delivery of 4,000 stands by September 30, 1799, and 6,000 more by September 30, 1800. Considering the fact that the New Englander had yet to tool his factory or recruit a trained labor force, this was an incredible promise. Whitney, however, had good reason to be impetuous. With a mounting debt incurred in numerous cotton-gin-patent litigations and his business on the verge of collapse, he urgently needed the credit that would be forthcoming with a large government contract. Particularly enticing was the promise of an immediate $10,000 advance. Better yet, the contract also stated that further advances would be made "at the discretion of the Secretary of the Treasury in proportion to the progress made in executing the contract." Whitney's motives were obvious. "Bankruptcy and

ruin were constantly staring me in the face," he wrote a friend. "Loaded
with a Debt of 3 or 4000 Dollars, without resources, and without any business that would ever furnish me a support, I knew not which way to turn.
. . .By this contract I obtained some thousands of Dollars in advance which
saved me from ruin."[1]

In the end, Whitney required nearly eleven years to execute his contract.
To forestall cancellation of the agreement—which most certainly would
have led to bankruptcy proceedings and dashed any hope for resurrecting
the cotton-gin business—he wrote numerous letters detailing plans, explaining difficulties, and pleading for patience on the part of the government
authorities. To strengthen his position, he also made many trips to the
Federal City. On one occasion early in January 1801, in the presence of
John Adams, Thomas Jefferson, and other dignitaries, he conducted a
dramatic demonstration of how the lock mechanism of one musket could
be exchanged with those from several others. Utterly fascinated by the
performance and by Whitney's glowing rhetoric concerning the benefits to
be derived from such a system, the government granted one extension
after another. Further advances accompanied each extension, so that only
$2,450 remained on the $134,000 contract when Whitney made his final
delivery on January 23, 1809. To many officials this seemed but a small
price to pay for the manufacture of arms with interchangeable parts.

So it was. But one might ask to what extent were Whitney's muskets
interchangeable? Here the evidence is clear and unmistakable: in several
collections there are specimens whose major parts will not exchange. "In some
respects," historian Robert Woodbury reports, "they are not even approximately interchangeable."[2] In fact, as late as Whitney's death in 1825, the
parts of individual lock mechanisms produced at his New Haven factory
were stamped with identifying marks to distinguish them from others in
the same batch—an unnecessary practice for the manufacture of truly standardized components. It is consequently difficult to escape the conclusion
that Whitney intentionally contrived his famous 1801 demonstration as a
stopgap measure.

Whitney's case provides a telling commentary on the undeveloped state
of the firearms industry during the early 1800s. Contractors generally were
not only tardy in making deliveries but were also remiss in living up to the
full letter of their agreements. Being in business primarily for profit, factory
owners as well as artisans had little compunction about covering up defects
and turning out inferior work, so long as such pieces would pass inspection.
This meant that thousands of faulty muskets were being delivered annually
to government agents who accepted them on little more than good faith.
By 1810 the problem had grown so serious that Colonel John Whiting of
the 4th Infantry reported the existence of over 10,000 defective contract

muskets in government arsenals. So poor was the quality of these weapons that Whiting recommended their disposal to markets in Africa and South America.

Although the shortcomings of private contractors may have been numerous, they were more than equaled by governmental ineptitude in setting acceptable standards for the manufacture of high-quality firearms. For more than two decades after 1792 the arms-procurement program floundered dismally, first under the Treasury Department, and after June, 1801, under the Department of War. Neither office possessed the staff nor the expertise to place the contract system on a sound administrative footing. In effect, this meant that each contractor, after being provided with a pattern piece and some vague instructions as to what constituted an acceptable weapon, was left mostly to his own devices in carrying out the order. Inspections were conducted, but, without the use of gauges and other accurate testing devices, much depended on the skilled eyes of the inspector. Because such skills varied markedly from person to person, the verification process tended to be haphazard and highly subjective in nature. Frequently contractors persuaded inspectors to overlook defective workmanship through appeals to friendship or in exchange for monetary "treats" and other gratuities. On other occasions, the Secretary of War simply abandoned protocol and allowed contractors to inspect and receive their own muskets on behalf of the government. This occured in December, 1808, when Henry Dearborn extended the privilege to Eli Whitney—barely six months after the New Englander had been reprimanded for delivering a large parcel of muskets with seriously defective parts. Such indiscretions served only to compound the difficulty of securing serviceable weapons for the United States.

On the eve of the War of 1812, Congress attempted to revamp the cumbrous army supply system by establishing three bureaus—the Quartermaster Department, the Commissary General of Purchases, and the Ordnance Department—whose primary functions were to assist the Secretary of War in procuring, inspecting, and distributing military equipment. Because the enabling legislation failed to clarify their relationship to one another or define adequately their respective duties, the activities of these agencies overlapped at many points during the ensuing war years, thereby perpetuating the same old problems that had plagued the army for two decades. Not until the fighting had ended did Congress take steps to remedy the numerous ambiguities and shortcomings inherent in the government's procurement program. On February 8, 1815, exactly one week before the Senate ratified the Treaty of Ghent, President James Madison signed a bill placing the entire responsibility for negotiating and supervising arms contracts under the direct jurisdiction of the Ordnance Department. The same bill also transferred authority over the national armories to the office of the Chief of Ordnance.

Though little noticed at the time, these actions set the stage for increased system and efficiency in the arms industry and paved the way for one of the outstanding technological achievements of the nineteenth century: the mechanized production of firearms with interchangeable parts.

The first Chief of Ordnance and the person most responsible for the department's early success was Colonel Decius Wadsworth. An experienced administrator and a strict disciplinarian, Wadsworth during the War of 1812 had almost single-handedly molded the Ordnance Department into a small, tightly knit organization which rivaled the Corps of Engineers in talent, competence, and dependability. His motto, "Uniformity, Simplicity and Solidarity," became guiding principles in the formulation of departmental policy and, as senior officer, he expected all who served under him to live up to this precept or suffer the consequences of transferal to less desirable duty. He accordingly surrounded himself with a group of bright young "soldier-technologists," the most able of whom were Captain Sylvanus Thayer and Major George Bomford. While Thayer left the bureau in 1815 and eventually became Commandant of Cadets at the United States Military Academy, Bomford spent his entire career in ordnance service, first as Wadsworth's chief assistant and later as head of the department.

George Bomford represented the first generation of West Point graduates who began to enter the ranks of the military establishment prior to the War of 1812. He exemplified the new breed of technically trained officers that older superiors both envied and admired. Urbane, intelligent, and persevering, he held great promise not only as an engineer but also as an effective administrator. Moreover, his marriage to Clara Baldwin, niece of the poet-statesman Joel Barlow and sister of a prominent Pennsylvania congressman, secured wealth, social position, and powerful political connections. Given these endowments, almost everyone knew that Bomford's star was rising and that one day he would succeed Decius Wadsworth as Chief of Ordnance. That day eventually came with Wadsworth's resignation early in June, 1821, and, from that time until Bomford's death in 1848, he presided over the affairs of the Ordnance Department with a sense of purpose and entrepreneurial skill rarely equaled in the annals of American military history. More than anyone else, he supplied the dynamic leadership which made ordnance one of the most respected branches of the War Department.

Upon receiving official instructions regarding the new status of the contract service and national armories in February, 1815, Wadsworth and Bomford proceeded to draw up an agenda which went far beyond mere administrative reform. Since thousands of arms had been damaged and rendered virtually useless in the war with England, their immediate concern was the production of cheaper, more uniform weapons, capable of being repaired in the field simply by substituting new components for those that had broken. Such a program required arms with interchangeable parts, a mechanical ideal which had persistently eluded the most skilled of artisans, including Whitney, for decades. Some means had to be found, therefore, to eliminate the innumerable variations that crept into guns made primarily by hand. In their search for a solution, Wadsworth and Bomford decided to adopt a new model (1816) musket, prepare rigidly standardized pattern pieces, and test their effectiveness under actual production conditions at the national armories. If the experiment proved a success, they reasoned, then the system could be extended to arms made by private contractors. Thereafter the cost and quality of muskets manufactured at Springfield and Harpers Ferry would be used as a yardstick in determining contract prices and in evaluating the work of contractors.

Although the uniformity idea looked promising on paper, neither acceptance nor practical success came easily. To some, the system presaged centralization under the military and the undesirable consequences that would inevitably flow from such an invidious association. To others, the problem of establishing industry-wide standards seemed illusory and beyond the bounds of administrative control, since manufacturing methods and inspection procedures differed so considerably from one armory to another. Too many variables had to be reckoned with. One officer voiced a common sentiment when he cautioned Colonel Wadsworth, "It is the easiest thing in the world to change the pattern at Washington and to make, in imagination, thousands of arms upon the new pattern; but it is far otherwise in the practice."[3] Other critics felt that the new system would be prohibitively expensive. It would not only require the painstaking preparation of numerous patterns and gauges, but also the construction of special-purpose fixtures and machinery. Moreover, once built, these implements had to be integrated with other units and coordinated with the total production process. This problem alone presented such a challenge that Roswell Lee, the magnetic and resourceful superintendent of the Springfield Armory, remained skeptical about finding any quick technological solutions. "It is difficult . . . to *please every body*," he reminded the Chief of Ordnance in 1817. "*Faults will really exist & many imaginary ones will be pointed out*. . . . It must consequently take some time to bring about a uniformity of the component parts of the Musket at both Establishments [Springfield and Harpers Ferry]."[4]

Much to the Ordnance Department's chagrin, Lee's prediction proved correct. Nearly thirty years would elapse before the national armories and arms makers generally possessed the technical capability of producing large consignments of weapons with interchangeable parts. Although the pace of change moved haltingly, neither Wadsworth nor Bomford lost hope, mainly because there were just enough glimmerings of success to auger well for the future. By 1819, for instance, the Springfield Armory—having mechanized several key operations and adopted a method of gauging components both during and after the manufacturing process—was producing smoothbore muskets substantially more uniform than those made during the War of 1812. During the 1820s John H. Hall, a New Englander working under special contract at Harpers Ferry, conclusively demonstrated that his patented breech-loading rifle could be made with interchangeable parts. In 1832 Simeon North, a singularly talented contractor from Middletown, Connecticut, added another dimension to precision manufacture when he successfully produced rifles whose parts exchanged with those made by Hall at Harper's Ferry. Yet, as impressive as these achievements were, numerous mechanical problems continued to plague the industry well into the 1840s.

As a whole, private contractors, many of whom harkened back to the diplomatic crisis of 1798, seemed particularly troubled by the uniformity system. Periodic inspections conducted by the Ordnance Department almost invariably revealed that contract arms were inferior to those made at the national armories. Repeated reports of flaws, subterfuges, and shoddy workmanship convinced more than one authority that such manufacturers as Lemuel Pomeroy, Asa Waters, and Marine T. Wickham could no longer meet the stringent requirements of the new technology. Confronted with mounting capitalization costs, more rigorous standards, frequent model changes, and the uncertainty of further government patronage, the attrition rate among contractors grew noticeably during the 1830s and early 1840s. For a time it appeared as if contracting would disappear altogether. While the Mexican War temporarily halted this trend, the makeup of the arms industry had changed markedly by mid-century. By 1846 only three of eleven major firms active in the 1820s still held government contracts. By 1856 all but one, the Whitney Arms Company, had gone out of business. Replacing them were larger, corporately organized enterprises headed by younger, more aggressive businessmen such as James T. Ames, Samuel Colt, Epiphalet Remington, Samuel Robbins, and Richard S. Lawrence. Unencumbered by old facilities, worn machinery, and lingering attachments to craft traditions, staffed by knowledgeable machinists, and spurred on by visions of infinitely expanding commercial markets, these "second-generation" firms availed themselves of the mechanical know-how accumulated over previous decades and carried interchangeable production to a heightened level of maturity.

Any doubts concerning the ability of these younger companies were quickly dispelled when Robbins & Lawrence of Windsor, Vermont, and Hartford, Connecticut's Samuel Colt, as well as several other American firms won international acclaim for the excellence of their products at the

London Crystal Palace Exhibition in 1851. Profoundly impressed by the quality of Colt's revolvers and the technical sophistication of six interchangeable rifles displayed by Robbins & Lawrence, the British government responded by dispatching two investigatory commissions to the United States between 1853 and 1854. While both delegations received instructions to examine and report upon the mechanical arts in America, only the famous three-man "Committee on Machinery," which embarked for New York in the spring of 1854 to study the so-called American System of interchangeable manufacture, possessed the power to make purchases. Upon visiting virtually every important machine shop and armory in the Northeast, the committee signed agreements with seven firms for the delivery of machinery valued at $105,379.50. The Ames Manufacturing Company of Chicopee, Massachusetts, made the largest sale, contracting for a large number of gunstocking machines and precision gauges worth $46,844.62. Close behind was Robbins & Lawrence which received orders for 138 machines, mostly millers, assessed at $46,455.60. Designed to produce components for the new Model 1853 British rifle-musket, the consignments of both firms were shipped to England in 1855. At the same time Her Majesty's government acquired the services of James H. Burton, former master armorer at the Harpers Ferry Armory, and several other American mechanics to set up the machinery and supervise manufacturing operations at the Enfield Armory near London.

In addition to the publicity they generated, the Crystal Palace Exposition, the purchases of 1854, and the subsequent parliamentary reports prepared by the British commissioners brought a new sense of pride and prestige to rapidly maturing Yankee arms makers. For the first time their products and techniques were considered equal to if not superior to those made in Europe. No longer did peers in England and on the Continent smugly dismiss the United States as a backwater nation of tinkers dependent on borrowed technologies.

Since machine tools and precision instruments represented the key ingredients of the American System, both foreign and domestic demand for these items increased. By the mid-1850s a number of American firms had adapted the techniques developed in the arms industry to the manufacture of metal products, most notably sewing machines. While orders continued to flow in from England, the governments of Russia, Spain, and Sweden initiated inquiries and sent observers to the United States. Encouraged by these overtures, American manufacturers actively sought to cultivate foreign markets. The most famous was Samuel Colt who, as early as 1853, had built a factory in London and established separate licensing agreements with arms makers in Belgium, Austria, and Prussia. Almost simultaneously other firms, such as the Ames Manufacturing Company, began to devote more and more of their resources to the production and commercial sale of machine tools. Indeed, the future of the machine trade looked so bright that a number of new, more specialized companies soon joined the field. Led by Brown & Sharpe of Providence, Rhode Island, and Pratt & Whitney of Hartford, Connecticut, their appearance paved the way for the establishment of a bona fide machine-tool industry in the United States.

In several respects the years between 1845 and 1855 mark an important crossroad in the annals of American industry. Among other things the decade witnessed the maturation of interchangeable methods in the firearms industry, their diffusion to other sectors of the economy, and the rapid growth of commercial machine building. Two generations of factory masters, artisans, and mechanics had participated in this broad-ranging development. So too had members of the Ordnance Department, though the extent of their contribution is often obscured by the inventive exploits of those more directly involved in the process of mechanization. Particularly significant are the activities of Colonel George Bomford, who for more than thirty years played a pivotal role in coordinating the affairs of private and public armories. To him much of the credit is due for relentlessly promoting uniformity in the face of persistent criticism and for encouraging an unprecedented spirit of cooperation among arms makers during the early nineteenth century. With Roswell Lee, he was instrumental in making the Springfield Armory a center for the acquisition and exchange of new ideas. Throughout the period, armorers and mechanics converged at the Connecticut Valley works to observe the latest techniques, compare notes, and discuss common problems. If they found a particular tool or machine useful, they could readily obtain drawings, patterns, and specifications from the superintendent. It is noteworthy, for instance, that all the gauges and machinery sent to England in 1854 by the Ames Company were based on patterns loaned by the Springfield Armory. Ames was only one of many companies that enjoyed the privilege of drawing upon this storehouse of accumulated knowledge. Such an "open-door" policy undoubtedly helps to explain the integrated character of the industry as well as the relative speed with which arms makers assimilated the new technology. It also accentuates the public-service orientation of ordnance institutions during the antebellum period.

While pursuing the engineering ideal of interchangeability, Bomford and his colleagues continually sought to systematize and improve other aspects of military production. A subject of pressing importance during the 1830s and 1840s concerned the dubious quality and erratic performance of artillery made of iron. Since 1801 civilian founders had supplied the army with cast-iron cannon and, for the most part, these weapons had served their purpose well. However, so little was known about the physical properties of ferrous substances that, whenever cannon burst, no one could adequately explain why. The fear and tension which attended such explosions, coupled with the fact that most European nations refrained from using iron as a construction material, prompted several Ordnance boards to recommend that the army revert to bronze until sufficient knowledge could be obtained and proper methods developed to insure the safety of artillerists equipped with iron cannon.

In order to bridge this technological gap, the Ordnance Department, during the early 1840s, instituted a research program aimed at gaining a greater understanding of the nature of iron. Among the earliest and most successful investigators was William Wade, a Pittsburgh iron maker and former assistant to Colonel Bomford, who returned to ordnance duty as a civilian employee in 1842. While serving as a government attending agent at several private foundries, Wade spent countless hours building testing machines and examining fractured samples of iron in an effort to establish correlations between their tensile strength, their specific gravity, and the durability of cannon constructed of such materials when subjected to continuous fire. In carrying out these studies, Wade was assisted by Captain Alfred Mordecai, an ordnance officer of considerable scientific merit, who gained prominence for extensive ballistic experiments conducted at the Washington [D. C.] Arsenal between 1842 and 1849. The most imaginative series of experiments, however, occurred at the Pikesville Arsenal near Baltimore where Campbell Morfit, a chemist at the University of Maryland and protégé of James C. Booth of Philadelphia, set out to determine the effects of carbon, sulphur, phosphorus, silica, and other substances on the quality of gun metal. Working closely with his old teacher, Booth, and Lieutenant Louis Walbach of the Ordnance Department, Morfit, between 1851 and 1855, submitted three reports which adduced metallurgical evidence corroborating the earlier findings of Wade. Together with the work of George Bomford, Daniel Treadwell, Thomas J. Rodman, and other contemporaries, these investigations yielded information which enabled founders to exercise far more control over the quality of their castings. Equally important for the growth of modern engineering, they represented an early attempt to enlist the tools of science on behalf of metalworking. By treating the technology of iron making in a scientific manner, members and associates of the Ordnance Department sought to substitute systematic research for cut-and-try empiricism. In doing so, they stood in the vanguard of those who were beginning to shed craft traditions for a more rigorous approach to the solution of technical problems.

The Civil War tested the American arms industry as never before. With the fall of Fort Sumter and President Lincoln's call to preserve the Union, the Ordnance Department faced the onerous responsibility of supplying an army of half a million men. Because the Harpers Ferry Armory had been stripped of its machinery and put to the torch by Confederate forces in the spring of 1861, the new Ordnance Chief, General James W. Ripley, sought to acquire weapons in Europe. In addition to forestalling the efforts of southern arms buyers, he reasoned that such a strategy would serve as a temporary expedient until the government's productive facilities at Springfield could be expanded and the contract system sufficiently strengthened to contribute to the war effort. Initially, Secretary of War Simon Cameron opposed the idea and delayed its implementation. But stark realities of battle, especially the depressing news from First Bull Run, soon changed his mind. By the end of July, 1861, Union agents were hustling off to Europe with the Secretary's blessing. Within a year they had returned with over 726,000 arms.

While the North continued to make foreign purchases throughout the duration of the war, the frantic search for weapons which accompanied the first fourteen months of the conflict eased after June, 1862. As early as January of that year Springfield was turning out 10,000 rifled muskets monthly, a number which exceeded the armory's entire product for 1860. By the end of 1865 the New England works had finished 815,139 pieces, a monumental feat in view of the fact that it had produced less than 700,000 from its establishment in 1794 to the southern exodus in 1861. This accomplishment, plus the delivery of 7,892 cannon, tons of ammunition, and well over 1.5 million small arms by private manufacturers in less than four years, justifiably convinced ordnance authorities that no other government agency had met the needs of the Republic "more fully, more promptly, or more satisfactorily" than did theirs during the war between the states.[5]

By 1865 northern industrialists had convincingly demonstrated that high-quality weapons could be produced in massive quantities. Yet no sooner had they begun to reap the harvest of their labors than the fruit withered on the vine. After Lee's surrender at Appomattox, Congress moved quickly to dismantle the nation's awesome war machine. In less than a year the strength of the army dwindled from more than a million men to a standing force of 57,000. Further reductions occurred during the next decade, eventually reaching a postwar low of 24,140 officers and enlisted men in 1877. Similar trends could be seen in fiscal affairs. By 1866, War Department appropriations had fallen precipitously from an all-time high of $1 billion in 1865 to $284 million. The next quadrennium brought even more decreases until, in 1870, the department's budget stood at a paltry $57.7 million.

One of the first agencies to feel the effects of financial retrenchment was the Ordnance Department. Faced with drastic budgetary cuts during the postwar period, Chief of Ordnance Alexander B. Dyer began to phase out existing contracts and to refuse the renewal of others in an effort to comply with current policy. Between 1865 and 1867 ordnance disbursements fell nearly 87 percent. Needless to say, the resultant drought in government spending worked serious hardships on the firearms industry. Firms which in 1861 had been encouraged, wooed, and in some cases, even hounded by officials to sign large government contracts now suddenly found themselves deprived of further patronage, saddled with high overhead costs in plant space and idle machinery, and abandoned to the whims of the marketplace. While three companies managed to receive contracts for the manufacture of breechloaders and several others made arrangements to do conversion work, these orders were hardly sufficient to sustain an industry which had been tooled to produce hundreds of thousands of weapons. To all intents and purposes the government discontinued the contract system, and it would not reappear until the eve of World War I.

Of forty-eight major arms contractors active during the Civil War, only eleven continued in the business after 1870. Many firms such as the Amoskeag Manufacturing Company of Manchester, New Hampshire, and the Bridesburg Machine Works near Philadelphia adjusted to the postwar situation by returning to old pursuits, including, among other things, the manufacture of textiles, textile machinery, locomotives, boilers, machine tools, and mill machinery of all kinds. Others sought to apply the techniques used in arms making to the development of new products, particularly sewing machines, typewriters, and bicycles. Less fortunate companies, encumbered with large debts and unable to stem the tide of intensified competition, went bankrupt and liquidated their holdings. A case in point is the Spencer Repeating Rifle Company of Boston, which ceased operations in 1869 and the following year sold its plant and machinery to the newly organized Winchester Repeating Arms Company of New Haven, Connecticut.

Amid this trend toward consolidation, a number of larger firms recognized the potential inherent in domestic and foreign markets and altered their strategies accordingly. The prospects overseas looked particularly promising, so much so that Colt, Winchester, Smith & Wesson, Remington, Ames, and the Providence Tool Company seemed blissfully indifferent about the possibility that they were contributing to international intrigue by exporting millions of dollars in munitions overseas. All told, some twenty-two countries, including distant China and Japan, purchased arms and ammunition from American manufacturers during the late 1860s and 1870s. The largest of these orders came in 1872 when the Providence Tool Company of Rhode Island contracted with the Turkish government for over 600,000 Henry-Martini rifles. At the same time Colt, Remington, and Smith & Wesson were busily stocking the arsenals of Turkey's perennial enemy, Russia.

Within five years those two nations would be at war for the fourth time in the nineteenth century.

Equally profitable was the export of gun-making equipment which, for twenty years after the Civil War, helped sustain arms manufacturers and stabilize the machine-tool industry in the United States. While Remington, Winchester, and the Ames Manufacturing Company shared in this trade, the most lucrative contracts went to two former Colt employees, Pratt & Whitney of Hartford, Connecticut. Between 1871 and 1875, for instance, Pratt & Whitney shipped over $2 million worth of machinery to Europe, most of which went to Germany for the production of Mauser rifles at the Royal Arsenals of Erfurt, Spandau, and Danzig. Frequently American firms provided technicians to set up machinery and instruct workers in its use. Like the sales of arms themselves, these transactions apparently played a part in heightening international tensions and accelerating an arms race in late nineteenth-century Europe. The degree of American involvement however, is still a matter of debate.

To a very real extent the Civil War ended a long period of mechanical creativity in the firearms industry. For fifty years private contractors, most of whom relied almost exclusively on government patronage for their livelihood, had worked closely with ordnance officers in pioneering the machinofacture of interchangeable parts. Besides highlighting the transition from craft to factory production and finding numerous applications in other technically related industries, the success of the American System underscored the importance of close-knit organization, mutual cooperation, and the cross-fertilization of ideas in the development of new methods. The acute conditions which followed the Civil War, however, appreciably altered, even reversed, this trend. With the discontinuance of the contract system and the consequent search for new markets, the last vestiges of openness and frequency of contact among arms makers virtually disappeared. Cutthroat competition, secretiveness, and intrigue became the order of the day. By the 1870s the arms industry had lost its integrated quality and ceased to be a dynamic force in American economic development.

Nowhere were the problems of the postwar era felt more severely than at government-owned installations. Since 1815 the Springfield Armory had made notable contributions to the mechanization of factory production and served as a clearinghouse for the acquisition and dissemination of all sorts of mechanical information. With the fall of the Confederacy the armory entered a period of technical amortization. Due primarily to tight budgetary constraints, but also to the fact that the machine-tool industry now possessed the ability to supply the mechanical needs of the age, a deemphasis on experimental work took place. Springfield gradually abdicated its position as a technical pacesetter and concentrated on the production of military firearms.

In many respects Springfield experienced a far gentler fate than the government's fifteen arsenals of construction. By 1867 hundreds of workers had been discharged from these establishments and production had come to a virtual standstill. The next few years brought further reductions, reaching a nadir with the Panic of 1873 and the depression which followed. By 1877 the situation had grown so serious that the War Department, in response to congressional inquiries, considered selling four of the five major arsenals on the east coast and confining manufacturing operations to one "grand arsenal" near New York City. Financial difficulties as well as a storm of political protest from the areas being affected forestalled implementation of this measure. Nevertheless, the War Department did dispose of fourteen smaller depots, either by direct sale or by transferral to other government agencies. Except for a trickle of goods from larger establishments such as Watervliet in upstate New York, the government arsenals confined their operations almost exclusively to the preservation and storage of military equipment.

For more than twenty years after the Civil War the Ordnance Department struggled to prevent serious impairment of the arsenal program. Yet, despite repeated pleas, protestations, and alternative proposals for financial relief, Alexander Dyer and his successor as Chief of Ordnance, Stephen V. Benet, utterly failed to loosen the purse strings of Congress. Deprived of adequate funding—indeed fighting to retain its staff and status as an independent army bureau—the fortunes of the Ordnance Department declined appreciably during the 1870s and 1880s. This, in turn, engendered a crisis of morale which drained the department of much of its vitality and *esprit de corps*. Uncertainty about the future, intensified by the lack of opportunity for advancement and constant rumors about imminent cutbacks in personnel, cast a "deadly pall" over departmental affairs.[6] Officers who only a few years earlier had engaged in significant research and entrepreneural activities became discouraged, cynical, and overly sensitive to outside criticism. In many cases thoughts of survival in an increasingly hostile environment seemed to absorb energies and derange daily routines. Experiments with various types of small arms and ferrous metals continued, but such work, having been divorced from the activities of private industry, moved haltingly and only so far as strict budgetary limitations would allow.

The results of this mélange of confusion, tension, and uncertainty became openly manifest during the Spanish-American War. To those charged with supplying the needs of over 260,000 men, nothing about the conflict seemed "splendid." By 1898 the United States lagged nearly a decade behind the military technology of Europe. The three most important developments of the age—magazine rifles, breech-loading steel artillery, and smokeless propellants—were only just beginning to be produced in large quantities at government arsenals and were not widely distributed among American troops until after the fighting had ended. Only regulars, for example, were issues new .30 caliber Krag-Jorgensen bolt-action rifles. The great majority of volunteers—some 200,000 strong—carried single-shot, black-powder Springfields, an arm which dated back to the late 1860s.

Historians frequently claim that conservatism in the Ordnance Department and ignorance within the army were responsible for the antiquated weapons used during the Spanish-American War. Though not without foundation, such assertions tend to oversimplify the situation that existed in 1898. Throughout the nineteenth century the Ordnance Department had acted in a very slow and deliberate manner when confronted with the adoption of new inventions. To have done otherwise would have amounted to an utter disregard for the technical prerequisites of large-scale production and a denial of the principles of uniformity, simplicity, and solidarity for which the department stood. General George Ripley's opposition to Abraham Lincoln's "champagne experiments" during the Civil War is often cited as a classic case of ordnance conservatism toward change. Yet one might well speculate about what would have happened to the Union supply system had Ripley indiscriminately introduced every invention brought to his attention by the President. Clearly the costs of such ventures would have been prohibitively expensive, to say nothing of how the proliferation of different model arms and ammunition would have complicated and, more likely than not, impaired the maintenance of uniform standards, quality control, and repair work in the field. In any event, there is no indication that members of the Ordnance Department opposed the introduction of breech-loading artillery, repeating small arms, smokeless powder, or other advances in weapons technology during the decades which followed the Civil War. If anything, they attempted to promote their adoption among comrades in the army who were skeptical of new and unfamiliar ideas. The real problem centered on resources rather than attitudes. Between 1869 and 1889 the Chief of Ordnance had to bow and scrape for every penny appropriated. Little could be done about developing, testing, and perfecting new inventions. There simply was not enough money. In this sense, the tight-fistedness of Congress rather than the narrow-mindedness of the Ordnance Office explains the armaments debacle of 1898.

Hard times breed pessimism, but frequently such experiences sharpen introspection which, in turn, can alter previous patterns of behavior. Such was the case with the United States Army between 1865 and 1914. Confronted with public indifference and lack of financial support, the military turned inward upon itself in search of new values and a strengthened sense of identity. It is more than just coincidence that the Ordnance Department's research and development activities slackened at a time when professional consciousness was beginning to emerge within the military establishment. While the officer corps affirmed its professional status, the theoretical structure of military "science" shifted from an emphasis on engineering to an emphasis on command. This was to have far-reaching implications not only for ordnance research and arms making but also for the entire spectrum of civil-military relations.

One of the earliest indications of impending change in military orientation occurred in 1866 when the Corps of Engineers relinquished exclusive control over the affairs of the United States Military Academy. Thereafter West Point's curriculum focused more on the art of war and less on technical and scientific training. The Academy, as one superintendent succinctly stated, was "no longer a school of engineering" but rather "an institution for the purpose of national defense."[7] Such feelings soon found expression in the teachings and writings of John Bigelow, Peter S. Michie, Arthur L. Wagner, and Emory Upton, all of whom opted for the emerging concept of officership based on the German professional model. Sensitized to the importance of strategy, tactics, discipline, and training, members of the regular army became increasingly committed to questions of an organizational nature.

The professionalization movement, of course, was not unique to the military. One of the most notable features of late nineteenth-century America is that the communities of science, engineering, and business were all undergoing similar transformations at precisely the same time. Professionalism by its very nature implies specialization, a sense of identification with an organization, and a certain amount of bureaucratic control. Being separate entities within the military establishment, the Ordnance Department, Corps of Engineers, and other bureaus had always exhibited a sense of collegiality often found lacking within other branches of the army. The difference between the old professionalism and the new was that the latter aimed at wiping out annuated distinctions and joining the officer corps under an all-encompassing system of command. While officers of the line certainly stood to benefit from this arrangement, the advantages of abandoning old loyalties and adopting new ones seemed less apparent to the Ordnance Department. For one thing the bureau had to surrender a certain amount of autonomy and decision-making power. More subtle but equally important, the new professionalism subordinated science and engineering to the needs of the line and, in the words of one writer, "extinguished the once-vibrant spirit of teamwork" which had characterized military-industrial relations since the days of George Bomford.[8] As the interests of national security increased and attitudes changed, the benefits of military technology found fewer and fewer applications in the civilian marketplace.

By 1900 the day of the soldier-technologist, well versed in science and committed to its peacetime uses, had largely disappeared. So too had the Jeffersonian notion of the military as subservient to civilian economic needs.

While the professional ethos gained a firmer foothold within military circles, the United States was rapidly emerging as an industrial power with expansive interests in international affairs. If most Americans sensed rather than recognized this prior to 1898, the war with Spain and the diplomatic events of the next nineteen years clearly fixed the country's new world role in public consciousness. Between 1900 and 1917 the army, mainly through the efforts of Elihu Root and Henry Stimson in the War Department and Leonard Wood as Chief of Staff, underwent a major reorganization aimed at transforming it into an effective fighting machine. During the same period the government's arsenals experienced a mild revival, though congressional appropriations fell far short of providing the support necessary for retooling and modernizing their operations. The five largest installations suffered chronically from obsolete equipment and rundown facilities. A survey taken in 1909 at the Watertown Arsenal near Boston, Massachusetts, for example, revealed that 40 percent of the machine tools in one shop were designed for carbon tool steels which dated back fifteen years or more. Machinery in other establishments could be traced as far back as the Civil War. The Springfield Armory was an exception, but neither Watertown nor its sister arsenals at Watervliet, New York, at Rock Island, Illinois, and at Frankford, Pennsylvania, were equipped for large-scale production on the eve of the First World War. One superintendent went so far as to characterize them as essentially jobbing shops whose work capacity did not extend beyond short-run requirements. Private firms such as the Bethlehem and Midvale Steel companies, of course, could and did supplement this work. Nevertheless, when the United States entered the First World War, only minimal preparations had been made for the conflict.

America's experience during World War I provides an apt illustration of how the momentum of technological change can alter existing institutional arrangements within a society. At least two generations had witnessed the lethal effectiveness of the machine gun and the precision fire of rifled artillery, but their amalgamation with automatic small arms, motorized tanks, aircraft, and other twentieth-century innovations formed an even deadlier combination, so different in degree as to constitute a difference in kind. By 1917, when the United States entered the conflict, the widespread use of mechanized weaponry had completely revolutionized the nature of warfare. Compared with earlier eras, military technology had become large, complex, and very expensive. At the same time the industrial prerequisites for producing such equipment had assumed far different proportions; so different, in fact, that traditional army procurement agencies could not effectively cope with the problems generated by massive mobilization.

Out of the wartime crisis emerged a new alignment between government and industry in which private businessmen played an active decision-making role. Such an arrangement contrasted sharply with former practices. For more than one hundred years the Ordnance Department and other army agencies had exercised exclusive control over the selection of contractors and the allocation of contracts. Under the new system adopted in 1917, however, civilians now shared in planning the munitions for war. Although military authorities swallowed this pill with trepidation, its bitterness was sweetened somewhat by the fact that the system worked. Nonetheless, the new military-industrial combination exacted a price. Quite unintentionally national defense had assumed a corporate character, subject to many of the same pressures of bureaucratization, centralization, and politicization found in other sectors of American economic life. Ironically the Ordnance Department, having done so much to foster the development of mass-production technology, became one of its earliest victims.

NOTES

1. Quoted by Robert S. Woodbury, "The Legend of Eli Whitney and Interchangeable Parts," *Technology and Culture* vol. 1, (1960), p. 239.
2. Ibid., p. 247. See also Edwin A. Battison, "Eli Whitney," in *Those Inventive Americans* (Washington, D. C., National Geographic Society, 1971), pp. 59-61.
3. *American State Papers: Military Affairs*, 2: 553.
4. Lee to Senior Officer of Ordnance, November 20, 1817, Letters Received, Record Group 156, Records of the Office of the Chief of Ordnance, National Archives, Washington, D. C.
5. Quoted by Robert V. Bruce, *Lincoln and the Tools of War* (Indianapolis, The Bobbs-Merrill Co., 1956), pp. 276-77.
6. Stephen V. Benet, comp., *A Collection of Ordnance Reports and Other Important Papers Relating to the Ordnance Department,* 4 vols. (Washington, D. C., Government Printing Office, 1890), vol 3, pp. 495.
7. U. S., Congress, Senate, *Report of the Commission . . . to Examine Into the Organization, System of Discipline, and Course of Instruction of the United States Military Academy at West Point,* 36th Cong., 2d Sess., 13 December 1860, S. Misc. Doc. No. 3, p. 148.
8. Clarence G. Lasby, "Science and the Military," in *Science and Society in the United States,* David D. Van Tassel and Michael G. Hall, eds., (Homewood, Ill., The Dorsey Press, 1966), p. 258.

JOHANNES R. LISCHKA

ARMOR PLATE: NICKEL AND STEEL, MONOPOLY AND PROFIT

In a basic sense, the military-industrial complex has existed as long as there were men who specialized in the fabrication of arms, and men who specialized in using those arms in combat. However, in the past twenty years, government and private concern about the relationship of defense contractors and the military establishment in the United States has increased markedly. This concern is real. It arose, to a large extent, from the fact that gigantic corporations built complicated weapons systems in close co-ordination with the military services at ever-mounting costs to taxpayers; and also from the fact that new weapons systems may be obsolete as soon as they have become operational, setting off a new round of appropriations, coordination, and spending.

Such matters relating to the military-industrial complex have been debated by academics, politicians, businessmen, military apologists, and clergymen. It is only recently that historians have sought to explain the origin of the military-industrial complex. Research to date tends to confirm the beginning of the complex in the period between 1862 and 1902, when the first armored vessels fought a naval battle and when the true prototypes of modern warships were completed. Throughout this period naval officers, industrialists, and congressmen had to create solutions to problems that were new and technologically challenging. The political and even the military questions are answered elsewhere.[1] It is the problem of technology, industrial combination, and profits that are of concern in this chapter.

Shortly after 1918 a great public outcry arose in the United States against the industrial complex that created the weapons used in World War I. These modern weapons had proved to be highly efficient killers of men. In the microcosm of the European trench war and self-contained battleship, the full impact of this efficiency could be seen by all who survived. Part of the outcry was directed toward a suspected worldwide syndicate of weapons manufacturers who were called collectively the "merchants of death." No one, however, seemed to have access to statistics that would prove the accusation of the protestors, and the manufacturers were silent on the matter. Their patience outlasted the criticism, and in 1936 Bethlehem Steel Company won a lawsuit brought against it by the Federal Government for "unconscionable profits on World War I contracts."[2] The outcry was stilled. And now a modern author can write:

The growing consumption of plates and sheets for other products than nails did not excite much comment as there was no spectacular product to be watched. They were used for one quite specialized use, which could not have used much steel although it generated a lot of excitement. This use was armor plate, and unlike the other types of plates, armor plate was a heavy product requiring heavy machinery to make. Entry was limited to the field of armor makers, . . . only the government was in the market for this product . . . a situation of bilateral monopoly was created between the government and armor makers which gave rise to much acrimonious debate. It may be wondered that anyone went into such a business, but considerations of national pride and national defense made the government supply inducements to a few steel manufacturers to make armor. . . .
The difficulty of making this kind of steel and the cost of the plant required may be gauged from the contract price of $536 per ton . . .and Congress became uneasy about the price. There followed a long series of negotiations, some double-dealing, and probably some cheating on contracts. But all that can be seen at this distance is the smoke of battle, not its precise outlines. . . .
Fortunately, the armor controversy was not of great importance. . . .[3]

Similarly, Bernard Brodie, writing in 1942 held:

The Krupp process called for enormously more care and accuracy in fabrication and more expensive materials. Consequently . . . the American armor producing companies offered to furnish it to the United States Navy at $545 per ton . . . .
One of the reasons for the high price of American armor was that a change in Navy Department specifications might require the scrapping of machinery which had only recently been provided. A million-dollar steam hammer at the Bethlehem Company was made virtually useless after it had been used to make only 5,000 tons of armor, because the government demanded that armor to be forged by press instead of hammer. The steel companies, therefore, sought to secure out of initial contracts both a complete amortization of their investment in equipment and a reasonable profit.[4]

Full disclosure of the question of armor and armaments manufacturers is not available, but some answers can be given now that were not within the scope of the protestors of 1918. Investigations reveal an interconnection of steel manufacturers, nickel monopoly, financial manipulation on both sides of the Atlantic, innovations, military need, and issues of national security. The reward of this complex of interconnections was millions of dollars in profits on the one hand, and the establishment of the United States as a major world, military, and industrial power on the other hand.

The question properly begins with the race in the late nineteenth century between the ordnance makers and armor makers. The armored vessel of war had been built prior to the famous battle of the *Monitor* and the *Merrimac* during the American Civil War; but this battle was the first war test of such vessels. The success of armor in that contest could not be argued, and naval engineers began using the concept of armor on all new warships with "sometimes bizarre styles in naval architecture."[5] The armor plate used was of wrought iron covering a wooden ship. This protection proved effective against the smooth-bore ship and shore guns of the time which used solid, round projectiles. Wrought iron was tough on impact by virtue of the large size and texture of its crystalline structure, but this trait also made it easy to puncture with a pointed projectile; and the next development was the rifled naval gun firing a conical, pointed shell.

The first rifled naval guns were only four-inch guns shooting a thirty-three-pound shell, but these were sufficient to puncture wrought iron armor. The answer to this threat by armor manufacturers was composite armor, a mechanical sandwich of hard-steel face and wrought-iron inner side, still covering a wooden hull.[6] Although the steel might shatter under a direct hit from the new shells, the tough wrought iron could hold the impact and thus keep the hull from being punctured. The armorers then increased the size of the gun, the size of the projectile, and the amount of powder driving the shell.

These developments took place almost simultaneously, bringing about a superiority for the guns. By 1889, however, the French were experimenting with nickel steel, and the armaments firm of Schneider et Cié patented an armorplate process using 4 percent nickel added to steel. This addition of nickel gave the armor a 5 percent resistance to impact over the composite steel-wrought-iron plates.[7] Two American steel firms, the Bethlehem Iron Works and the Carnegie Steel Company, were licensed to produce the Schneider armor in the United States. Meanwhile H. A. Harvey, an American metallurgist, in 1891 patented a process whereby the exterior surface of the armor could be hardened for an inch of depth by placing the red-hot plate in contact with powdered carbon. The Harvey process for producing "cemented plate" increased the resistance of armor to twice that of wrought iron, and one-and-a-half times that of composite armor.[8]

Naval guns had by this time increased to 16.25 inches, firing armor-piercing and explosive shells of 1,800 pounds that were able to penetrate over 34 inches of wrought-iron armor at ranges in excess of 1,000 yards.[9]

The German Krupp works had perfected a decremental hardening method in 1894, whereby the cementing process on nickel steel was carried out very thoroughly on the face, while the inner surface of the plate was as tough and fibrous as wrought iron. This process was immediately adopted by the world's armor-plate makers.

Thus, by 1894, just thirty-two years after the *Monitor* and *Merrimac* battle was fought in 1862, the world's naval vessels had undergone greater change than at any prior period in history, and naval guns had reached a size and power that could not be enlarged because of recoil pressures on the vessel itself.

The race between ordnance and armor was virtually at an end, yet the right combination of armor thickness, ship size and speed, number, placement, and size of guns, were still problems that were being debated. All of this discussion provided those companies engaged in the armor-plate industry with an opportunity to make money, since the race was now between governments. The leaders competing to have the world's most modern navy included England, France, the United States, Germany, Japan, and Russia, but there were also many smaller nations buying warships; some only gunboats, but all using armor plate. Changes in armor and ordnance were assured in this new race for naval superiority. These changes also assured an increasing demand for nickel steel plate.

The world's armor-plate manufacturers and their suppliers of nickel for this product can be seen as two distinct groups for the period 1885–1901: the Canadian-American group and the French-European group.

Three United States companies were manufacturing armor plate in 1900. The Bethlehem Iron Works and Carnegie Steel Company began making armor as early as 1889, both having access to the Schneider nickel-steel patents. Midvale Steel Company entered the field in the late 1890s, selling armor only to the United States government, while the other two manufacturers had built a large export trade as well as receiving domestic contracts from the government.

All nickel used in United States production of armor was a product of the Sudbury Ontario mines, worked solely by the Canadian Copper Company. Nickel was discovered in Canada as early as 1856, but no mining was begun until the need for nickel had driven the world market price to $.60 a pound, thereby making the mining of the 4 percent nickel-content ores a profitable venture.[10] The increased demand was a result of the use of German silver as the basis for the electro-silver-plating industry that had been begun in a small way in Birmingham, England, in 1844, and as a result of the adoption of nickel for use in coins by many countries. Much speculative activity took place in the Sudbury area, but only the Canadian Copper Company

ultimately emerged with control of the mines and the market. The owners
of Canadian Copper Company were United States businessmen not connected with either the steel or nonferrous metal markets, but only interested
in a well-paying investment. The promoter of the corporation, S. J. Ritchie,
had been previously associated with lumbering interests in the carriage-
making trade, and was thus able to bring capital from men in these industries to back his mining venture.[11] Canadian Copper Company was originally
formed to mine copper, but the complex Sudbury ores, high in nickel content, could not be smelted by the methods of copper-ore smelting then
used. The Canadian ore required a new method, and thus a new plant for
economical recovery of the nickel and copper contained in it. Sudbury ores
were mixtures of sulphides and sulphates of iron, copper, and nickel. The
initial process after mining the ores was to deliver the ores to belt con-
veyors and . . .

After rocky material had been removed by hand-sorting on belts and
tables, the ore was taken. . .to the roast yards where most of the sulphur
was removed by its own combustion. This was done by piling heaps of ore
upon a foundation of cordwood sufficient to maintain a fire for about sixty
hours. The burning cordwood ignited the sulphur, which then continued to
burn, sometimes for three or four months or more, until all but ten or
eleven percent of the sulphur had been consumed. From the roast yard the
ore passed to the blast furnace, which removed further rocky matter, thereby increasing the proportions of copper and nickel in relation to the iron
and sulphur. The product of this [was] called "matte," consisting usually
of about thirty-five percent combined nickel and copper. . . .[12]

The directors of Canadian Copper began searching for a solution to
refining the Sudbury matte into copper and nickel. Their discussions led
them to believe that the answer was to be found in the United States, where
"Americans are so much more ready to alter their plant and undertake any
new thing of the kind than the Europeans, that . . . we shall be able to do
better in the United States."[13] The result of these deliberations was an
extraordinary contract entered into by Canadian Copper and the Orford
Copper Company in 1890. Canadian Copper was to supply all of its matte
to the Orford Company, which in turn would buy matte only from Canadian
Copper. Orford, under the progressive leadership of Robert M. Thompson,
had developed a successful method of refining the ore matte of the Canadian
mines, whereby all of the constituent elements were saved.[14] The contract,
to run for five years, was apparently entered into by Canadian Copper out
of necessity forced by the patented extraction method of Orford's, as
well as considerations of keeping the Sudbury district free of competition.
Under the contract, Canadian Copper could be assured that no other mining
company could have access to the Orford process, and therefore no mines
could be dug profitably in the region.

Orford, in turn, was supplying the United States armor-plate manufacturers with nickel under long-term contracts at a fixed price. These contracts kept the nickel accounts for the Canadian-American monopoly; and although world nickel prices fluctuated considerably during this period (1890-1900), the contract prices to the steel companies were firmly held.[15] Orford also sold matte (not refined nickel) to Joseph Wharton, an American refiner who had begun the Bethlehem Iron Works. Wharton's nickel production was being sold to Bethlehem, as well as overseas. Wharton's nickel was purer than that of Orford, and most of his production was being sold to Merton and Company in England for use in the German silver trade. It seems that his sales to Bethlehem were a consideration of his former connection with the company and also of the fact that he was not supplying enough nickel to make any appreciable difference to Orford. Hence, the relation between Wharton and Orford seems to have been good and no price-cutting seemed to have been present.

European armor manufacturers were being supplied with nickel by a French corporation, Le Nickel, which held a monopoly on the New Caledonian nickel ores. Le Nickel was financially controlled (as were the mines of New Caledonia), through stock and first-mortgage bonded indebtedness by the House of Rothschild, bankers whose influence also extended to many of the steel companies producing armor plate. The New Caledonian ores were being shipped to France as ore, with both the matte process and the refining being finished 12,000 miles from the mines. However, the monopoly position of Le Nickel and the financial control held by Rothschild closed out other sources from entry into this European market, and artificially supported prices for nickel could be held until 1896.[16]

British manufacturers of armor, as well as other users of nickel in Great Britain, received supplies from H. H. Vivian and Sons, Ltd., a refiner of smelting ores supplied by Le Nickel, and also by Henry Merton and Sons, Ltd., a wholesale metal sales agency that was selling refined nickel bought from Le Nickel and from Joseph Wharton. Both Merton and Vivian held the European prices established by Le Nickel. Unable to directly control the British market, Le Nickel maintained the artificial price of continental nickel quotations through indirect means by agreement with Wharton and by financial inducements extended by the Rothschilds in the form of assistance to the British suppliers.[17]

Thus a balance was reached about 1900 whereby European manufacturers were being supplied nickel by the French monopoly controlled by the Rothschilds and were supplying armor plate to their home governments and other European and foreign governments within their normal trade areas while American manufacturers were being supplied by the Canadian-American nickel monopoly and in turn selling armor plate to the United

States government and exporting to other nations in the United States sphere.

The situation changed rapidly, however, in both the nickel and armor-plate industries. The first change to take place was the sale of Canadian nickel in Europe. Mining and refining of Sudbury ores into finished nickel exceeded United States demands by 1895. Orford then began a price war with Le Nickel to dispose of overproduction. World prices fell from $.60 a pound in 1891 to a low of $.26 in 1896.[18] This price decline caused a substantial reduction of profit and stock-market value of Le Nickel shares. A secret agreement was arranged in 1896 between Orford and Le Nickel that conceded approximately one-third of the European market to Orford, that fixed the minimum price of nickel, and that named Merton and Sons as the sole agent for Canadian nickel on the Continent. This agreement, coming on a rising nickel demand, allowed continued increase of the Sudbury mining, and assured profit to both Le Nickel and Orford. The agreement was honored by both companies until it was canceled by the formation of the International Nickel Company in 1902.

European armor manufacturers formed a cartel in 1900 fixing the price of armor plate at about $540 per ton. This price was attractive to both Bethlehem and Carnegie, and they began actively bidding and selling to European governments. Considerable agitation ensued in the United States, since American firms were selling to the United States government at a price agreed to among themselves of between $500 and $600 a ton, while selling overseas at considerably less. Several investigations were undertaken by the government to determine the basis for this price discrepancy, and possibly much of the subsequent excess-profit controversy began as a result.[19]

Meanwhile, Andrew Carnegie, primary stockholder of the Carnegie Steel Company had tired of business and was seeking to sell his holdings. Carnegie, a Scottish immigrant to the United States, had parlayed a $2,500 investment in 1864 to a $500,000,000 steel company by 1900. One of the primary reasons for this success was the delegation of authority by Carnegie to capable and loyal men. Among the men managing the Carnegie Steel Company in 1900 were Charles M. Schwab, Henry C. Frick, Ambrose Monell, and William E. Corey.[20] These men were also stockholders in the Carnegie Steel Company. They therefore had a real interest in the future direction of the company when Carnegie sold his controlling interest. It was Schwab's idea, apparently pushed by Carnegie, that the company should be the integral part of a combination of other steel firms to form a holding company producing and selling all the products made of iron and steel.[21] This suggestion was conveyed on several occasions to John Pierpont Morgan, the most important banker in the United States; but Morgan was not interested in steel at that time. He had invested heavily in various railroads between 1870 and 1900, as well as having underwritten many bond issues for industry and governments. Morgan knew that the large capital requirements of the steel combination being discussed would exceed any that private industry had ever seen. He also knew that any combination as large as the one being suggested by the Carnegie executives would necessarily entail a large inflation of value (watering) of the stock to gain the stock transfers required by the transaction.[22] For several months in late 1900 Morgan remained unconvinced of the feasibility of the plan.

It has been held that Morgan was finally persuaded to accept the plan when Schwab gave an after-dinner speech on December 12, 1900, "and the youthful Carnegie president swept the financier off his feet and along with him in the flood of his oratory."[23] However the case may have been, Morgan was convinced that he could underwrite the transaction by the end of December. Carnegie agreed to sell his holdings through an exchange of Carnegie Steel stocks and bonds wholly in the bonds of the new corporation, and agreements were reached for the stock transfers of the other involved corporations. The combination, the United States Steel Corporation, with Schwab as president, was incorporated under the laws of New Jersey on February 25, 1901, with all agreed-to stock transfers completed by March 29, 1901.

The total capitalization of the new corporation was $1.4 billion, a very large amount for the time. Of this capitalization about one-half was inflated value, and J. P. Morgan Company as underwriters received a paper profit of just under $100 million for its services.[24] U. S. Steel was a totally integrated company. It produced steel from the mines to finished, assembled product, owning all of the mines, transportation, furnaces, mills, machine shops, and warehouses necessary to its products.

The important point is that United States Steel now owned the Homestead Works of the Carnegie Steel Company, one of the three plants in the United States producing plate. This plant continued to produce armor plate, but capacity was greatly increased. The Morgan bankers now had control of almost one-half the armor-plate capability of the United States.

On March 28, 1902, one year after the formation of U. S. Steel, the International Nickel Company was formed under the New Jersey Holding Company Act. The new company was funded on an authorized capital of $24,000,000 in stock, both preferred and common, and $12,000,000 in 5-percent-first-mortgage bonds. The business of the company was to exchange International Nickel stock for the outstanding stock of the Canadian Copper Company, the Orford Copper Company, the American Nickel Works, the Anglo-American Iron Company, the Vermillion Mining Company, the Nickel Corporation Ltd., and Sociéte Miniéré. These seven corporations enjoyed an absolute monopoly on the Canadian nickel ores and the Canadian-

American nickel production as well as a part of the New Caledonian ore fields and a share of the European nickel market. In the stock transfer that was effected under the laws of the corporation, $8,912,626.09 was exchanged in 6-percent preferred stock; $8,912,626.09 in common stock; and $9,890,836.51 in first-mortgage bonds, or a total paper transaction of $27,716,088.69.[25]

The only two companies operating at the time of acquisition were the Canadian Copper Company and the Orford Company. Their joint value at the time of stock transfer was approximately $10,000,000. The rest of the capital stock was paper value (water) that was injected into the transaction by the funding underwriters, J. P. Morgan and Company. It can thus be seen that Morgan was able to control the new nickel corporation with no cost to himself, and a net paper profit of about $7,000,000.[26] By early 1902 the Morgan interests held control of the Canadian-American nickel industry as well as the Homestead armor-plate mill.

The next link in the chain of the Morgan control over the armor-plate industry is not as clear as the two cited. In the fall of 1901, while still president of United States Steel, Schwab bought Bethlehem Steel Company for $7,500,000, apparently in order to realize profits in a merger of several steel companies proposed by E. H. Harriman. This merger never materialized, and "realizing that his position as president of one steel company and owner of a competing concern was an ambiguous one, he asked. . .J. P. Morgan to take the property off his hands at the price he had paid for it. This Morgan consented to."[27] The following spring Schwab repurchased Bethlehem from Morgan for $10,000,000 and sold it through a stock transfer to the United States Shipbuilding Company, a holding company organized to unite a number of companies for shipbuilding much as U. S. Steel had been organized to produce steel. Under the transfer agreement Schwab received $10,000,000 in preferred stock, $10,000,000 in common stock and $10,000,000 in first-mortgage bonds—or a paper profit of $20,000,000—an indication that there was over two-thirds water in the stock of the ship-building company.

Schwab resigned as president of United States Steel in April, 1902. It has been held that he was not satisfied with the job because of the restraints imposed on the presidency by the huge size of the company and the necessity of group decisions on all vital points of policy. There is, however, also an indication that he was in poor health and simply wanted to retire and rest.

On July 1, 1903, the United States Shipbuilding Company was declared bankrupt. Schwab was particularly involved, because his bond holdings made him the chief creditor of the comapny. The various companies of the defunct shipbuilding corporation were organized into a new holding company, the Bethlehem Steel Corporation, formed on December 10, 1904.

Bethlehem Steel was now funded with a capital of $15,000,000 in preferred stock, $15,000,000 in common stock, and $3,000,000 in bonds. Shareholders and bondholders of the shipbuilding corporation were able to exchange shares with the new company at less than par. It is obvious that some of the water was thus shaken out of the shipbuilding holdings (as well as all of the creditors except the original bondholders of Bethlehem Steel Company), but the new corporations's stock was still about one-half water.[28]

Schwab assumed the presidency of Bethlehem Steel Corporation at this time, and built it into an armaments enterprise that was ultimately "the American Krupp works."[29] There is no further indication that Morgan controlled Bethlehem *directly*, but the connection of Schwab to U. S. Steel, to the Homestead Works where he was manager until 1897, and to the resources of J. P. Morgan and Company cannot be denied.

The final link in the control of the armor industry by Morgan was the purchase of the Midvale Steel Company in September, 1915. Midvale had been producing armor since the 1890s, but was selling only to the United States government because the president of the corporation had two daughters, one of whom was married to an Englishman and the other to a German. No matter to which of these countries he might sell armor, he would be sure to offend a family member.[30]

The purchase of Midvale was officially made by W. E. Corey (former president of U. S. Steel), Ambrose Monell (president of International Nickel), A. C. Dinkey (president of Carnegie Steel Division of United States Steel), and H. C. Frick (former president of the Carnegie Steel Company). Dinkey became president of Midvale Steel Company, while Corey became president of the Midvale Steel and Ordnance Company, the parent holding company composed of the Midvale Steel Company, the Worth Brothers Iron Company, and the Remington Arms Company.[31] The new holding company began at once to build armor and armaments for the allied countries in Europe. The enterprise was formed because the mills of both Bethlehem and U. S. Steel were behind on war-goods orders and Midvale had already been engaged in the armor business, although on a limited basis.

There seems to be little question that the funding of the new armaments company was underwritten by J. P. Morgan and Company. Midvale Steel had been a useful competitor to the other two companies. It had been allowed to take part in profitable United States government contracts, and did not interfere with export trade, yet it had, by example, proven that no monopoly existed in the armor industry.

A similar example can be shown in the nickel industry. While International Nickel held a monopoly when it was formed in 1902, a new company was being started by Ludwig Mond, a British chemical manufacturer. Mond had discovered and patented a new process of nickel refining while engaged in chemical research in 1889. His process, using a previously unknown reaction between carbon monoxide and nickel, was more efficient than the Orford process, but he was unsuccessful in attempts to market it to either Canadian Copper or to Orford. His demands in stock and cash would have amounted to control of either corporation and were thus rejected.[32] By 1902 Mond Nickel Company had been organized and had bought mining properties in the Sudbury district. Mond's efforts were not restricted in any way by International Nickel; in fact, he was offered as much of the market at the then-current price as he could fill. It seems that Mond proved to be a useful competitor. His production was small compared to International's, yet his presence in the industry was used time after time to prove that there was no monopoly held by International Nickel.[33]

Both Mond and International Nickel sold their product overseas through Merton and Sons, and a connection existed between Merton, International, Morgan, and Rothschild; but the lines of connection are not clear. In 1902, before Monell had been chosen, Charles Schwab offered the presidency of International Nickel to Henry Gardner, a partner of Merton and Sons, "the wise and trusted advisor and friend of the successive heads of International Nickel, particularly in the shaping of European Commercial policies."[34]

It can be seen from all of the above cases that J. P. Morgan and Company controlled the United States armor-plate industries as well as the nickel supplies vital to them. Morgan's control was financial and the rewards were great. In each case shown it can be seen that Morgan and Company realized very large profits from the underwriting of various industrial combinations. Much more money was earned, however, through the growth in value of the common and preferred shares in the corporations under Morgan's control. This growth in value was a direct reflection of the profits earned.

It is worthwhile to look at these profits for the years 1903–18. Table 1 lists the profits for International Nickel.

Because of the great need for nickel-steel armor in World War I, it can be seen that profits rose correspondingly in the later years. The total profits shown need to be compared to the actual investment of International Nickel of $9,800,000.00 For the total period average annual net profits are computed to be 51 percent of the investment using 12¢ per pound base, and 75 percent of the investment using the 18¢ per pound base.[35]

Table 2 lists the profits of the armor-plate manufacturers. These include Bethlehem, United States Steel, and Midvale. Once again, the wartime needs are reflected in the increases in tonnage and profit to be noted from 1914–18.

For these three corporations the actual investment was $728,000,000 in the period studied. This investment includes all of the facilities of the corporation: those used for armor as well as those used for all other steel production, because no separate amounts have been published for various

Table 1.

Nickel Production in pounds, International Nickel with profits realized. (Earnings are approximate)

Year	Pounds of Nickel[a]	Profit @ 12¢[b]	Profit @ 18¢[c]
1903	14,000,000	$ 1,680,000	2,540,000
1904	10,000,000	1,200,000	1,800,000
1905	20,000,000	2,400,000	3,600,000
1906	22,000,000	2,640,000	3,960,000
1907	22,000,000	2,640,000	3,960,000
1908	20,000,000	2,400,000	3,600,000
1909	26,000,000	3,120,000	4,680,000
1910	38,000,000	4,560,000	6,840,000
1911	34,000,000	4,080,000	6,120,000
1912	44,000,000	5,280,000	7,920,000
1913	50,000,000	6,000,000	9,000,000
1914	46,000,000	5,520,000	8,280,000
1915	64,000,000	7,680,000	11,520,000
1916	82,000,000	9,840,000	14,760,000
1917	84,000,000	10,080,000	15,120,000
1918	92,000,000	11,040,000	16,560,000

Notes: a. The production figures are from Main, *Canadian*, pp. 62,65. His figures are given in tons. These have been changed into pounds to allow for the computation.
b. The 12¢ per pound profit is the figure used by International in its dealings with governments, particularly with the Canadian government in the fight against taxes on exports.
c. The 18¢ a pound profit is computed by taking the average cost of the mining, smelting, and refining process and subtracting it from the average world selling prices for the period. Some years it may vary from these figures.

functions. For this reason, the average annual profit over the period based on Profit "A" (computed at a cost of $296.89 per ton) is only 18 percent of the investment, and Profit "B" (computed at a loss of $244.27 per ton) is only 36 percent of the investment. These profits would be presumably

Table 2.

U. S. Production of Armor Plate. Includes Bethlehem, U. S. Steel, Midvale Steel. Tonnage includes Domestic and Foreign sales. Profit is computed using only Domestic Price.

Year	Nickel (tons) in armor[a]	Total Armor Plate (tons)[b]	Profit "A"[c]	Profit "B"[d]
1903	4.5	1,125,000	$ 56,250,000	112,500,000
1904	2.5	625,000	31,250,000	62,500,000
1905	5.0	1,250,000	62,500,000	125,000,000
1906	5.5	1,375,000	68,750,000	137,500,000
1907	5.5	1,375,000	68,750,000	137,500,000
1908	5.0	1,250,000	62,500,000	125,000,000
1909	6.5	1,625,000	81,250,000	162,500,000
1910	9.5	2,375,000	118,750,000	237,500,000
1911	8.5	2,125,000	106,250,000	212,500,000
1912	11.0	2,750,000	137,500,000	275,000,000
1913	12.5	3,125,000	156,250,000	312,500,000
1914	11.5	2,875,000	143,750,000	287,500,000
1915	17.0	4,250,000	212,500,000	425,000,000
1916	20.5	5,125,000	256,250,000	512,500,000
1917	21.0	5,250,000	262,500,000	525,000,000
1918	23.0	5,750,000	287,500,000	575,000,000

Notes:

a. Armor tonnages are computed from nickel purchased by the corporations from International Nickel for the period. Actual production figures are unavailable but may vary from those shown.

b. A government survey in 1907 found that the production cost of armor was $244.27 per ton (profit B above); but held the "full cost" was $296.89 per ton (profit A above). Production cost "includes the price of all raw material, cost of labor, cost of upkeep of plant, the current repairs, salaries of superintendents, and interest on capital. Full cost includes in addition taxes, insurance, and a host of items which cannot be readily itemized." (Berglund, "The U. S. Steel Corporation," pp. 146-48). The columns above reflect these two "costs."

c. An average selling price of $346.00 a ton is assumed. Prices varied from $545.00 and up in the early period, but leveled out to near the average in 1907 and remained fairly constant after that date.

d. The above totals include exported armor plate, and much of the exported armor sold for more than the average used here. Current world prices paid for armor in 1907: (Krupp Cemented Plate)

Japan	$400.00	France	$572.00
Austria	557.00	England	681.00
Italy	550.00	U S A	346.00
Germany	450.00		

much higher were we to have access to the total investment of only armor facilities within the corporations. Even at the rates of return on investment shown above, however, the corporations engaged in armor manufacture show rates of approximately twice the national average of 7 percent to 9 percent for all industries over the period.

Looking at these figures, it is apparent that the nickel-steel cartel was effective in its control of the armor industry, and that it was thus able to command large profits from government contracts. While a sum of this profit was paid to shareholders in dividends, a far larger amount was retained by the corporations as reserves and for new plant. It seems that the large profits from the armor trade stabilized the value of the common and preferred stocks of the corporations, and brought the par and book values together. This tended to remove the large amounts of paper value that had been injected into the corporations when they were formed.

After 1918 all three of the combinations underwritten by J. P. Morgan and Company, United States Steel, Bethlehem Steel, and International Nickel were in good financial condition. Much public controversy over the large profits continued, however, leading directly to the Budget and Accounting Act of 1921. This Act set up a system of defense-contract inspection and negotiation, set up an excess profits tax, and set up a reorganization of contract policies. It effectively limited cartel abuses in subsequent defense spending. It seems doubtful that United States manufacturers or bankers will again realize profits as large as those realized in the armor industry. But without the profits in the period of 1903-18 the corporations studied would have been in financial difficulty. The large amount of inflated value of their stocks, had it not been removed by the war profits, would have caused a lack of public confidence and possibly insolvency during the Depression of 1929. This did not happen, and the steel corporations, America's largest industries, survived the Depression. Thus, the merchants of death served an important function in the economic maturity of United States industry.

NOTES

1. See especially B. Franklin Cooling, "The Formative Years of the Naval-Industrial Complex: Their Meaning for Studies of Institutions Today," *Naval War College Review*, XXVII, March/April, 1975, pp. 53-61.
2. See article on "Charles Michael Schwab," in *Dictionary of American Biography*, XXII, p. 603.

3. Peter Temin, *Iron and Steel in Nineteenth Century America* (Cambridge, Massachusetts, The M. I. T. Press, 1964), pp. 228-29.
4. Bernard Brodie, *Sea Power in the Machine Age,* (Princeton, N. J., Princeton University Press, 1941), pp. 129, 237-38.
5. Cooling, op. cit., p. 54.
6. Brodie, op. cit., p. 218.
7. The usual proportions in modern nickel steel are: .35 to .5 percent carbon, 3.5 to 4 percent nickel, 1.5 to 2.5 percent chromium, .4 percent manganese and .15 percent silicon. O. W. Main, *The Canadian Nickel Industry* (Toronto, Canada, University of Toronto Press, 1955), p. 19.
8. Cemented armor could be made from either nickel steel or merely carbon steel. According to Brodie, there was a price difference of $145 a ton between the two (p. 219). This is possibly explained by the many more steps of manufacture required by the nickel steel- - -these were, "casting the low carbon ingot, stripping the ingot, removing the scale, rough-machining, carbonizing, scaling, reforging, annealing, machining, bending, tempering, rectifying, finish machining, and erecting"; in all 14 operations. Louis E. Brown, "Millions for Naval Armor- -The Remedy," *Scientific American,* 109,110 (August, 1913).
9. Brodie, op. cit, p. 222.
10. Main, op. cit., p. 33 ff.
11. D. M. Le Bourdais, *Sudbury Basin* (Toronto, Canada, The Ryerson Press, 1953).
12. Ibid., pp. 49-50.
13. Main, op. cit. p. 16.
14. John F. Thompson and Norman Beasley, *For Years to Come: A Story of International Nickel of Canada* (New York, G. P. Putnam's Sons, 1960), pp. 81-101.
15. Typical of the price quotation reports of the period; "The price of refined nickel in New York remained practically constant throughout the year—the quotation being 'large lots, contract business, 40 to 45 cents per pound. Retail spot from 50 cents for 500 pound lots up to 55 cents for 200 pound lots.'" *Canadian Engineer,* 20, 447 (January-June, 1911).
16. Main, op. cit., p. 19. There is ample evidence that a close connection existed between the Rothschilds and J. P. Morgan, but only hints are found, no clearcut definition of the connection. See in particular Horace L. Wilgus, *A Study of the United States Steel Corporation in its Industrial and Legal Aspects* (Chicago, Callaghan & Company, 1901), p. 8, and F. L. Allen, *The Great Pierpont Morgan* (New York, Harper & Brothers, 1949), pp. 38, 116-18, 223.
17. Main, op cit., p. 19. See also Thompson and Beasley, op. cit.
18. Ibid., p. 37.
19. Abraham Berglund, "The United States Steel Corporation," in *Columbia University Studies in History, Economics, and Public Law,* XXVII, no. 2 (New York, The Columbia University Press, 1907), pp. 145-49.
20. The development of the Carnegie system of management selection, as well as short biographies of these men is found in James H. Bridge, *The Carnegie Millions and the Men Who Made Them* (London: Limpus, Baker & Company, 1903).
21. Arundel Cotter, *The Authentic History of the United States Steel Corporation* (New York, The Moody Magazine and Book Company, 1916), p. 14.
22. The New Jersey Holding Company Act of 1889 allowed the formation of large combinations. All those combinations in this chapter were organized under this Act. Allen, op. cit., pp 158-160.
23. Cotter, op. cit., p. 15.
24. Morgan's profit came in three ways: payment in stock for the underwriting, commission on other stock transactions, and commission earned in a second bond issue of $50 million that was issued in May 1902. Cotter, op. cit., pp. 50-51.

25. Thompson and Beasley, op. cit., p. 143.
26. Main, op. cit., p. 45.
27. Arundel Cotter, *The Story of Bethlehem Steel* (New York, The Moody Magazine and Book Company, 1916), p. 6.
28. Ibid., pp. 10-12.
29. See article on "Charles Michael Schwab," in *Dictionary of American Biography,* XXII, p. 602.
30. "The Steel Trust's New Rivals," *The Literary Digest,* 51 (July-December, 1915), p. 948. The president of Midvale was not named in the article.
31. Ibid., p. 947.
32. Johannes R. Lischka, "Ludwig Mond and the British Alkali Industry: A Study in the Interrelations of Science, Engineering, Education, Industry, and Government," unpublished Ph. D. dissertation, Duke University, 1970, pp. 197-99.
33. Main, op. cit., p. 67.
34. Thompson and Beasley, op. cit., p. 145.
35. My colleagues in Economics and Finance have urged me to calculate the return on investment by using the present value formula:

$$I = \frac{1}{(1 + i)^n} \; ;$$

however, the discount (i) would have to be quite large for the profits shown, and depreciation and the time value of money in the period studies are not as important as they are today. My thanks to Dr. James Rinehart and Dr. Richard Wallace, Francis Marion College.

HENRY C. FERRELL, JR.

REGIONAL RIVALRIES, CONGRESS, AND M I C; THE NORFOLK AND CHARLESTON NAVY YARDS, 1913–20

In the twentieth century, a diverse set of causes prompted the predominately agrarian southern states to acquire the manufacturing and supply facilities that eventually realized the present large share of federal military expenditures. On occasion, to obtain the necessary investment capital, the skilled personnel, and continuing federal contracts, coordination was required between private corporations and congressional leadership. However, in the expansion of navy yards at Norfolk, Virginia, and Charleston, South Carolina, politicians, embodying arguments of frugality, efficiency, and avoidance of "greedy capitalists who have the Government by the throat...," utilized federal funds contrary to the desires of private corporate interests to construct federally owned manufacture and service complexes that employed federal salaries to train and maintain an adequate labor force.[*]

Among the congeries of factors that emerged during the years 1913 and 1920 to enlarge federal navy yards at Norfolk and Charleston, United States Senators Benjamin Tillman and Claude Swanson provided the primary political catalyst. The 1912 election of Woodrow Wilson led these southerners prematurely to anticipate prompt application of patronage to both cities. However, before the schemes of commercial and realty elements within these venerable South Atlantic ports became a reality, Tillman and

(*) A shorter version of this chapter was presented at the thirty-seventh annual meeting of the Southern Historical Association, November 18, 1971. The author gratefully acknowledges the critical suggestions offered him by Professor Joseph F. Steelman of East Carolina University and Professor Monroe Billington of New Mexico State University.

59

Swanson needed to dominate the decision processes that molded national naval policy. They contrived positions of influence through the formation of a regional alliance, founded upon the willingness of the Secretary of the Navy, North Carolinian Josephus Daniels, to cooperate with his neighboring politicians. This compact and its insuing achievements support the contention that the national Progressive Movement was in part a series of regional struggles for competitive advantage within the framework of the federal government.

Concurrently, having attained influential contacts within the Navy Department, Tillman and Swanson blended their views on the proper role of government and decisively influenced the course of the naval renaissance during the Wilson Administration. Motivated by a populistic mistrust of private corporations, in concert with Daniels, they argued that government manufacture be developed as the basic supply source for the navy. It was fortunate for the projects of both senators that their general arguments supported their particular contentions for government manufacture to enhance the navy installations at Norfolk and Charleston.

The phases of naval development during the presidency of Woodrow Wilson directly affected the promotion of the Norfolk and Charleston yards. Partisan and factional politics dominated the first phase from 1913 through 1914, that featured the Navy Department as merely a fresh federal patronage source, denied the Democrats by constantly recurring Republican congressional majorities and presidents. During the second period, 1915 to 1917, the prospect of being imminently awash in the chilling tide of a general Europea war compelled an evolving solicitude for naval planning that denied Tillman and Swanson the luxury of indulging in their parochial political pursuits, but permitted the opportunity to shape grander designs from which Norfolk and Charleston might benefit. Events moved them to embrace a national perspective with respect to naval policy that encouraged them to advocate government industries to meet the emergency. The final years, from 1917 to 1920, covered American participation in World War I and its immediate aftermath in which the plans of the second period were initiated, altered, and eventually abandoned in the detritus of war.

At the time of Woodrow Wilson's presidential election, Benjamin Tillman, South Carolina's senior senator, calmly anticipated the award of either the chairmanship of the Senate Interstate Commerce Committee or Committee on Appropriations. Tillman, in his sixty-sixth year, suffered infirmities that partially muted his "pitchfork" tongue, but, as Francis Simpkins has emphasized, his pen still sparked with the rudeness that reflected "the genuine rustic" qualities of his nature. Having witnessed in the Senate the efficiency of Republican organization, he assumed that the Democrats could perform as smoothly in their majority position with a Democratic president. However, following the summer of Wilson's nomination, a "chaotic condition" developed within the Senate, owing in part "to the retirement of the old leaders and the failure of new ones to appear. . . ." Tillman mistrusted the younger, grasping Democratic senators as he did business interests or the Republican party. He conjectured that these young "jackasses" had "played the Devil" in the organizing caucus, but his senatorial associate, Thomas Staples Martin of Virginia, jolted the one-eyed South Carolinian by bartering the majority leader's post for chairmanship of the Committee on Appropriations. Tillman salvaged from the wreck of his hopes the chairmanship of the inconsequential Naval Affairs Committee, and thoroughly aroused against the schemers sponsoring Norfolk Navy Yard as well as those of northern bases, he cynically renewed his determination to outfit Charleston with a "first-class" navy yard.

Aware of Tillman's disgruntlement toward Virginia, the state's junior senator, Claude A. Swanson, as the third-ranking Democrat on Tillman's naval committee, ardently pursued political credits in the Virginia Tidewater by maintaining and expanding, if possible, the Norfolk naval base. Despite only three years in the Senate, the suave fifty-one-year old politician had been a congressman from 1893 to 1906 and a leader of the free-silver movement in Virginia, associated with the William Jennings Bryan wing of the party. As governor of Virginia, Swanson had demonstrated an exceptional ability to handle legislative bodies and fashioned a series of significant reforms. His sponsorship of a rural free delivery of mail and federal aid to highway construction, as well as a political stance opposed to the machinations of corporations exemplified his rural origins. His breeziness often misled usually shrewd observers when calculating the depth of his intellect and the texture of his sagacity. An extremely ingratiating person, Swanson most efficiently accomplished political projects in Washington by directly contacting reluctant bureaucrats. However, despite Thomas Martin's benevolent concern on appropriations, Swanson apprehensively considered the prospects of Norfolk Navy Yard upon assessing the attitudes of Tillman and the new Secretary of the Navy, Josephus Daniels.

Daniels had very little firsthand knowledge of the navy. As a successful editor he possessed few attachments with corporate interests that had permeated the naval politics of the previous Taft administration, and his progressive leanings, carried from North Carolina to Washington, were intensified by national politics. Distrustful of business influences, Daniels would reject what he assumed to be their agents, "machine" politicians, both groups having convinced him of their perfidy during the 1912 presidential campaign. Temporarily holding similar grievances, Wilson instructed his navy secretary that political appointees be not only Democrats but that their birthplace, residence, "the wing of the party" and politicians with whom they had been "affiliated" be additional considerations. As a preconvention sponsor of Champ Clark, Swanson had been roughly handled by insurgent Virginia Democrats who identified with Wilson's candidacy and who labeled Swanson and Martin "machine" politicians. These elements now surged forward to post claims for patronage prizes. Virginia's senators feared their influence and scrambled in the Senate for defensive positions. These circumstances had encouraged Martin to seize the Appropriations Committee over Tillman's aspirations. Developing factionalism within the party created more stormy moments among Democratic senators and, after three months of feuding, Tillman observed that every day demonstrated "more and more that the Democrats in the Senate are almost helpless in the hands of the Republicans because of lack of leadership."

Disorganization of the majority party disturbed the committees in the backwaters of the Senate. In October, 1913, Tillman pleaded with the ineffectual majority leader, John W. Kern, to enlarge the number of Democrats on the Naval Affairs Committee. The balance of eight Democrats to seven Republicans bred difficulties for the South Carolinian, as he could not rely upon the attendance of his Democratic colleagues or their votes on any given issue. In January, 1914, after the Senate steering committee refused his request, Tillman desperately sought Daniel's aid, complaining that the Republicans were active and perceptive. Senator Henry Cabot Lodge "is very adroit, and always attends and with his experience he can manipulate things before the committee. . . ." Suspicion among Democrats continued as Wilson postponed patronage appointments. Daniels irritated Swanson and Tillman by promoting marine officers from North Carolina, then issuing more difficult requirements for other candidates. Symptomatic of the distrust between the southerners, Swanson feared that Tillman would influence Daniels to remove the Norfolk recruiting station to Charleston.

During the first Wilson congress, the 63rd, party unity declined in the second and third sessions, as only the tariff and foreign-policy issues attracted the disjointed Democrats to a high level of party unity. Under the best of circumstances Democrat support for naval legislation as a party measure had been erratic, and the lackadaisical voting patterns of the previous two congresses continued throughout the 63rd. Only by incorporating indirect and individual paths to preferment did Tillman and Swanson achieve their goals during the first years of the Wilson administration. Not until the spring of 1915 were naval appropriation bills treated as party issues with any considerable hope of favorable results. Even then outspoken opposition arose from some Democratic leaders.

Swanson and Tillman intervened separately in the daily fleet operations. Swanson requested Daniels to alter repair schedules to allow the Virginia yard, rather than northern bases, to refit destroyers. These projects furnished steady employment for skilled mechanics between new ship-construction orders and provided arguments for the appropriation of additional maintenance funds. Over the objections of Virginians, Tillman shifted gunnery practice from Lynnhaven Bay to Charleston, whereupon the presence of the fleet encouraged business, enticed tourists, and engaged the navy yard in unaccustomed activity. As an additional benefit, Charleston property owners received payments from the federal treasury for alleged damages from vibrations of artillery blasts. Modified repair schedules and exploding shells did not suffice, and more costly designs were forthcoming.

Daniel's decision in 1913 to inspect southern navy yards boosted Norfolk. In a series of studies, authored by special commissions of officers investigating the potential of various sites, Norfolk received the preferred recommendation over other southern ports. Hampton Roads offered unmatched natural assets—proximity to Washington, excellent rail connections, safety from hurricanes, adjacent coalfields, and astute politicians to sponsor its cause. Previously, Republican administrators had maintained the yard as the only major facility south of Philadelphia, and navy officers favored Norfolk as a port of call. By 1913 machinery was well worn, docks were in ill repair, and Republican secretaries had resisted increasing the wages of Norfolk yard workers to match those of their northern counterparts. The nearby presence of Newport News Shipbuilding and Drydock Company hindered yard development. In 1913, singular in the South, the company could build modern dreadnoughts, and, since 1911, the *Texas* had been under construction there. Local interests debated seeking competing facilities in the government yard, as the company experienced sufficiently stern competition from northern builders in bidding on federal contracts. However, events and Norfolk business interests soon solved Swanson's quandry as to which channel to follow.

A few days prior to Woodrow Wilson's inauguration, the retiring Taft regime awarded to northern yards three battleship contracts. With Newport News facilities swamped by the *Texas*, Swanson and other irate Democrats realized that, if any other contracts for the dreadnoughts were to be obtained by southern yards, the construction of additional docks capable of handling the behemoths was imperative. While united against the Republicans, accusing them of collusion, the obvious solution evaded the contentious Democrats. Consideration was given to forming civilian companies chartered by the government to construct ships. However, dissatisfaction with private construction mounted as armor-plate prices soared. Despite its Southern origins, the *Texas,* after its inspection, proved less than satisfactory. Assistant Secretary of the Navy Franklin Roosevelt suspected that naval inspectors were lax with the contractors, and Tillman believed that, when the officers were conscientious, they had been removed by skulduggery. The South Carolinian cut through the tangle by recommending the development of federal construction facilities at Charleston as a measuring stick to assess the true nature of private construction costs.

The general political atmosphere, hostile to private corporations, allowed the southerners to renew investigations of the armor-plate "trust" and to argue that lower costs with superior results would be obtained in government-owned navy yards. In May, 1914, Swanson encouraged Assistant Secretary Roosevelt to request construction at Norfolk for a navy dry dock capable of repairing the dreadnoughts. Concurrently, Josephus Daniels awarded new ship contracts to government navy yards, despite anguished objections from the private contractors, including Newport News Shipbuilding and Drydock Company. Daniels replied that his "first duty was to the Navy as a whole, and that in all matters relating to navy yards my duty is [then] to the Government yards as superior to that of the private yards."

Daniel's commitment to the expansion of government yards encouraged Tillman in his struggle to outfit Charleston. Recruiting allies within the Navy Department, he approached Roosevelt with the plea that Charleston "has been suppressed and discriminated against in every possible way," not only in pay scales but in the award of repair contracts. Upon the recommendation by Roosevelt that the Norfolk yard be expanded, Tillman observed the political footprints of the Virginia senators and categorized their capacity for treachery as equal to northerners when the distribution of navy yard appropriations was at hand. While the lack of facilities prevented Charleston from successfully bidding against northern yards for new-ship construction, Tillman did make use of a special 1913 navy committee study that recommended Charleston as an emergency base for the fleet, a port for destroyer squadrons and torpedo boats, the manufacturer of certain standard articles for ship repair and equipage, a home for elderly destroyers, construction site for tugs and barges, and a training station for machinist mates.

These proposals produced some practical benefits in Charleston. Tillman notified the mayor of the city that Cyrus S. Radford, "a pioneer in organizing. . .the manufacture of clothing. . .at the Philadelphia Navy Yard" was en route to South Carolina. The Senator instructed local officials to be alert, to show Radford available buildings, and to emphasize that potential employees, who would be "mostly women, of course," would accept lower wages than those paid in the North. To another booster, he cautioned secrecy to avoid northern interests scotching the plan. Tillman promised: "After the thing has started and taken root so that it cannot be smothered at the beginning," he would offer more support publicly. Incorporating the argument of budget savings, the obligation to respond to the public aversion toward greedy corporations, and the necessity of a government yardstick to measure changes by private contractors, Tillman and Swanson encouraged government manufacture and yard development at the expense of private interests along the eastern seaboard.

During this period, the hard edges of earlier antagonism between Swanson and Tillman softened. The weekly Monday morning committee meetings increased personal contact and produced quickened political demands that forced closer cooperation. Common viewpoints surfaced as Daniels fell into an easy relationship with the two senators. In Tillman's case, his chairmanship compelled it. In Swanson's situation, Daniels recalled the Virginian as an eager young congressman, waiting to gather patronage prizes from Daniels, Grover Cleveland's chief dispenser of political favors in the Department of the Interior. The bright work of former comradeship having been burnished, similar cultural backgrounds and a mutual distrust of business interests and Republicans led these men to emphasize their populistic attitudes and progressive proclivities. While an attitude more favorable to Charleston and Norfolk permeated the office of the Secretary and the southern yards grew sleek from his attention, this navy triumvirate, growing more accustomed to the mantle of leadership, altered the general policies of the navy as well.

As proposals were submitted, projects developed, and special commissions favored Norfolk and Charleston yards, Daniels and the two senators perceived that complexities and delays characterized the tradition-encrusted naval bureaucracy. Controversy over wage rates at Norfolk Navy Yard continued, and Swanson involved Assistant Secretary Roosevelt in the hassle. The Virginian petitioned the youthful New Yorker, directly responsible for the yards, to abandon regional discrepancies and institute a national wage scale. The introduction of the Taylor System of time-work studies created further difficulties among yard employees, and Roosevelt again was summoned to investigate alleged irregularities. Despite a Democratic administration, the navy proved to be intransigent toward change. As early as January, 1914, Tillman observed that the "Navy needs shaking up and reorganizing. . . ." Daniels became dissatisfied with the "aids" system of departmental organization. Roosevelt discovered that great difficulties were often presented by the conservative admirals when they were faced with novelty or innovation. Tillman suspected that the department was "under the control of old employees, who are mostly republican [sic]." For these Democrats, a political reordering of the navy became a necessity. To establish direct control through personal loyalty Tillman and Daniels promoted Victor Blue, North Carolinian by birth and South Carolinian by residence, to the key personnel post, Chief of the Bureau of Navigation.

Tillman successfully sponsored another South Carolinian, Samuel McGowan as Paymaster. Within the department Swanson's connections were considerable, exemplified by his association with Josiah S. McKean, who eventually became assistant for material in the Office of Naval Operations, and Virginians David W. Taylor and Robert S. Griffin in Construction and Engineering respectively.

After August, 1914, the general European war stimulated the movement for organizational reform. Supported by increased public apprehension, Daniels, aided by Swanson and Tillman, on the Senate committee, seized the opportunity and strengthened the Secretary's control of the department by tying the position of Chief of Naval Operations to the Secretary's apron strings. Distrustful of certain officers, Daniels admitted that "I have gone as far as is safe, consistent with civilian control, in giving the chief of operations large powers." Emphasizing his suspicions of the officer class, Tillman noted that "our Navy is permeated. . .with egotism and self-sufficiency enough to sink it." Swanson questioned the assumptions of some naval officers and their advocates: "Is the Navy created to give promotions to officers? Is it created for the purpose of making an officer an admiral, a captain, or a lieutenant?" To insure his influence, Daniels appointed a Georgian, William S. Benson, former yard commandant at Philadelphia, as Chief of Naval Operations, knowing him to be personally more dependable than his predecessor, Bradley A. Fiske. A certain result of these arrangements allowed Swanson and Tillman to adjust naval appointments to benefit Norfolk and Charleston.

One personnel assignment of considerable consequence was that of yard commandant. At Norfolk or Charleston the position required a politically supple officer, alert and active, with the capacity to compose reliable estimates for construction bids and the ability to coax visiting commissioners and dignitaries to support yard improvements. These commandants echoed local voices urging yard expansion and used the political advantages available through the offices of the senators. During the initial shipbuilding programs of 1913 and 1914, Swanson obtained bids submitted by other navy yards and forwarded them to Norfolk for comparison and future reference. Tillman reassured the inutile Charleston commandant and detailed for the officer the procedures to follow and the deadlines for submission of construction bids. Fearing the yard had been intentionally staffed in 1915 by an incompetent, Tillman instructed Victor Blue of the Navy Department to appoint a commander at Charleston "who has some common sense and discipline, not merely a society ornament. . . ." Both senators influenced appointments, promotions, and other aspects of personnel affairs through their associations.

Despite shrill questions concerning the condition and strength of the nation's sea power hurled by some politicians and preparedness leaders during the autumn and winter of 1914, Tillman and Daniels hesitated to plunge into an emergency building program. Tillman fancied that "when the German and English fleets do meet and half of their battleships are destroyed and sunk, our little Navy would be very respectable." In February, 1915, with partisan accusations of unpreparedness peppering his coattails, Daniels refused to launch upon an immediate building program without adequate planning: "We ought not to go too fast now until we learn more about what the European War will teach us. . . ."

Tillman, Daniels, and Swanson appeared to endorse ships that were lighter and speedier than the conventional dreadnoughts sponsored by the steel companies and elements of the navy's officialdom. Tillman observed: "Battleships seem to be the darling project in every naval officer's mind." The construction of the smaller ships could be handled in southern yards and this influenced their decisions to a degree. Concurrently, the importance of the Naval Affairs Committee grew in 1915, following a reorganization of appropriations procedures; Swanson and Tillman more easily increased the items requested for their favorite navy yards, as a five-year plan for naval construction evolved.

Walking on political cat's feet, as opposed to Tillman's clattering demands, Claude Swanson developed a sophisticated lobbying technique that eased him into the center of navy policy making. Swanson, through congressional sources, suggested a new survey of Norfolk and, between 1915 and 1917, a series of Navy Department studies were written to the specifications and aspirations of interests at Norfolk, both within the navy yard and the propertied community. The recommendations proposed that repair facilities be shifted to construction work, capable of building a "modern dreadnought." In October 1915, the so-called Roosevelt Board report placed on record the Assistant Secretary's high regard for Norfolk's strategic position, while censuring "the shortsighted policy of past years, which has prevented us from having proper buildings and equipment. . ." as "an amazing instance of inefficiency and maladministration." A fire at the yard increased its inadequacies and, in the summer of 1916, a second commission headed by Josiah S. McKean and John A. Lejeune urged the acquisition of the bankrupt Jamestown Exposition property for training grounds, marine barracks, fuel storage, fleet stores, submarine and aviation bases, and piers. Placed within the framework of navy planning during this period, these proposals, owing to their existence in the files of the department, became the initial blueprints for immediate expansion upon the declaration of war in April, 1917.

During 1916 Tillman encountered obstructions in entering his plea for a modern dry dock at Charleston. He fought the idea expressed in appropriations debates that Charleston "is not at all accessible" and that the "channel has to be dredged constantly." He attempted to bludgeon Daniels into the fight by applying the "pitchfork" and railed before the cherub-faced secretary at what he considered to be the prejudice of "naval officers against Charleston." Tillman threatened to undertake the deepening of the channel and extension of the dry dock "without depending upon your [Daniels'] cooperation." In August, frustrated by his counterpart in the House of Representatives, Lemuel Padgett, whose opinions of Charleston were shaped by an admiral opposing the establishment of federal munitions facilities at the port, Tillman refused any compromise during the conference committee's deliberations. Finally, he relented, allowed Daniels his "four battleships" and other increases, and expected as his reward $700,000 to be assigned by the Secretary for yard improvements in South Carolina. Part of the arrangement included Padgett's acquiescence to a general study of southern ports to select a major yard facility south of Cape Hatteras. The arbitration of the August crisis gave evidence of Claude Swanson's expanding influence with both Daniels and Tillman.

During 1916 the increased number of personnel assignments and construction projects often puzzled the aged and ailing Tillman, and he reached the conclusion that on the Naval Affairs Committee he needed an associate, similar to Victor Blue in the Navy Department, to handle the multiplying developments of the preparedness program while the senator attended specifically to Charleston. To secure a development project where competing public and private interests were involved required a combination of associations within the House of Representatives, on appropriations committees, among navy officers and clerks, and with fellow senators. Claude Swanson met his needs. The senators agreed not to disagree over appropriations for their particular yards. The impact of Swanson's personality softened some of the partisan lines that Tillman had molded within the Naval Affairs Committee; Swanson's insinuating nature permitted compromise with northern politicos, evidenced by the major Navy Bill of 1916, shaped by Swanson, Tillman, and Henry Cabot Lodge, Boston's yard spokesman and Republican leader. Swanson performed as floor handler for the bill as well. After Wilson's reelection, Tillman, relaxing in South Carolina, informed Daniels that he suspected that "Swanson is very busy about the Navy Department and I presume that he is looking after Norfolk; he can not do too much for Norfolk to suit me."

Swanson may have masterminded the study of southern harbors in order to enhance Charleston with official recommendations. The affair was carefully structured, incorporating the argument that, in the event of a naval war in the North Atlantic, a southern port would offer a superior defensive position for repair and safe harbor. The commission carefully investigated southern sites from New Orleans to Wilmington, North Carolina, and in December, 1916, recommended Charleston. As the senior officer on the commission was James M. Helms, former commandant at Charleston, Tillman had observed its progress "with keen interest." The freshly completed report was rushed to the Navy Department in order to be included in the 1917 appropriations bills. At this point the gossamer strands of the plot parted under the pressure of criticism. Sensitive to accusations circulated during the previous presidential campaign that the South had received excessive amounts of federal patronage, Daniels hesitated, and the House Navy Committee, staffed with other southerners, lobbying for their favorite yards, scuttled the proposal. In a midnight conference committee meeting, Tillman refused to admit the defeat of the dry-dock scheme, and Swanson alone was able to convince the South Carolinian to permit passage of the navy appropriations bill without funds for Charleston. However, the projected plans for Charleston's elevation to major status were filed in the Navy Department and, as in Norfolk's case, would be rushed to implementation during the excitement and alarms of war.

In the struggle for federal funds, whether immediately successful or delayed by countervailing forces, these southerners shaped a regional alliance while broadening their vision of public service and emerged as men capable of uniting and leading others from self-serving goals to wider areas of statesmanship. These schemes offered a pattern devoid of the utilization of large business interests and sponsored instead government manufacture of textiles, munitions, and armor plate accompanied by ship construction. This provided their constituencies, relatively undeveloped industrially, with major federal funds; but, contemporaneously, corporate interests were denied influence as well. Daniels emphasized that government ownership and direction reduced costs substantially. Swanson believed that among the "people who manufacture projectiles today, whether. . .good or. . .bad, the main idea that prevails . . . is the profit made from the sale. . . ." As to the constitutional issue, Tillman observed to President Wilson: "Some fossils in the Senate—Democrats, I am sorry to say—have been debating. . . the constitutional power of Congress to manufacture nitrates. . . . They make me sick."

In June, 1917, Swanson and the new Senate Majority Leader, Thomas S. Martin, through wire-pulling in the House, amended the navy appropriation bill to provide funds to purchase the Jamestown Exposition property, following the recommendations of the 1916 report that proposed the site for major navy development. The two Virginians were successful only after Wilson and his Cabinet were recruited and able lobbying work was performed by Captain Josiah S. McKean. Even after calling upon such prestigious voices, the act to develop Norfolk Navy Yard as one of the major military installations of World War I would have failed but for the persistence of Swanson, the prestige of Martin, and the conviction of Josephus Daniels. Besides bailing out realty investors in the bankrupt Exposition Company, the decision permitted Wilson to condemn the area "if the purchase price" was not regarded by him "as fair and reasonable." Daniels again received from what he termed "partisan sectionalists" stinging accusations of gross administrative favoritism toward the South.

The turmoil of war prevented a satisfactory fruition of the plans of earlier years. Business interests were enrolled during the emergency while Daniels attempted to hold their profits to 10 percent. But eventually this guideline was abandoned. As the navy hastened to launch the urgently needed destroyers for convoy duty, the department suspended bidding on contracts. Instead, navy officials oversaw all aspects of construction in the private yards. This offered Tillman opportunity to harass what he called the "Navy Clique." When the Admiral in charge, Washington L. Capps, appeared not to favor Charleston harbor with sufficient construction orders, Tillman accused him of "sectionalism" and pledged " to make him feel it in every way possible as long as I am in the Senate." Although in poor health, Tillman urged Acting Chairman Swanson to rectify the situation, and two months later, despite Daniels' pleas to the contrary, Capps resigned, pleading failing health.

The accelerated pace of war production produced major alterations in the life of Norfolk and thrust the city and its environs from the nineteenth century into the growth, confusion, and sprawl of the twentieth. Following the heightened activity, simmering labor problems boiled over into strikes within the navy yard. An observer in Norfolk warned Assistant Secretary Roosevelt that "the pressure. . .is getting too great. . . ," and work stoppages occurred that eventually involved Swanson, Daniels, Roosevelt, Wilson, and Samuel Gompers. Overcrowding produced friction between whites and blacks, and Daniels proposed establishing a cordon between the enlisted men and the "so-called colored section" in Norfolk, as some sailors, he observed, "make themselves exceedingly objectionable and a considerable feeling of resentment on the part of colored citizens has been excited." Other social problems, such as organized prostitution and incipient street riots bedeviled the authorities.

Although not designated for major development until January, 1918, Charleston benefited from wartime expenditures. As Tillman lay ill with his final sickness, Swanson husbanded the South Carolina port through appropriations debates. The government clothing factory at Charleston survived to flourish in the hothouse of war. The number of employees was increased, but when black women were hired, turmoil erupted. Daniels solved the problems by housing the two races in separate buildings. The major appropriations of 1918 initiated projects to deepen the channel sufficiently to serve heavy ships and build a large dry dock. The advent of peace and the return of Republican majorities stopped the expansion in midstride, but the navy yard with its destroyer ways, training facilities, storage houses, pattern shop, power plant, hospital, and nearby Marine training camp were retained, surviving for another age.

Corporations moved to develop new plants in the Norfolk area. In Newport News, the Shipbuilding and Drydock Company increased the number of employees by twentyfold, and issued $400,000 weekly in wages. The port's bank deposits increased $7,000,000 in 1918 over 1917. Correspondingly, the influence of the general manager, Annapolis graduate Homer L. Ferguson, grew and his company obtained over $9,000,000 in federal funds to provide facilities for ship construction. Business and government continued to mix in the port areas as federally financed roads, piers, and bridges accompanied by government housing, water, and sewer projects, received impetus. A stunning prosperity, beyond the harbor boosters' earlier imagination, resulted.

Tillman and Swanson were both aware of the intrusion of large business aggregations in the affairs of the navy. Writing his Virginia colleague in February, 1918, Tillman was convinced that "powerful interests were at work all along the line to prevent an effective and actual reform to be carried. reform as you and I understand the word." In 1919, following the death of Tillman and Swanson's senior Virginia colleague, Thomas Martin, the return to Republican congressional majorities aided in the resurrection of northern influences that thereafter severely limited Swanson and Daniels.

The economic consequences of the growth of the Charleston and Norfolk naval complexes were extensive. Navy and Marine Corps establishments, complete with military and civilian payrolls, service industries, supply needs, and utilities requirements, became the major single economic factor in Norfolk and comparatively so in Charleston. The expenditure of federal funds in the erection and maintenance of these bases and similar ones in the remainder of the South marked the third major incursion of northern economic power into the South within two generations. Unlike the military invasions of the 1860s and the establishment of northern capital's dominance over southern commercial and agricultural interests in the years following, southern congressmen and local leaders held a significant part in the decision procedures that led to the application of federal funds during the Wilson years. The outlay of tax revenues attracted a great variety of private industry, retail establishments, and commercial banks that helped free southern business interests from utter dependence upon northern investment capital and led to the development of a mature industrial and commercial economy for the port areas. Initially desired as patronage, the navy yards and other military bases gained additional economic dimensions that, by 1919, inspired a close alignment of private interests seeking public funds.

The political primacy of the yards became a reality locally in the years after their development. The tidewater realty, commercial, and banking combine vibrated to any conjecture concerning the future of the yards. These groups insisted that the permanent stations should be considered as holding, with older agrarian and commercial interests, equal title to the attention of city and state politicos. Tillman, Daniels, and Swanson forged a regional alliance that benefited the home state constituency of each. Nationally, personal associations and friendships were constituted that affected naval developments decades into the future. Assistant Secretary of Navy Franklin Roosevelt obtained insight into the nature of political leadership, committees, and personalities as well as observing the congressional strategies of Daniels, Tillman, and Swanson. The admirals acquired political techniques that they had heretofore shunned, being tutored by Daniels, Swanson, and the other politicians of the era.

However, the circumstances that allowed Daniels, Tillman, and Swanson to sponsor government-owned facilities for manufacture at the expense of private enterprise were unique prior to World War I. Had Charleston or Norfolk contained extensive private heavy industrial interests, Tillman and Swanson would have been unable politically to support many of the government programs for manufacture, instead allowing the Navy Department to satisfy its needs through contracts with private business. With the exception of Newport News Drydock and Shipbuilding Company, these political pressures were absent for the most part as the ports were principally commercial prior to the war. The three southerners sponsored government manufacture as a means of avoiding the high costs that contracted supplies demanded. The trio reflected the southern agrarian tradition that viewed suspiciously the machinations of corporate wealth upon the government. Their attitudes were sharpened by earlier Populist campaigns and later Progressive attacks against business "trusts." Derived from their world view and political necessities of the moment, Tillman, Daniels, and Swanson presented a reasonable alternative to the eventually standard and expensive twentieth-century procedure of material procurement that World War I initiated.

DANIEL R. BEAVER

THE PROBLEM OF AMERICAN MILITARY
SUPPLY, 1890-1920

The First World War has long been labeled by historians an important
turning point in western history, an event that disrupted the stable political-
military world of the nineteenth century and introduced a chaotic era of
large-scale incorporated violence. During the Great War the organizational
and technological capacity to bring whole societies into a war effort actually
existed. The terrible spiritual and material costs of the first eighteen months
of battle marked the end of an age of limited war for limited objectives.
Unbounded objectives inhibited the possibility of a negotiated settlement,
brought increased military production programs and caused every warring
European power to integrate its economic and military organizations in
ways previously considered unwise, immoral, or both. After the war it
might be expected that the powers would make massive alterations in their
war-making establishments to incorporate the changes that had occurred
during the conflict. However, only modest modifications were made, suggesting that human institutions tend toward equilibrium, that they maintain
at least an illusion of continuity in the face of the most serious challenges,
and that, when they do affirm the necessity for changes, they move glacially
to blunt their effects and incorporate them into traditional structures.

This essay is a modest test of that hypothesis, an attempt to show how
the drama of institutional modification played itself out in the United States
Army between 1890 and 1920. It is directed primarily at the military supply
organization, for it was there that the challenge of change was most clearly
articulated at the time. The story involves the development of internal
War Department mechanisms to shape supply policy and manage supply
activities in light of the experience of the Spanish-American War. It includes
a description of a broader organizational enterprise by the military and, as

the need for cooperation was accented by the approach of war in Europe, by concerned nonmilitary interests to bring the industrial might of the nation to the support, initially, of national preparedness and, later, of the American war supply program. It analyzes the institutional changes that the men of that day incorporated into traditional military supply structures at the end of the war to meet changed conditions as they understood them and raises some question about the appropriateness of "industrial-military complex" as a useful device to describe that early twentieth-century American experience. In the process it contends that other popular terms like "turning point" are also too imprecise and value-laden to describe a profoundly complex set of circumstances through which men in institutions, under tension from within and from without, slowly, incrementally, adjust themselves to new realities.

In the nineteenth century American policy makers might have reviewed the European war that erupted in 1914 as just another indication of "old world" corruption and decay. But new circumstances—the roots of which lay in new power relationships brought about in part by the emergence into world politics of Japan, Germany, and the United States in the last decade of the nineteenth century— made such a response to the great European war improbable. Japan, engaged in a massive military and naval modernization program, cast covetous eyes upon the China mainland. Germany was on the move in Africa and the Far East. The United States, its interests renewed in the Caribbean, in Latin America, and the Pacific, had already clashed with Germany in the Samoan Islands and with Japan in China before the Spanish-American War. The changed foreign-policy situation required, or so it seemed, increased American military power and Washington inaugurated a substantial naval building program, coastal-defense modernization, and a moderate army reequipment program which brought the War Department for the first time in a generation to reconsider its relationship to the American business community.

American enterprise had been transformed since the Civil War. By 1885 the organization most characteristic of American industry was the corporation; both vertical and horizontal trusts had appeared and commercial and investment bankers, through the use of investment credit, had gained control of major sectors of American industry. The Panic of 1893 catalyzed the latter movement and the late 1890s and early twentieth century witnessed the emergence of giant combines such as United States Steel, International Harvester, the DuPont Company and, of course, Standard Oil. John D. Rockefeller wrote at that time:

This movement was the origin of the whole system of modern economic administration. It has revolutionized the way of doing business all over the world. The time was ripe for it. It had to come though all we saw at the

time was the need to save ourselves from wasteful competitive conditions.
The day of combination is here to stay. Individualism is gone, never to
return.[1]

Reports of the United States Industrial Commission and, later, findings
of the Pujo Committee showed that the consolidation of American business continued through the first decade of the twentieth century. It became
clear to the informed public that the age of *laissez-faire* was ending. American industry and finance were incorporating and institutionalizing on a
national even an international, basis. Some men, like Woodrow Wilson,
feared the corporation. Others, like Theodore Roosevelt, gloried in the
potential they believed it had, if properly directed, to improve national
life.

The corporate structure bred a new kind of business executive, a new
creed of industrial efficiency and a new "American system" of doing business. American industry since the Civil War had been known for rapid
growth rather than for achievement in factory management and production
technique. Efforts to improve manufacturing methodologies were initiated
by Frederick Taylor and his associates through what they termed the science
of industrial management. The time-study system introduced by Taylor, as
well as his very important discoveries of the use of high-speed tool steels,
paved the way for increased American industrial efficiency and foreshadowed
more sophisticated techniques that would change even the physical appearance of American factories by the 1930s. Great mail-order houses like
Montgomery-Ward and Sears-Roebuck revolutionized retailing. Their mer-
chandising innovations—especially those involving functional organization
to expedite rapid procurement and efficient delivery of products—symbolized
the new American way. Awareness of the value of statistical data grew, and
agencies quickly appeared to interpret such material for industrialists, financiers, and government officials hungry for everything that would help
describe the country, its economy, and its society. The work of the United
States Industrial Commission, the Tariff Commission, the National Monetary
Commission, the National Commission on Country Life, and myriad state
and local agencies provided vast amounts of previously undigested information of great potential economic and social significance. The Brookings
Institute, for example, in the prewar years funded a number of important
projects such as the New York Municipal Research Bureau. Gifted statistical
analysts like William F. Willoughby were retained to recommend desirable
reforms which would rationalize public and private organizations and make
them efficient and effective.

The military was significantly influenced by the organizational revolution symbolized by the new "American system." After the Spanish-American War the army encountered a set of conditions that tended to bring it

nearer the mainstream of American political and industrial life. Indeed, the institutional dynamism in the army was characteristic of the reform momentum of the progressive era. Under forceful leaders like Elihu Root, William Howard Taft, and Henry Stimson, the War Department moved to meet its new responsibilities. The Corps of Engineers undertook the largest federal peacetime enterprise in American history up to that time by completing construction of the Panama Canal. The Signal Corps built telegraph and telephone systems in Alaska. Army officers gained experience in contemporary government when serving as administrators in the Philippines, Puerto Rico, and the Canal Zone. The mission undertaken by the War Department after 1900 to defend the Philippines presented new strategic and logistical problems. Conflict with Germany or Japan was a real possibility and the army for the first time had to plan for a ground war at long range with a first-class power. In 1903 command of the army was reorganized and a corporate general staff was formed to bring the internal structure of the American army into line with contemporary organizational theory and to control and integrate planning for new and potentially dangerous military contingencies.

The new army management structure contained many ambiguities, the most important of which, for this essay, involved the command relationship of the General Staff to the chiefs of the War Department supply bureaus who, historically, had been virtually independent of any control—even that of the Secretary of War. During the Civil War, for example, Ordnance Chief Brigadier General James W. Ripley resisted innovations in weapons development and maintained his independence even in the face of presidential intervention. Permanent assignment of bureau personnel to Washington and especially bureau control over War Department contracting created influence with the Congress which the chiefs had used effectively in past struggles within the department.

Every chief of staff before 1916 insisted that the bureau chiefs were under his command, but the bureau chiefs vigorously resisted such authority. They insisted that they were perfectly capable of meeting the new supply needs of the army. They were aware that some form of industrial-mobilization planning had to be undertaken, and between 1903 and 1914 they reorganized and revitalized their own bureau activities in line with the most recent administrative theories. The Quartermaster, Pay, and Subsistence bureaus, for example, were combined into a militarized Quartermaster Corps. The Ordnance Bureau experimented with advanced shop-management techniques including the "Taylor System" to increase the efficiency of its arsenal operations. As the War College developed mobilization plans, each bureau chief drew "shopping lists" which coincided with War College directives. These exercises culminated in the 1915 mobilization plan for arming and equipping an army of a million men. But individual bureau planning was never integrated into any kind of coordinated procurement program and, when the United States entered the First World War, the issues of command and control inside the War Department were still unsettled.

It took the outbreak of the Great War to bring certain other issues to public attention. The army was organizationally and functionally isolated inside the federal bureaucracy and had only limited contacts with the private industrial sector of the nation. Since the days of Alexander Hamilton the nation had resisted a great nationalized military production plant. Congress had opted on three separate occasions in the nineteenth century for a mixed system of military procurement. The army relied upon its own resources for much of its supply in time of peace and purchased only certain special items from civilian producers. The Quartermaster Bureau, for example, manufactured army uniforms at its Philadelphia depot, but contracted for wagons and horses on the open market. Although the Ordnance Bureau relied on Colt, Remington, and Smith and Wesson for certain small arms, it maintained a substantial production capacity in its own arsenal system. Until the middle 80s it contracted for gunpowder and artillery tubes on the private economy, but manufactured its gun carriages and limbers "in house." After 1890, however, it reduced its reliance on private manufacturers by developing a modest capability to produce tubes and smokeless powder in its own plants. Without the navy's compelling need for large private industrial capacity, the army bureau chiefs neglected private producers, concentrated on modernizing their own manufacturing facilities, and made little effort to coordinate their potential emergency demands with the productive capacity of the nation.

Concern about such liaison was expressed as early as 1908 when talk began about a Council of Public Defense which might coordinate industrial production and transportation with military needs, but it was not until the Naval Consulting Board was established during the "preparedness campaign" of 1915 that government leaders, businessmen, prominent civilian experts, and soldiers began to discuss in earnest the broader questions of coordinating national defense.

By 1916 three important positions had emerged concerning the emergency production of war material and the control of economic mobilization. The business community and most civilian management experts believed that the supply side of any war effort should be run by an independent agency. William F. Willoughby, representing expert opinion, wrote in the *New Republic* in May, 1916, that a "Department of Public Defense" should be created, functionally organized, with its business aspects completely separate from its war-making functions. The army insisted that such division of authority was impossible and advocated exclusive control of procurement and supply by the War Department. A third view, supported by those elements in the country determined to "take the profit out of war," and concerned about the threat of a "military-industrial alliance," resurrected again the time-worn proposal to place all munitions production in public hands—in other words, a nationalized munitions industry.

The discussion over industrial preparedness culminated in 1916 in the appointment by Secretary of War Newton D. Baker, of the Kernan Board to investigate and make recommendations concerning possible effects of public and private production of munitions on the nation, and the creation, through a rider attached to the National Defense Act of 1916, of a Council of National Defense (the CND) composed of appropriate cabinet members with an advisory commission of management experts to link the government with the business community. The Kernan Board recommitted the army to the proposition that the government should rely upon the private sector for supplies and munitions in the event of an emergency rather than build a government munitions industry. The question of who should control industrial mobilization remained unresolved. Secretary Baker perceived the CND simply as an advisory agency to the War Department. In his *Annual Report* for 1916 he wrote:

Power is given to the Council to select a director who will be the executive officer and an adequate appropriation is made for the employment of expert and clerical help so that there will be established in Washington as an agency of the government a central body which will catalogue the resources of the nation and create such relations between our industrial and commercial agencies as will equip them to respond instantly to any call from the government.

Baker optimistically continued:

It may well be that some part of the work of the Council having a purely military usefulness will not be needed, but the general effect of such a plan in operation will be to produce more heathful and harmonious relations between the government and business and to give to the great industrial and commercial enterprises of the country a national and patriotic aspect which will both keep the country prepared should emergencies arise and stimulate business and industrial methods throughout the country.[2]

2

When the United States entered the war in April, 1917, it had been decided that private industry would provide the vast majority of the military's requirements. But no clear supply-control mechanism existed inside the army and, aside from the appointment of the Advisory Commission of the CND, nothing had been done about directing the industrial war effort. At the War Department, bureau chiefs charged off in a bustle of dedicated activity. Quartermaster General Henry Sharp, in particular, moved with great effectiveness to secure initial supplies for the army. Most equipment delivered from American sources before the end of the war was contracted during the spring and summer of 1917. Every bureau engaged in frenzied internal expansion and reorganization. There was no lack of vitality. In fact, it was the unrestrained activity of the bureau chiefs that led to virtual nationwide industrial and transportation paralysis in the winter of 1917–18. By December, 1917, as the army program expanded and absorbed a greater and greater part of national production, the question of who would direct and control the national supply effort could no longer be sidestepped. Pressure for an independent government supply department similar to the British Ministry of Munitions mounted from all sides and finally erupted in January, 1918, into a political crisis which threatened the Wilson administration's control of the war effort.

Secretary Baker, convinced that the army must exercise ultimate control over its own supply, strove to reform the War Department from within, and in doing so precipitated a three-cornered struggle among the General Staff, the Assistant Secretary of War, and the bureau chiefs, who still clung to their traditional independence even in the face of potential disaster. The internal conflict was symbolized by the struggle of Chief of Staff Peyton C. March, Quartermaster General and Director of Storage and Traffic George W. Goethals, and Assistant Secretary of War Benedict Crowell to impose their wills on the bureau chiefs. Although all three opposed an independent Ministry of Munitions, March and Goethals were convinced at the time that the direction of the supply program should rest with the General Staff. Crowell believed that all business activity should be separated from military control and concentrated under him in the Office of the Assistant Secretary of War. In retrospect, Crowell's efforts were doomed. He did not have the confidence of the Secretary of War. March and Goethals, who respected each other and loathed Crowell, had Secretary Baker's complete support. Goethals moved rapidly, after his appointment in December, 1917, to bring all procurement under military control. He knew supply had already proved a burying ground for military reputations and he was determined that his place in history as the builder of the Panama Canal must not suffer. By late April, 1918, Goethals had brought procurement, storage, and transportation under the supervision of the General Staff Division of Purchase, Storage and Traffic.

The P. S. and T. emerged, ironically, from an effort by Assistant Secretary Crowell to bring control of procurement under his office. The "committee of three," which Crowell appointed in April, 1918, to investigate the supply situation, rejected his plan for a separate supply administration in the War Department and instead strengthened Goethals' hand. Goethals brought together a notable array of experienced and talented executives, including Robert Thorne of Montgomery Ward; Gerard Swope of General Electric; Robert E. Wood, a friend of the General's from the old canal days; and the irrepressible Hugh "Iron Pants" Johnson. Goethals grimly fought off Crowell's increasingly frenzied efforts to control the supply function. The "victor of Panama" insisted that he reported only to Chief of Staff March and Secretary Baker. Crowell may have had the better theoretical argument, but at the time personality and desperate need were more important than theory. By October, 1918, Goethals' division of the General Staff had taken virtual control of military supply procurement in the United States.

Meanwhile, mobilization of the private sector remained a confusion of half measures. The Wilson Administration was loathe to act precipitously. The steps which were being taken would not only determine the organization of the emergency military-industrial machinery; they might also shape the postwar political-economic structure of American society. Creation of the General Munitions Board in April, 1917, and its successor organization, the War Industries Board (WIB) in July, 1917, by the CND did not represent an agreement to centralize control of the war effort. In fact, between January and March, 1918, the Army reached into certain early civilian agencies and incorporated whole sections directly into the War Department machine. And subsequent events revealed no consensus. Industrial managers like Walter Gifford of American Telephone and Telegraph saw in the WIB an opportunity to organize the whole economy along corporate lines for the future. Secretary of the Treasury William McAdoo saw the WIB much more narrowly as a temporary agency to control industrial mobilization in the emergency. Secretary of War Baker was determined that the army's access to supplies must not be impeded and saw the WIB as an information-gathering and liaison institution to put the army, with its critical marketing list, in touch with the appropriate producing units in the society. At least until April, 1918, army representatives paid very little attention to the WIB. It was not until March, 1918—when President Wilson, as part of his broader struggle to retain political control of the war effort, appointed Bernard Baruch chairman—that the WIB became effective at all; and then its chairman was a facilitator rather than, as he later claimed, a director.

Baruch did revitalize the board, but it was not until Goethals made Hugh Johnson Director of Purchase in the P. S. and T. that the War Department and the business community were linked usefully for the first time. Combined committees of the War Department and the WIB assessed requirements and established new priorities. Unused plants were located and new facilities developed. The WIB organized the country into twenty-one production zones. Influential businessmen were named, usually with the advice of local chambers of commerce, to regional advisory committees within each zone.

The regional committees quickly displayed independent initiative, informing army supply agencies of unused plant capacity and providing the WIB with information about plant conversion and new construction. But organizational momentum rested with the War Department. By war's end many regional advisory committees were acting as lobbyists but with the army bureaus, not the WIB. As Franklin D. Crabb, chairman of a regional advisory committee in Kansas City, wrote in September, 1918:

We find from experience that it will be absolutely necessary for us to have a regional representative in Washington, D. C. in order for us to secure any business for our manufacturers.[3]

The army was in the saddle, its demands for the moment more significant than any technocratic ideology or even traditional politics. In July, 1918, Samuel Vauclain, president of the Baldwin Locomotive Corporation and Chairman of the Locomotive Committee of the WIB, stated well the real relationship between the War Department and the WIB:

The Secretary of War says "We want those locomotives; now you get them." By George, we will have to get them whether domestic business stops or not because the first business today is to fight this war. It does not make any difference what else there is.[4]

3

Examination of a single project in a single bureau shows how the same fundamental issues emerged at lower levels of American war administration. Study of the Ordnance Bureau's artillery program shows that the bureau had the same problems in coordinating its own internal activities that the General Staff encountered in trying to supervise the work of the War Department generally and indicates how ineffective the ordnance planning process was. The story of ordnance and the private sector can also be told with very little direct reference to Baruch and his associates, reinforcing the view that the WIB was unable to curb even the army's most outrageous demands for material and that wartime relations between the army, civilian "experts," and the WIB crowd were always ambiguous, often hostile.

The Ordnance Bureau, in dealing with other War Department agencies and with the business community, had a record of independence, even intransigence, stretching back into the nineteenth century. And its antics during the years before the Great War gave little indication that it would change its ways. Chief of Ordnance, Major General William B. Crozier, an able engineer and a recognized authority in artillery design, was an outright opponent of the general staff system and labored mightily to keep the staff out of what he conceived to be exclusive Ordnance Bureau business. After his appointment in 1901, Crozier quickly gained control of all army ordnance activity. Convinced that technicians knew best what combat troops required, Crozier arrogated to himself the duties of the Board of Ordnance and Fortification to pass on the effectiveness of army artillery and ran the bureau like a feudal fief. A study of his *Annual Reports* for the prewar years and his testimony before congressional committees reveals Crozier as something of a know-it-all who had great difficulty following any directives except his own.

The ordnance program was in large measure undefined when the United States entered the war. In March, 1917, Crozier was ordered to prepare an ordnance project for an army of one million men. Crozier knew the difficulties. He had warned in 1915 that it would take two years to deliver new artillery equipment to the line. The government arsenals at Watertown and Watervliet and the powder plant at Picatinny had to be expanded. The Ordnance Bureau, unlike the navy, had only a small group of civilian producers with which it had established relations before the war. The largest and most efficient of them were fully committed to Allied production. Trained commissioned and enlisted personnel were unavailable, and machine tools of all kinds were in short supply. On the basis of existing tables of organization and equipment, Crozier reported, he could equip such a force with an adequate mobile artillery if it was not deployed abroad until 1919.

But the early movement of the American army to France made extraordinary measures necessary. After the arrival of the Allied war missions in Washington in April, the General Staff hurriedly drafted plans for the American Expeditionary Force (AEF). On May 26, Major General John J. Pershing and a headquarters staff were ordered to France and by the end of the month the War College had concocted a tentative scheme to place an army of a million men on the European continent by the end of 1918. On June 9, 1917, General Crozier received the following memorandum from the Chief of Staff:

Referring to information conveyed by you to a committee of the War College Division of the General Staff that the French government would be able to deliver to this government five seventy-five millimeter field guns and carriages daily commencing August 1, and two 155 howitzers and carriages daily commencing October 1, 1917, and that ammunition therefore could be provided, the Secretary of War directs that you enter at once into arrangements to procure this material. The ammunition caissons and other vehicles necessary to equip complete units should be obtained from French or other sources. The French type of ammunition should be used with the above material and our corresponding types not too near completion—three inch guns and six inch howitzers—should be chambered and bored to receive the same ammunition. Arrangements should be made to obtain the French ammunition for the service of these cannon in war. The construction of our own type should be continued with modified chamber and bore because there is no prospect otherwise of obtaining within the necessary time the number of cannon required for the successful prosecution of the war.[5]

The planning process continued during the summer and early autumn of 1917. The General Organization Project of July, 1917, formulated by a joint board of officers from the War Department and Pershing's staff and approved by Secretary Baker in October, 1917, as the "Thirty Division Plan," increased the strength of every army unit and called for the addition of new corps and army artillery organizations. Crozier was called upon to procure more 75-millimeter and 155-millimeter guns. Even heavier weapons— 8-inch and 9.2-inch howitzers, 155-millimeter howitzers, 12- and 16-inch guns and howitzers—were required as well. The ordnance chief renegotiated the Franco-American artillery protocol and persuaded the British government to provide additional heavy mobile artillery. With the initial artillery crisis apparently under control, the War Department looked ahead. In October, 1917, Crozier was ordered to prepare plans on the basis of the new tables of organization and equipment to arm an additional thirty AEF divisions with artillery from American sources alone by the end of 1919.

During the summer Crozier expanded the bureau substantially. The administrative offices were enlarged. An equipment division, an inspection division, and a supply division were established. A special nitrates division was formed to expedite smokeless powder production. AEF requirements were translated into production projects in the equipment division, while the distribution of ordnance materials was controlled by the supply division. Inspection, which traditionally had been decentralized through officers at various government arsenals, was centralized in the Office of the Chief of Ordnance. Government arsenals set to work round the clock. General Crozier stated in his 1917 *Annual Report* that the ordnance program was progressing satisfactorily. Expansion of departmental personnel was approximately 50 percent completed and "suitable arrangements" were being made for securing the remaining personnel required. He reported also on the "very cordial and useful cooperation" which was "being given by our allies in regard to field-artillery material" and stated that every possible opportunity was being taken to press the manufacture of "some foreign designs in this country with vigor."

If the war had stabilized in October, 1917, there is every probability that Crozier, with French and British help, could have muddled through. But the chaos and disorganization of the war effort at home and the disastrous change in battlefield conditions in Europe proved insurmountable. Like the other bureaus, Ordnance had gone into the market pell-mell during the summer of 1917. Competition with other bureaus had driven prices sky high, while the determination to "get the job done" had brought ordnance officers and their counterparts in other agencies all over the country to overload existing facilities and to ship indiscriminately to ports of embarkation all the war material they could lay hands on. Ironically, it was the zeal of officers single-mindedly determined upon the success of their own bureaus which was responsible for the paralysis of the war effort during the winter of 1917–18. And Crozier became a sacrificial goat. His prewar antagonism and arrogance toward "staff and line" left him few friends in the army and his defensiveness during the early hearings of the Senate Military Affairs Committee in December, 1917, lost him what support he had left in the Congress. On December 19, 1917, he was kicked upstairs to a newly created "War Council" and the former chief of Ordnance Supply Division, Brigadier General Charles B. Wheeler, became acting chief of the bureau.

During his first week in office Wheeler was handed a cable from General Tasker H. Bliss, the American military representative at the Inter-Allied Munitions Council, recommending a selective new munitions program to replace the balanced ordnance program of 1917. The Bliss cable read in part:

The representatives of Great Britain and France state that their production of artillery—field, medium and heavy—is now established on so large a scale that they are able to equip completely all American divisions as they arrive in France during the year 1918 with the best make of British and French guns and howitzers. The British and French ammunitions supply and re-serves are sufficient to provide the requirements for the American army thus equipped at least up to June, 1918, provided that existing six inch shell plants in the United States and the Dominion of Canada are main-tained in full activity. With a view, therefore, first to expedite and facilitate the equipment of the American armies in France, and second, to securing the maximum ultimate development of the ammunition supply with a minimum strain upon available tonnage, the representatives of Great Britain and France propose that the American field, medium and heavy artillery be supplied during 1918 and as long after *as may be found conven-ient from British and French gun factories* and they ask (a) that the Ameri-can efforts be immediately directed to the production of propellants on the largest possible scale and (b) Great Britain also asks that six inch, eight inch, and nine point two shell plants already created for the British service in the United States shall be maintained in the highest activity and that large additional plants for the manufacture of these shells shall at once be laid down.[6]

The Secretary of War, the General Staff, and the Ordnance Bureau all either misread or rejected the essence of the Bliss memorandum. Fear of an Allied collapse which would leave the American army without an artillery could explain the decision. An understandable patriotic outrage that the army of one of the most highly industrialized nations in the world should be dependent upon others for its artillery could be another explana-tion. Pure administrative chaos which prevented planning and contracting from being coordinated could be a third explanation. In any case, the interallied program of December, 1917, was simply superimposed upon the existing ordnance program. The revised project increased artillery, smokeless-powder, and shell requirements out of proportion to any foreseeable need and virtually doubled the 1919 program.

The Ordnance Bureau had been continuously modifying its organization, but the December crisis brought a complete top-to-bottom remodeling. General Wheeler called upon an outstanding civilian manager, Guy E. Tripp, chairman of the board of Westinghouse Electric, who was already associated with the bureau, to develop a new bureau-control system. Tripp's recommendations, adopted on January 14, 1918, called for a functional reorganization of the Ordnance Bureau. Washington had become a national choke point, Tripp claimed, and to relieve the situation he recommended in accord with existing managerial theory, a system that would establish intermediate organizations at other points in the country to handle the overwhelming mass of routine work and stimulate production while the bureau in Washington concentrated on policy decisions.

The Tripp plan followed the conventional "managerial wisdom," and divided the Ordnance Bureau into Engineering, Procurement, Production, Inspection, Supply, and Nitrates Divisions. The Engineering Division determined types of ordnance, produced and distributed blueprints and operating manuals and was responsible for research and development. The Procurement Division, the contracting element of the bureau, was the contact point between the Ordnance Bureau, the General Staff, and the great civilian emergency boards. It placed all bureau orders with government arsenals and with private contractors. The greatest innovation was the Production Division, which Tripp headed himself. He established a number of production districts, each under the supervision of a hand-picked production manager with considerable authority to make on-the-spot decisions, whose orders were, by every known means "to aid, stimulate, and accelerate" manufacturing to meet the increased requirements of the 1919 program. Tripp's idea caught on and soon every ordnance division chief in Washington appointed district managers who reported directly to Washington. The Supply Division continued to store, ship, and issue all ordnance materials to troops, while the Nitrates Division expedited the expanded smokeless-powder program. All operations were coordinated through a new Supply Control Section in General Wheeler's office.

There is no evidence that the Tripp System worked any better than the Crozier System. It had two basic flaws characteristic of functional organizations. First, the various division managers at the district level were coequal and submitted all disputed decisions to the Chief of Ordnance's Office. Second, members of the Supply Control Section in Wheeler's office who adjudicated and coordinated such matters were not members of any of the functional divisions and had no independent access to information which would make sound decisions possible. A glaring example of the control problems occurred in the notorious case of the Dodge recuperator contract. An inherent conflict between the Production Division with its concern for speed and the Inspection Division with its concern for quality led to the difficulties. In the spring of 1918, the Dodge plant in Detroit was pushing hard to increase production of recuperators for 155-millimeter howitzers. The plant superintendent approached the district ordnance production manager for advice. The finished machining on the outside of the sleigh of the recuperator was done by a big form cutter on an Ingersol milling machine, he said. When the cutter became dull, considerable time was required to sharpen it. If tolerances could be relaxed just a bit, the cutter could be used for a longer period without regrinding and production would increase. The production manager agreed. The local inspection manager was concerned and complained to his division chief in Washington, but the Supply Control Section, when it was handed the problem, supported the Production Division. When the sleighs were attached to the rest of the recuperator assemblies and joined to the gun cradles at the Sandy Hook proving grounds, it was found that they interfered with the rivet heads at the bottom of the cradles and the recuperator failed to return the gun to battery. The rivets had to be chipped off with air hammers. Weeks of assembly time were lost as all of the recuperator mechanisms had to be reground.

The bureau was still plagued by the lack of a reliable list of bidders. Nobody knew what manufacturers could really meet their contract obligations. A midwestern firm, known for years as most reliable manufacturers, bid for a contract to produce carriages for 155-millimeter howitzers. An officer who followed the case through to its dismal conclusion left the following reminiscence:

This company had a very excellent reputation as manufacturers. . . . It had grown from a very modest beginning to one of the first of its kind in the country over a period of forty years under the management of two very able brothers. These two men were very affable gentlemen and gave the impression of being thoroughly confident of the ability of their very conservative organization. . . . Their representative who came to Washington and secured their contract was one of the most accomplished salesmen I have ever seen. In a short time it became clear that this firm had no idea of how to proceed with its task. It lacked machinery and personnel and its contract amounted to about ten times the annual business it had ever done before. The brothers sublet the planning of the work to a company of efficiency engineers which apparently botched the job completely. After six months it became clear that the company could not meet its contract and, under protest and upon the suggestion of the Ordnance Department, the firm placed a shop superintendent and general manager chosen by Washington in charge of the work. Matters did not materially improve and finally the plant was commandeered and management turned over to one of the company's chief competitors. These competitors tore the company literally to pieces, reorganized the shop along their own production model and by the time they completed all their arrangements the armistice fortunately put an end to the war.[7]

It was Clarence C. Williams who deserved whatever credit there was for cleaning up the ordnance mess. When General Wheeler was ordered overseas in April, 1918, General Williams, AEF Chief of Ordnance, was transferred to the United States to head the Ordnance Bureau. He found ordnance business in Washington in chaos and Tripp depressed and in a purple funk. Williams had a field soldier's perspective. He is alleged to have said on one occasion that the job of the Ordnance Bureau was to serve the men in the field. "If the fighting men want elephants, we get them elephants." Unlike Crozier, Williams had a clear understanding of the need for central direction of all military supply. Also, unlike Crozier, he had a shrewd sense of political realities inside the War Department. Under Williams' direction the Ordnance Bureau eliminated overt opposition to General Staff direction and cooperated, although at times grudgingly, with March and Goethals. Williams' tactics allowed the Ordnance Bureau to retain considerable independence and escape being swallowed up by the P. S. and T.

Williams struck immediately at the flaws in the Tripp System. In mid-May he established the Estimates and Requirements Division which took the place of the Supply Control Section and brought coordination to the artillery program. He called weekly meetings of division heads to create some measure of administrative coordination. A new program section in the Estimates and Requirements Division checked on the status of contracts and production of component parts. In mid-June he made district production managers district ordnance chiefs and delegated to them the power to implement all basic policy decisions. According to ordnance historians Williams had a galvanizing impact. As district ordnance chiefs were usually well-known members of regional business communities, relationships between them and the Ordnance Department grew more intimate. In each line of ordnance work local manufacturers formed associations which established contact with the district chiefs and later with the regional advisory committees of the War Industries Board. Contractors got prompt payment for completed items, enabling them to turn the money back into new work. The district engineering managers accelerated operations by interpreting specifications and handling minor changes. The district production men exerted themselves to remove obstacles and stimulate output by seeing that manufacturers were provided with shipping orders, priorities, raw materials, coal and lubricants, gauges and machinery.

Williams could do everything except regain lost time. The war ended "too soon." Ordnance labored like Hercules, but the most heroic efforts produced little finished artillery or ammunition. Less than 3 percent of contracts made before mid-December, 1917, had been delivered at the end of the war. The whole program was out of balance. The 75-millimeter shell production, for example, included 30,600,000 primers and 26,800,000 shell cases, but only 12,000,000 fuses, 13,900,000 shell bodies, and 10,900,000 boosters. Carriages, limbers, and guns were still lying around waiting for recuperators. Repair kits and replacement parts were utterly lacking. While the Ordnance Department and American industry huffed and puffed, the AEF fought the war with foreign artillery and ammunition.

The post-armistice reorganization of the Ordnance Department charac-terized, in the changes that were rejected and the innovations that were in-corporated, the ambiguities of the war experience. Williams, in his *Annual Report* for 1920, attempted to put the best possible face on things. He wrote in glowing terms of the cooperation the army had secured from the nation's industrialists and suggested that an ordnance advisory board of civilian experts be created to help plan for the future. He pointed out the large number of reserve officers who were familiar with current bureau practices and recommended a program to maintain a pool of trained reserve officers. He proposed that the Ordnance Bureau maintain an up-to-date list of civilian bidders and that Congress provide funds for educational contracts to familiarize manufacturers with artillery production in case of emergency. His single most significant recommendation was that the Crozier System of ordnance development "by technicians" be changed and that the using branch should have the final word on the weapons they would be required to employ in the field.

Among themselves ordnance officers declared that working with the business community during the war had brought one headache after another, and all the Ordnance Bureau could show for its effort was a mass of obsoles-cent equipment and a vast supply of deteriorating powder and artillery ammunition. Many officers blamed Tripp and the civilian experts whom they insisted should never again be allowed to tamper with the bureau. One ordnance officer summed up his feelings about the war performance of civilian industrial management experts as follows:

In reading over the various histories of the ordnance districts and the various histories of the production of ordnance articles one cannot fail to be im-pressed with the evident desire of the writers to hang garlands around the necks of all who were in any way connected with munitions production through the war, regardless of the results obtained. This of course is more or less to be expected as a result of the victorious ending of the war and a desire to produce the "a good time was had by all" feeling among all the personnel concerned. If, however, this attitude on the part of these writers is not properly discounted. . .one is likely to [receive] a really false impression as to the efficacy of the work on which so many billions of dollars was expended during the war. . . .[8]

4

Discussion of the problem of military supply continued into the postwar period. It was only part of the debate over general military policy which, in turn, was intertwined with the struggle over the Treaty of Versailles. The paramount issues involved the future of the current centralized War Department supply system and the locus of control over future emergency economic mobilization. The chief opponents of centralized supply were the bureau chiefs, who argued vehemently against any institutional changes that would continue the wartime restraints on their independent stature in the War Department, General March favored continuing the P. S. and T. and even insisted that future economic mobilization should be controlled exclusively by the General Staff. Goethals agreed with March that the supply services should be centralized and militarized, but he advised that the agency should be separate from the General Staff and have its own special cadre of military professionals—experts in procurement and production. Assistant Secretary of War Crowell continued to believe that control of supply and industrial mobilization should be in the Office of the Assistant Secretary of War. March, Goethals, and Crowell might disagree on where power should be placed within the War Department, but they agreed wholeheartedly with a statement made by James R. Douglas, a young Ph. D. in political science from the University of California at Berkeley, who had been a member of the P. S. and T. during the war:

It is vital to the efficient organization of the army and its proper preparation for wartime burdens that some sort of supply directing agency be continued [to] direct, supervise, and coordinate under the Chief of Staff and the Secretary of War, the activities connected with the supply of the army. It is essential that this fact be recognized by Congress when it takes up the task of military reorganization. All prejudices should be laid aside. The principle of centralized control and supervision and decentralized administration and operation is coming to be accepted as unassailable even by the chiefs of the supply bureaus themselves no matter what disagreements they may have as to its manner and methods of execution. The United States is facing many problems during the coming few years. No one knows how great a part the army will be called upon to play in meeting these problems. The size of the army, no matter what world conditions may augur to the contrary, will be small. Small in size, it should be organized in such a way most nearly approaching perfection, on a line capable of immediate expansion when war shall come. Experience, one of the few factors capable of salvage from the wreakage of the present war, points unquestionably to a centralized system of control of army supply.[9]

Businessmen like Baruch supported Crowell on internal War Department matters, but insisted that coordination of national mobilization should be vested in a civilian agency similar to the War Industries Board. Indeed, in their attempt to persuade the Congress that such an agency should be created they made claims for and created myths around the WIB that were entirely out of keeping with its rather modest wartime performance.

To call the arrangements provided by the National Defense Act of 1920 a "complex" is a misnomer. There was neither an integrated military-industrial machine nor any clear doctrine of economic mobilization shared by the army and the business community; and, instead of charting a new course, Congress merely modified the National Defense Act of 1916. The power of the General Staff in the War Department was modestly increased, but the P. S. and T. was abolished and a centralized supply system for the army was rejected. On the surface, at least, it seemed that Congress had reestablished the traditional bureau system. The legislation did place responsibility for industrial procurement planning in the Office of the Assistant Secretary of War; but army program planning, which required a most delicate awareness of the relation of civilian priorities to military needs, was located in the General Staff. The Crowell, March, and Goethals plans were melded in such a way as to divide responsibility and limit the effectiveness of the War Department in any future crisis. Little was said about the future of the old Council of National Defense. Although those sections of the 1916 legislation which referred to it were not repealed, the agency and its advisory commission were allowed to atrophy. Apparently most congressmen, if they thought about it at all, preferred to bypass permanent institutional change and jerry-build an emergency structure modeled on the "WIB myth" in the event of another major conflict.

The formal appearance of institutional continuity was in part illusionary, for decisions had been made at every level during the war which linked irreversibly, if informally, the War Department establishment and the business community. The army and business could not be insulated from each other as they had been before the Great War. The interdependence of a technological society prevented such mutual exclusiveness. Important personal relationships like those of Hugh Johnson with Bernard Baruch and Robert E. Wood with Robert Thorne could not be undone. The Kernan Board 1916 recommendation to follow traditional policy and to rely upon the private sector for military equipment in crisis rather than to create a nationalized munitions industry was reaffirmed in 1920. It brought in its wake need for cross-institutional communication and planning that resulted in creation of the Army-Navy Munitions Board in 1922 and founding of the Army Industrial College the following year.

Only prophets or fools believe that they can foretell the precise contours of the future. Even after the fact it is difficult to tell the one from the other. Most people admit that they see ahead only dimly and, accordingly, plan through compromises embodying consensus and calculated risk. The National Defense Act of 1920 was just such a compromise, a classic example of institutional incrementalism. In its provisions it paralleled other actions of the postwar Congress. If the assumptions of the contemporary majority which rejected any necessity for radical departures in foreign and military affairs were correct, the legislation was prudent and appropriate. If, as a minority insisted, world conditions had been misjudged and future necessities misperceived, the compromise of 1920 would be found wanting. Similar issues would soon rise, probably again in some dramatic context, demanding immediate and potentially more disruptive resolutions.

NOTES

1. Thomas C. Cochran and William Miller, *The Age of Enterprise: A Social History of Industrial America* (New York, Harper, 1961 edition), p. 143.
2. U. S. War Department, *Annual Report, 1916,* (Washington, D. C., Government Printing Office, 1917) I, pp. 38-39.
3. Ltr. F. D. Crabb to E. E. Gibbs, September 14, 1918, War Industry Board, Resources and Conversion File, Requirements Division, WIB, Record Group 61. National Archives and Records Service (NARS), Washington, D. C.
4. Statement of Samuel Vauclain, Chairman of the Locomotive Committee of the WIB, July 11, 1918, WIB Records, Ibid.
5. Memorandum, Chief of Staff - Chief of Ordnance, June 9, 1917, Ordnance Historical File, Record Group 156, NARS.
6. Ltr., Tasker Bliss to Newton D. Baker, December 5, 1917, Records of the Supreme War Council, Record Group 120, NARS.
7. Draft Paper, "The Problem of Requirements: What an Ordnance Officer Should Know," June 22, 1922, Ordnance Historical File, RG 156, NARS.
8. Ibid.
9. James R. Douglas, "The War's Lessons with Regard to the Supply System of the Army," June 1919, Records of the Chief of Staff, US Army, Record Group 165, NARS.

The history of military-industrial relations suffers from the crudest conceptual foundations. Much of what has been written has been polemical or sensational. This short list hopefully eliminates most of that kind of literature and contains only the best and most readable books and articles on the period. An excellent set of general introductory essays on the First World War and institutional change is Jack Roth ed., *World War I: A Turning Point in Modern History* (1967). There is no account of American industrial-military relations for the entire era. A general overview can be garnered from consulting James A. Huston's *The Sinews of War: Army Logistics 1775-1953* (1966). Broader military problems are brought into focus in Russell F. Weigley's *History of the United States Army* (1967). Staff developments throughout the prewar period are surveyed in Otto L. Nelson's *National Security and the General Staff* (1946) and Paul Y. Hammond's *Organizing for Defense: The American Military Establishment in the Twentieth Century* (1961). There are a number of well-written and provocative accounts of the role of the corporation in American life in the twentieth century. Among the best are Alfred D. Chandler, *Strategy and Structure* (1962); and James Weinstein, *The Corporate Ideal in the Liberal State 1900-1918* (1968). Other attempts to integrate the rise of the corporation into the American main stream are: Robert Wiebe, *The Search for Order 1877-1920* (1967); Gabriel Kolko, *The Triumph of Conservatism, 1900-1916* (1963); and Samuel Hayes, *The Response to Industrialism, 1885-1914* (1957).

The war period itself resulted in a flood of controversial accounts. The most important of those contemporary books which illuminate the debate between businessmen, management experts, and soldiers were: Peyton C. March, *The Nation at War* (1932); Bernard Baruch, *American Industry in the War* (1921); William C. Crozier *Ordnance and the World War* (1920); Benedict Crowell and Robert F. Wilson, *How America Went to War* (6 vols., 1921); William F. Willoughby, *Government Organization in Wartime and After* (1919); and Grosvenor Clarkson, *Industrial America in the World War* (1923). The newer books are Robert D. Cuff's fine study, *The War Industries Board: Business-Government Relations during World War I* (1973); Edward M. Coffman's first-rate work, *The Hilt of the Sword: The Career of Peyton C. March* (1966); and Daniel R. Beaver, *Newton D. Baker and the American War Effort 1917-1918* (1966). Also useful are the introductory chapters of two excellent books in the *United States Army in World War II* series: Constance M. Green, Harry C. Thomson, and Peter C Roots, *The Ordnance Department: Planning Munitions for War* (1958); and R. Elberton Smith, *The Army and Economic Mobilization* (1958). Two unpublished doctoral dissertations, Harvey A. DeWeerd, *Production Lag in the American Ordnance Program 1917-1918* (1940), and John K. Ohl, *The Military Career of General Hugh Johnson* (1971), are quite valuable. Among the more significant recent articles on the war period are Paul.A. Koistinen, "The Military-Industrial Complex in Historical Perspective: World War I," in *Business History Review* (Winter, 1967); Robert D. Cuff, "A Dollar a Year Man in Government: George N. Peek and the War Industries Board," (loc. cit.); and Daniel R. Beaver, "George W. Goethals and the Problem of Military Supply," in Daniel R. Beaver, ed., *Some Pathways in Twentieth Century History* (1969).

ANNE TROTTER

DEVELOPMENT OF THE
MERCHANTS-OF-DEATH THEORY

Devils and devil theories are probably as old as mankind, for devils, like gods, are born of need, Although their descriptions, motives, and methodology differ, they are alike in one respect—each is responsible for a particular evil. As mankind has become more sophisticated, the nature of the devils has changed. Modern man is too well educated scientifically to believe that a volcano erupts because a capricious god was not fed enough nubile young virgins. He is less sophisticated, however, when it comes to other, more complex, but equally beguiling ideas which affix blame for social calamities on human devils rather than mythical scapegoats.

Nowhere is this more apparent than in the matter of wars and war scares. A very comforting myth has evolved through the years to account for mankind's penchant for self-destruction. War can be blamed squarely on two elements of society that are limited in number, highly visible, and unloved—the munitions makers and their associates, the international bankers. These devils have come to be known collectively as the "merchants of death," although the term is quite often applied to the munitions makers alone. Fear and suspicion of the arms industry dates back to biblical times, but the term was popularized in the mid-1930s by Helmuth Engelbrecht and Frank Hanighen in their best seller, *The Merchants of Death,* and by the famous Nye Committee operating in the same period.

According to the so-called merchants-of-death theory there is an international munitions industry whose various parts conspire together to control Government officials and, through them, the destinies of nations in such a way as to maximize profits at the expense of human lives. In time of peace when profits are low, the theory runs, the companies stir up hostile feelings and/or wars among various nations, arm the combatants, and fill the corpo-

93

rate coffers. This pattern of activities is both frightening and oddly reassuring to the believer. It says to him that there exist specific evil men who are directly responsible for wars; who have, if you like, sold their souls to the Devil for profit, as Dr. Faustus sold his for youth. Although in the past these men were not recognized for what they are, they have now been identified and can be controlled. And once they are controlled or destroyed, war will occur only rarely if at all.

In the 1930s the United States became the first nation as a whole to accept the theory as a truism and to apply it historically to our experience in World War I. The method adopted for handling this newly isolated evil was very American. Beginning in 1935, Congress passed a series of neutrality laws forbidding the sale of munitions and the lending of money to belligerent nations. Alas, like Demon Rum before it, war did not go away.

Clearly the generation of the 30s went too far in its enthusiastic acceptance of the merchants-of-death theory as the explanation for war. Still, there is a certain logic to this as it had recently rediscovered the old progressive thesis that corporations charged outrageous prices and used the profits to manipulate local, state, and Federal governments to their own advantage. The merchants-of-death theory simply expanded the anti-business feelings brought on by the Depression.

Yet there were obvious reasons to be wary of the munitions industry. Three specific charges are usually made against the arms makers by their critics and each has a measure of truth to it. First, they are disturbers of the peace. Desiring war as a means of enrichment, the companies become an active force constantly encouraging strife, lobbying against programs for world peace and disarmament, fomenting war scares, and stirring up international suspicions so that nations are easily incited to war. Second, they are disloyal. The armorers have banded together in an international network of interlocking ownerships and reciprocal agreements for the exchange of information and technical assistance. By doing this in peacetime, each violates the loyalty it owes to its own nation and government. In wartime the continuation of the network amounts to treason. Third, they are profiteers. Bids for government contracts are frequently collusive and dishonest. Their prices are exorbitant; profits, excessive.

Each charge can be supported by specific incidents of antisocial behavior. For examples of the first, disturbing the peace, one has only to look at the case of H. H. Mulliner, director of the Coventry Ordnance Works, who helped to create the Anglo-German Naval Race of 1909, or the activities of William Shearer, who was sent by certain American steel companies to disrupt the Geneva Disarmament Conference of 1927. Lastly, it can be easily demonstrated that various arms firms have helped to create or increase tensions in Latin America throughout this century.

The charge of disloyalty is much more complicated. There is no question that the alleged international network does, in fact, exist. The munitions industry is similar to all other large businesses in so far as peacetime marketing techniques and operations are concerned and in having a global base. To paraphrase Eisenhower's Defense Secretary Charles Wilson, "What's good for General Motors is good for DuPont, Krupp, and Vickers." Only the products are different. This is the crux of the problem, for the weapons and technical expertise supplied by the munitions firms in one country to those in another may end up being used against the respective countries. For example, during the early part of World War I, a number of field guns used by the German army on the Western Front had been purchased from Vickers prior to 1914. Thus an English firm had inadvertently supplied some of the very weapons which were destroying a generation of British youth. Whether the system continues unabated or in modified form in wartime is another problem, one which merits a good deal of study on its own. There is, for example, the question of whether hostilities invalidate a properly drawn peacetime contract. Vickers and the British government disagreed about this throughout World War I and for years thereafter.

Thirdly, the charge of profiteering is often used in connection with the munitions industry. Obviously many American companies made gigantic profits from their war orders. The problem is to determine what part of that profit was excessive, what was based on volume, and what was earmarked to convert operations to peacetime output. In addition, there is neither a generally accepted nor even a working definition of the term "profiteering." As late as the middle of World War II, Congress vaguely defined profiteering as making an unconscionable profit on a product. The economists provide no better definition. Critics and defenders of the industry used their own definitions or feelings on the subject. During the late 1920s and 30s, the general public came to consider any record of large corporate wartime profits as *prima facie* evidence of profiteering during the Great War. They never stopped to consider the basic problem of what constitutes a fair profit in a capitalist economy or that it is necessary to have these companies during an emergency.

The question of profits became even more confused as at least a part of the public was worried about another, noneconomic aspect of the "munitions problem." They were convinced that it was wrong for companies to profit from the production of equipment or projectiles designed solely to destroy human life. The complexity of dealing rationally with certain aspects of profiteering can be seen by two unraised questions: Is the man who works on the assembly line as guilty of antisocial behavior as his employer? and, At what point in the production of munitions does it become immoral to make a profit? Cotton as well as steel is essential to the making of a bullet. How do you judge the farmer whose prices rise in war-time? These are problems which require serious thought. However, few people wanted to delve deeply into basic matters and settled instead for a simple stereotype. Those who owned the munitions companies were merchants of death, deserving of moral opprobrium. Given the emotions usually engendered when the subject of munitions is mentioned, this is not surprising.

In order to understand more fully the acceptance of the merchants-of-death theory not only by the depression generation buy by those that have followed, it is necessary to put the thesis into historical perspective. Fear of and concern about the role of the private munitions makers as disturbers of the peace is essentially Anglo-American. Its origins are English; its development, American.

An island nation, England relies on a large navy for protection. As the bulk of that fleet has always been privately constructed, the English have had a naval-munitions industry for literally hundreds of years. Traditionally shipbuilding, commerce, and defense have been so interrelated that no one questioned costs, prices, and profits. Then, in the mid-nineteenth century, astute politicians such as John Bright, Richard Cobden, and William Gladstone started examining the relationship of invasion scares to naval budgets to profits.

Richard Cobden in particular was disturbed by the pattern of steadily increasing Admiralty budgets at a time when England was clearly master of the oceans. In 1861, he published the classic *Three Panics, An Historical Episode,* which examined the invasion scares of the previous twenty years. He pointed out certain common factors: the enemy was France; newspaper editors and/or military heroes helped to stir up fears; no real attempt was ever made to ascertain the seriousness of the threat; after generous naval appropriations were voted, the threat subsided. Cobden carried his line of thinking even further. He and Bright started to voice the suspicion that the patriotism of many who loudly demanded a stronger navy was grounded in stock prices and edged in gold. It was, they reasoned, in the arms industry's interests to promote spending. The only ways to do it were to play on natural fears where they existed and to create them where they did not. In other words, they had arrived at a primitive merchants-of-death theory.

The role of newspapers in aiding the big navy interests was amply demonstrated by the panic of 1884. In May, Lord Northbrook, First Lord of the Admiralty, informed the House of Lords that the Royal Navy was in such superb shape that he would not know what to do with any additional funds if they were voted. Only a few weeks later William T. Stead, the super patriotic editor of the *Pall Mall Gazette,* published a series of articles "proving" that England was utterly defenseless and in grave danger of imminent invasion by the French who were secretly building vessels. Newspapers across the country quickly ran their own scare stories and demanded protection regardless of cost. As current unemployment was high, businessmen added their voice to the general hue and cry. Bowing to public pressure, the Admiralty asked for emergency funds to reinforce the fleet. Appropriations were duly raised as were taxes.

By 1900 English critics had discerned a definite pattern to the industry's activities and were looking at corporate relationships to society and government. They accepted almost as natural law the role of the industrialists in agitations for increased defense spending. They recognized that many of the same men were members of patriotic societies devoted to supporting the navy or expanding the Empire, the latter naturally depending on the former. Of greater concern was the fact that so many "right" people owned stock in arms companies. Numerous Members of Parliament had such investments as did wealthier members of the nobility, gentry, and officials of the Church of England. Retired officers found positions as advisors or directors of companies such as Vickers, Whitehead, or Cammell-Laird, where they proved to be excellent contact men at the Admiralty and War Office. Men with similar interests often owned, either in part or outright, the newspapers which played an important role in whipping up public demands for an ever larger navy. When all these voices clamored in unison, it required a very strong prime minister to resist.

Critics could find patterns where they wished, but they could not convince the general public that the government was manipulated for the benefit of the arms makers. Not even the popular playwright and fervent socialist, George Bernard Shaw, could raise public ire. His *Major Barbara*, produced in 1906, dramatically presented the now-classic portrait of the munitions maker. One of the play's protagonists is Andrew Undershaft, a highly successful purveyor of death, who is openly pleased when he improves his products and boasts of his willingness to sell to anyone who can pay his price regardless of race, ideology, or color. In fact he is delighted to supply quality goods to both sides in a conflict. At one point in the play he brutally asserts that he and the other armorers *are the government* (italics mine); that there will be peace or war as they see fit; that when dividends need to be raised, national honor must suddenly be defended. Americans in the 1930s would revere Shaw as a great prophet, but to contemporary English audiences the play was merely another of Shaw's amusing productions. They listened to the clever lines, yet paid no heed to the warnings about the cupidity of munitions makers. Not until after the revelations of the so-called Mulliner affair in 1910 would the public begin to be concerned.

H. H. Mulliner was the managing director of the Coventry Ordnance Works, a firm whose fortune rested on government orders. In 1909, when things were not going as well as he thought they should, Mulliner decided to convince the proper authorities to increase the naval budget. He told friends at the Admiralty about his "secret intelligence" that the Germans had speeded up their shipbuilding program and within a few years would have enough dreadnoughts to effectively challenge England. The ships and their large gun mountings were allegedly being produced by Krupp, a company whose name automatically inspired fear. When the story was leaked to the press, public emotions were inflamed. Soon crowds were gathering in London and elsewhere chanting, "We want eight [dreadnoughts] and we won't wait!" Denials by Krupp and Berlin only made matters worse. Parliament upped appropriations by over two million pounds, which paid for four dreadnoughts among other things. Viewing British actions with alarm, Germany increased its spending. The Anglo-German naval race had begun.[1]

The story did not have a happy ending so far as Mulliner was concerned. When Coventry received few orders, he wrote a series of letters to the *Times* in January, 1910, detailing his role in creating the scare, which he naturally regarded as a patriotic gesture designed to shore up the navy. His honesty was too much for company and country. He was fired. His replacement? A retired admiral who was from a "good" family. As a result of Mulliner's self-confessed activities, the company lost favor with the Government and did not receive another contract until 1913.

Despite Krupp's demonstrable innocence in this case, the English public was now solidly convinced that the company was inherently wicked. Thus, prior to World War I this family and its company had come to personify evil. Nothing has ever erased the stigma.

Throughout Europe concerned men were beginning to view with alarm the expansionist activities of their domestic munitions industries[2] and to put their fears into writing. This coincides with the flourishing of the peace movement on both sides of the Atlantic during the decade prior to the Great War. There were literally hundreds of local, national, and international peace societies. Their basic goals were the establishment of permanent international arbitration machinery and general arms limitation. To attain these goals they had to arouse the public. Increasingly the peace societies turned to the printed word. They produced thousands of inexpensive broadsides, pamphlets, and books dealing with various aspects of the peace question.

After 1910 a growing number of the publications attacked the munitions makers and their marketing techniques. Given the size of their shipbuilding industry and the individual's freedom to voice criticism, it is not surprising that the English led the attack.[3] Perhaps the most significant work was *The War Traders,* by George Perris, for his well-reasoned approach appealed to a wider audience than most. Admittedly the popular readership was limited, but this book and similar works spread among an articulate sector of the European intellectual community the idea that the munitions makers were a threat to peace. Increasingly it was believed that the armorers had become too powerful, too greedy, too unconscionable to be controlled. Nationalization of the munitions industries was the only solution.

Initially neither the idea of the basic villainy of the arms makers nor the proposed nationalization of the industry made many converts in the United States for several rather obvious reasons. First, there simply was no really large industrial combine that primarily depended on munitions sales for its existence. Even if arbitrarily lumped into a single unit, the American firms still were not large enough to influence the national economy, much less foreign policy. Second, nationalization runs counter to the traditional American belief in free enterprise. Finally, attacks on the industry in Europe were often led by avowed socialists, a group whose influence was very limited in this country.

Early in this century the DuPont company had been taken into court for Sherman Act violations in connection with its dominance of the powder industry and there had been revelations of collusive bidding on government armor-plate contracts. Neither attracted much public interest. Prior to the First World War people just were not interested in the subject. Few specifically American anti-munitions industry materials were published.

The situation changed between 1914 and 1918. Fear and distrust of the arms makers began to develop particularly among the progressives, who were both articulate and respected enough to influence public opinion. Progressives, like socialists, regarded war as economic in causation and beneficial only to their domestic villains, the big businessmen and the bankers. In the fall of 1914, progressives had applauded Secretary of State William Jennings Bryan when he barred loans and credits to belligerents. Great was their irritation when his successor, Robert Lansing, rescinded the order in 1915. They vigorously opposed the Wilson Administration's military-preparedness program, arguing that both were clever ploys of the munitions moguls and bankers to get us into the European conflict. Once preparedness was enacted, they demanded that the program be paid for by those who would benefit the most from it. In 1916 Congress responded by passing a special munitions tax, the only one aimed at a specific industry. The following year it was supplemented by a war excess-profits tax, frankly designed to soak the rich.

The worst fears of the progressives were realized in April, 1917, when Wilson's request for a war resolution was heartily endorsed by business and financial leaders and the stock market rose markedly. Steel and munitions companies in general found intervention an increased boon to their already thriving operations. Bethlehem, United States Steel, and DuPont occupied particularly enviable strategic industrial positions as they mass-produced goods essential both to direct military operations and to other types of wartime production. Therefore they were able to earn unprecedented profits. Their profits made them special targets for criticism both during the war and in later years. Of the three, DuPont was the most vulnerable, for it emerged from the war with a $90,000,000 surplus in its treasury that was mainly derived from the sale of powder and explosives, products with purely military uses. To the public of the 1930s, DuPont would become the greedy company whose bloated profits were stained with blood, while the steel industry was largely ignored. This is doubly ironic, since DuPont was one of the few firms to reduce its prices during the war and it was the steel industry which had been justly condemned for profiteering by President Wilson and the War Industries Board.[4]

After the Armistice in November, 1918, domestic economic controls were abandoned; Americans turned their backs on war-related problems and settled down to enjoying normalcy. Throughout the 20s popular literature on the subjects of profiteering and the munitions industry was scanty. In general the public was not concerned with such topics, although there were some exceptions. Bernard Baruch, former head of the War Industries Board, and spokesmen for the newly formed American Legion presented separate programs to prevent profiteering in future wars and demanded that Congress take positive action on the problem. The results were several long-forgotten and always-ignored hearings, the establishment of the Industrial College of the Armed Forces, and a lackadaisical investigation of alleged corporate war frauds by the Justice Department. Nothing was accomplished.

The lack of action occasioned no comment because of an underlying public belief that businessmen must be shrewd operators who knew how to drive hard bargains. Even in retrospect there was little criticism of them for their cleverness. Besides, the newly prosperous America could afford to ignore or forgive any nefarious business practices as they were mistakes of the past. Mistakes, moreover, which would not be repeated, for America would never again permit herself to become involved with a degenerate, quarrelsome Europe.

In 1917 this nation had launched a great crusade to save democracy and to reform Europe. By the mid-1920s it had become obvious that neither had occurred. Crusaders by the thousands turned into cynics and isolationists. The feeling of alienation was bolstered by historians who began to reject the Versailles war-guilt thesis that Germany alone was responsible for the conflict. This new idea set a current of doubt in motion. The more one suspected the purity of Russian, French, and English involvement in the war, the more inclined one was to question the wisdom and motives of those who had guided America into battle at their sides. Was the Wilson Administration guided less by idealism than by other, unspecified, factors?

One answer to that question was propounded by Harry Elmer Barnes. In 1926 he published *The Genesis of the War* in which he propounded radical ideas and applied them to American involvement. After placing most of the war guilt on Russia and France, Barnes then blamed propaganda, loans, and purchases for tying us to the Allied cause. Taking advantage of the situation, the unneutral Wilson and his warmongering assistants had used the submarine issue to get us into the war. The Barnesian theory found a ready-made market among those who had found the postwar world disillusioning despite domestic prosperity. Over the next decade a host of books along similar lines were published and met with equal or greater acceptance.

As the 1930s began, many thoughtful people were convinced that our participation had been unjustified, a mistake, and was in large measure responsible for current economic difficulties—an idea reinforced when European nations defaulted on their war debts. Others were all too aware that everything had gone wrong in their world but did not know why. Both groups were certain that "someone" in the business community was responsible for the deplorable state of affairs, foreign and domestic. After all, the businessman had been paid in full and grown rich off the war, while the public was now being cheated on debt payments and hit by economic disaster. To make matters worse, the process seemed to be starting again as the very nations which had defaulted were rearming themselves for yet another conflict and turning to American manufacturers to help supply them. The public mood was one of frustration, fear, and anger; all that remained was to identify the specific villains.

Into this atmosphere stepped Gerald Nye, a brash young senator from North Dakota with a deep-seated distrust of Wall Street finance and large-scale industry. He initiated an investigation in order to prove the theory that munitions makers and bankers were responsible for American intervention in 1917 and for wars in general. Once he validated the theory, he could then sponsor legislation to keep the United States out of future wars and to destroy the domestic munitions industry. In the process he would emerge as the champion of peace which would enhance his reputation in the senate and secure him a place in history.[5] Designed to capture the public's attention and interest, the hearings were highly sensational. Often there was a "revelation" before lunch for the evening papers and another in the afternoon for morning editions. The Nye Committee concentrated on exposing unethical conduct by bankers and arms makers in peace and war. From the fall of 1934 to the early spring of 1936 the nation was treated to revelations of corrupt corporate practices involving bribes, government favors, high prices, secret worldwide marketing agreements, the exchange of patent information and other activities the committee deemed counter to the national interest. The public watched with glee as company officers appeared before hostile senators to answer questions about how they ran their businesses. They bought and read a growing number of publications detailing the evils of the private munitions industry. They listened as Nye delivered impassioned speeches attacking the greed of the arms makers and the dominant financiers as *the prime cause of war*. Each reinforced the other and whipped up emotions. It is not surprising that in the general excitement few people noticed that the committee had failed to substantiate its thesis. The public had found its villains and that was all that mattered.

The biggest villain of them all was DuPont which, like Krupp, was both a firm and a family. Thus it was possible to personalize evil to an infinitely greater degree than with United States Steel or the Electric Boat Company, which were run by anonymous officials. People had no trouble identifying the four DuPont brothers as to who they were and what they did. They were genuine, in-the-flesh merchants of death. This same sort of personalization occurred when J. P. Morgan testified, as he embodied the rich financier whose loans to belligerents earned him a fortune and involved his country in the war. The fact that the committee failed to prove this was irrelevant. In the persons of Morgan and the brothers DuPont evil had appeared in human form.

The Nye Committee's final report placed the blame for American entry squarely on the domestic munitions makers, bankers, and exporters, who had had enormous investments in the war. In their unrestricted pursuit of profits, they had convinced the nation that it was essential to support the Allied war effort. Once prosperity was tied to that effort, there was no alternative but intervention when the cause seemed on the verge of collapse. Wilson was carefully exonerated by the committee as a victim of circumstances.[6]

Now that the devils were identified, they had to be exorcised. The public demanded stringent legislation. Congress responded by enacting a series of neutrality laws that provided a foolproof formula for staying out of future wars. According to the statutes, once the President declared that a state of war existed anywhere in the world, there could be no sale of munitions and no private loans to belligerents. These laws offered eloquent testimony to America's basic disillusionment with Wilsonian involvement in international affairs and to the general acceptance of the theory of war proffered by Nye.

The results were almost disastrous, since the neutrality laws unfortunately were tailored to fit the problems of World War I and not present realities. The laws failed to take into account Hitler or the plight of weak, poorly armed nations which were defenseless against the attack of wealthier, well-armed invaders who could purchase from the United States crucial, but non-munitions goods such as oil, scrap metal, or cotton. The net effect was to put us on the side of the aggressor in Europe.[7] Despite the legislation's drawbacks, there was widespread public support for it. The 30s were a decade of disillusionment, isolation, and bitterness. No matter who suffered, we were not going to be drawn into another European conflict. Americans felt betrayed because the war to end all wars had failed to achieve its objective. The writings of revisionist historians led many people to question the motives for our entry into the First World War. Nye Committee revelations of wartime profiteering and fraud, which would have had little impact in the prosperous 20s, took on a new meaning in the Depression-ridden 30s when the mood of the nation was decidedly anti-big business.

A growing trend toward interpreting history in the light of economic interests also made Nye's conclusions more readily acceptable than they would have been in the past. The committee and various authors popularized an overly simplified view of war as resulting from the activities of the munitions industry and its confederates. Had the American public been less disillusioned by the last war and less afraid of approaching European conflicts, the merchants-of-death theory would have found a far less receptive audience. It provided a simple solution to the complex problem of remaining neutral in a world which was about to explode in new wars.

Insofar as it influenced American foreign policy, the theory's effective life-span was roughly 1935–38. During that last year it became apparent to all but the most dense that Hitler and not the private munitions industry was the true menace to Western civilization. For more than two decades thereafter the theory lay dormant. In his farewell address of 1961 President Eisenhower voiced his concern about the growing military-industrial complex and its impact on American society. He was warning the nation that, among certain corporations, labor leaders, military officers, high-ranking bureaucrats, and others, there existed a community of interest which exerted a steadily increasing influence on domestic and foreign policies. A few years later young anti-Vietnam protestors would simplify the idea and adopt it for their own. The devil this time would be Dow Chemical not DuPont, but the thinking would be the same. It would be left to older, more sophisticated men to examine the complicated problem raised by Eisenhower, work which is currently under way.

NOTES

1. In 1935 the British Government established a Royal Commission to investigate the private manufacture of and trade in munitions. Almost without exception the opponents of the arms makers cited the Mulliner case. The Commission hearings may be found in the Public Record Office—T181/1-177, London.
2. On April 18, 1913, a leading German socialist, Dr. K. Liebknecht, rose in the Reichstag to launch an impassioned attack on his native domestic munitions industry. Similar attacks can be found by reading the records of almost all European parliaments.
3. The British Museum has an extensive collection of material published by various peace groups. The best collection of comparable American material is in the Swarthmore College Peace Collection, Swarthmore, Pennsylvania.
4. Alfred Chandler, Jr. and Stephen Salsbury. *Pierre S. duPont and the Making of the Modern Corporation* (New York, Harper and Row, 1971) provides the best corporate study. US Senate. Federal Trade Commission. *Report on Profiteering 1918.* Senate Report .248. 65th Cong., 2nd Sess., 1918. The attacks on DuPont are so numerous as to defy a complete listing. Among the more popular are: George Seldes, *Iron, Blood, and Profits* (New York: Harpers, 1934); Helmuth Carol Engelbrecht, *One Hell of a Business* (New York, R. M. McBride and Co., 1934); Engelbrecht and Frank C. Hanighen, *Merchants of Death* (New York, Dodd, Mead and Company, 1934). None of these books deal with DuPont exclusively, but they serve to increase public suspicion of the company. Magazines of the period 1934-37 are filled with attacks on the arms industry as even a casual glance at the *Reader's Guide to Periodic Literature* will attest.
5. The two best monographs on Nye and his Committee are: Wayne S. Cole, *Gerald P. Nye and American Foreign Relations* (Minneapolis, University of Minnesota Press, 1962); and John Wiltz, *In Search of Peace* (Baton Rouge, Louisiana State University Press, 1963).
6. US Senate. *Hearings of the Special Committee Investigating the Munitions Industry,* 40 parts. 73rd Cong., 2nd Sess.; 74th Cong., 2nd Sess., 1934-36. The 9-part committee report is Senate Report 944, 75th Cong., 2nd Sess., 1926.
7. An outstanding monograph dealing with this problem is Robert A. Divine, *The Illusion of Neutrality* (Chicago, University of Chicago Press, 1962).

ALLISON W. SAVILLE

THE NAVAL MILITARY-INDUSTRIAL COMPLEX, 1918-41

The military-industrial complex for naval technology in the interwar period was one of shifting relationships, which had marked the past. The immediate earlier period had witnessed increasing domination by the navy over that mixed conglomerate. The great 1916 "Navy Second to None" construction bill and funding which accompanied it accelerated that trend. Thereafter, the navy amazingly with congressional support, vastly expanded its design, production, and construction facilities. This was made possible by funding that resulted in increases in the staffs and work load of the design section in the Navy Bureau of Construction and Repair, at the Naval Gun Factory in the Washington Navy Yard, and of construction and repair facilities at existing and newly acquired naval shipyards. Yet quality and, in the 1930s, quantity were to beguile this navy attempt to dominate the military-industrial complex. Neither its capabilities, funding, nor facilities were sufficient for the task. And the last decade of the period marked the gradual return to a more balanced, more equitable, more profitable, and successful system with private industry again sharing the tasks.

That rather little of the 1916 naval bill saw completion and that the navy never achieved its long-sought position as the prime naval power of the world until well into World War II were both hallmarks of the interwar period. While large numbers of flush-deck, four-piper destroyers, the *O, R* and *S* class submarines in that program, were completed late in the war period and thereafter through 1924, only eight of the battleships and the ten light cruisers of the *Omaha* class commissioned. Britannia continued to rule the waves. The period, under the aegis of successive naval disarmament treaties, witnessed a severe cutback in authorizations for new battleships, battle cruisers, destroyers, and auxiliary vessels until well into the 30s.

Emphasis, limited primarily by budgetary restrictions, was upon prototype aircraft carrier, cruiser, and submarine classifications into the early 30s.

Fewer private prime contractors figured in the design, construction, and repair chores within the military-industrial complex until 1933 (with the navy largely filling those functions). Yet much of the general format of the old military-industrial complex procedural system remained as before. The navy had for decades delineated the ship and item specifications for everything in the Naval Establishment. The three technical bureaus, Construction and Repair, Engineering, and Ordnance, assisted the Navy General Board in drawing up the preliminary and contract specifications for all shipyards and manufacturers. Contracts were then awarded on the basis of the 1861 "low bid" Revised Statute 3709 for private industry or else allotted to navy manufacturing and construction installations, in both cases often accompanied by navy designs from the technical bureaus. In these years, however, naval appropriations generally carried congressional riders, mandating that navy yards or government arsenals produce all material unless excessive costs and time loss resulted. And stringent limits on profit-taking were also set by law. Vessel construction itself did not always follow that pattern, but the net effect was to limit severely the industrial side of the complex until 1939. In addition, whether at naval plants or private sites, naval supervisory staffs and inspection teams, scattered around the country, supervised production and played a large role in the procurement process, including testing and formal acceptance. But coordination was poor in that each of the technical bureaus—Ordnance, Aeronautics, Engineering, and Construction and Repair—inspected entirely independently of one another until 1927.

The whole operation hinged neatly upon congressional authorization and funding of programs recommended to it by the Secretary of the Navy as drawn up by the Navy General Board, with the Bureau of the Budget and the navy's own Bureau of Supplies and Accounts often controlling the flow of appropriation monies. Until 1933 those were "bare-boned" authorizations and, after 1921, separately appropriated funds. Neither the War Plan fleet requirements, the great 1916 "Navy Second to None" goal, the parity with Great Britain which displaced it following the Washington Naval Agreement of 1922, nor even a successful over-age-ship replacement program could be fulfilled. Republican-dominated politics and policies effectively throttled down on the Big Navy goal of yesteryear. The likes of President Harding's speech of July 27, 1923, to the Seattle Press Club were to have a wooden ring to them down through the next decade: "I have just reviewed the Pacific Fleet; it is equal to first in all the world. It is covenanted. . .that our Navy shall retain that first rank." A far better index of the dismal realities was in the lengthy surveys of the naval situation done by Admirals Eberle and Hepburn in 1925 and 1940 respectively, in the annual General Board "Are We Ready?" assessments, and in the War Plans "Estimate of the Situation" series in the naval records.

The sharp budgetary cuts, which began in 1919, and the Washington Naval Treaty of 1922 were the harbingers of "times of trouble" for the navy. A large part of the 1916 program was canceled and scrapped, and the massive fiscal 1920 naval construction program implement for 12 battleships, 16 battle cruisers, 6 carriers, 30 scout cruisers, 108 destroyers, 233 submarines, 284 minesweepers, 18 tenders, 2,080 aircraft, 156 dirigibles, and 24 rigid airships never was seriously considered by the Congress. The shore establishment likewise suffered. There would be no new battleship contracts until 1937, none for new carriers between 1922 and 1930. Constriction, not expansion of the navy, reflected deliberate national policy. The impact on the old MIC was soon felt. One history of Bethlehem steel admits that its shipyards subsisted on repair contracts and civilian pursuits during this time. Others were not so fortunate. The great Cramp Ship and Engine Company of Philadelphia and Bath Iron Works of Maine went out of business.

Turning to ship classes, the Congress appropriated funds to modernize most of the battleships, five of those contracts going to the Philadelphia Navy Yard, for example. This "half-a-loaf" measure resulted in eliminating most of the heavy British-styled cage masts in favor of tripods, conversion to oil-fired boilers, fitting of aircraft facilities, and ordnance changes, including re-gunning and increasing of gun elevation to allowable limits under the treaties. The battleship force was stabilized at fifteen under the allotted Washington Treaty ratio until the expiration of the holiday on such construction in 1936. That was the year of the onset of the new worldwide naval race. The navy thereafter sought five new classes of battleships, totaling seventeen ships, designed between 1935 and 1938. All were larger and faster than their predecessors. They ranged in displacement from 35,000 to 58,000 tons, carried 16-inch guns and sagely, in anticipation of the air-power threat, heavy antiaircraft batteries. Only ten were constructed, with two of the *Iowa* class and all five *Montana* class falling prey to cancelation in the 40s. The long-dormant, specialized skills of private industry for naval construction and high-quality material were ill-prepared for the task or the volume ahead.

The two-ship *North Carolina* class of 1937 reflected the postwar navy design influence. The New York and Philadelphia Navy Yards undertook their construction. Thereafter, overwhelmed by the volume of new general naval construction, the navy opted to private designs for the four units of the 1938 *South Dakota-Indiana* classes. New York Ship Building Company of Camden (NYSB) designed and built the *South Dakota* and provided

Bethlehem Fore River of Quincy with the design for the *Massachusetts* to be constructed there. Similarly the Newport News Ship Building Company of Virginia carried out the design and construction of the *Indiana* and transferred a set of plans to the Norfolk Navy Yard for the *Alabama*, the last vessel in the class. General Electric or Westinghouse turbines and Babcock and Wilcox (BW) or Foster Wheeler boilers powered these four-screw ships, whereas GE and the New York Navy Yard supplied the turbines and BW the boilers for the *North Carolina* class. The two electrical giants, GE and Westinghouse, also fairly well shared contracts for steam-turbine generator equipment and electrical switchgear in virtually all classes of ships for this period. Gradually the Bethlehem, Midvale, and Carnegie-Illinois Steel corporations were brought back into the battleship armor field after 1937. The next classes of battleships, the six *Iowa* class and projected five *Montana* class, 58,000-ton giants of 1939–40, were exclusively navy design and construction projects, suggestive of the wartime pattern of the military-industrial complex wherein the navy concentrated its efforts on battleship, carrier, and submarine construction to the limits of its own facilities and left other classes of vessels as almost exclusive enclaves of private suppliers, save for a share of the ordnance for them.

The one new major ship type in the interwar navy was the aircraft carrier. The first of these, the *Langley*, resulted from the conversion of an old fleet collier at the Norfolk Navy Yard which was commissioned in 1922. It was the first turbo-electric-drive ship in the navy. Ponderous, slow and ugly, she was no match for the trim, fast British carriers of wartime vintage. But she did yeoman service as a developmental, seagoing platform for the infant Naval Air Service. This guinea pig gave way to the first fleet carriers, *Lexington* and *Saratoga*, converted after 1922 from two battle cruisers slated for scrapping before completion. They were commissioned in 1927 at Bethlehem Fore River and New York Shipbuilding, Camden, respectively. These 33-knot, General Electric turbo-electric-drive ships, the longest (909 feet) ships in the world for a decade, served as vital developmental carriers for the evolution of tactical air doctrine and carrier evolution, and as testing vehicles for plane-arresting gear, palisades, catapults, etc.

Two years elapsed following the commissioning of these ships before the Congress authorized another carrier, the 14,5000-ton *Ranger*, built by Newport News Ship Building. Her small displacement betrayed an attempt by the navy to secure as many carriers as possible within the 135,000-ton allotment permitted by the Washington Naval Treaty. With the navy planning to put the *Langley* aside, it would utilize the tonnage remaining beyond the 66,000 for the *Lexington* class for five small *Ranger* types. Despite the sizable 769-foot flight deck and 86-plane capacity, the type was overcrowded and underpowered. Deck conservation devices like the overside beam outrigger park system (i. e., parking planes on I-beams extending outboard of the flight deck edges) served to increase plane carrying capacity, but not overall efficiency of the carrier. Even before *Ranger* commissioned in 1934, the navy decided to adopt a minimum displacement of 20,000 tons for fleet carriers in order to overcome the inherent debilities of the smaller type. Out of this decision came the two authorized in 1933, the 19,900 ton *Yorktown* and *Enterprise,* again awarded to Newport News.

A strange twist developed at this stage. With the Navy Bureau of Aeronautics coaching the design section of Bu C&R in carrier-type evolution, Bu Aero faced the unpleasant task of returning to another small carrier, because there were now just 14,700 tons remaining in the American treaty allotment. The 14,700-ton *Wasp* contract went to Bethlehem Fore River in 1935. She was completed in 1940 after numerous construction and trial problems. It was an approximate *Ranger* repeat, with similar debilities, but was vastly superior to the *Langley,* reclassified as a seaplane tender in 1937.

This apparently completed American carrier construction limited by choice to six. The new London Treaty of 1936, however, brought on open escalation of all classes since Japan, which neither attended nor signed, was already carrying out a vast fleet-expansion program. Still not until 1938 did the navy secure funding for another carrier, the *Hornet,* a 20,000-ton repeat *Yorktown,* which Newport News completed just before the outbreak of war. The final prewar orders for carriers came in 1940 with appropriations for eleven long- and short-hull *Essex*-class vessels, on a standard displacement of 27,000 tons. Seven were awarded to Newport News and four to Bethlehem Fore River (the latter using its own design), thus confirming those two firms as the prime civilian construction contractors for fleet carriers by the beginning of war. For these World War II fleet carriers the navy abandoned the practice of allowing the shipyards to supply their own turbines. A standardized Westinghouse type was adopted to mate with the near navy-wide favorite, BW boilers. Finally, one might mention the construction or conversion of an escort carrier series for Britain, beginning in 1939. These were to give numerous private shipyards in the country much experience with the class of vessel, ultimately for our own escort types, which numbered over one hundred and in the main were private yard conversions of their own merchant-ship products.

Cruisers, along with carriers, were a great rage of major naval powers in the interwar years. All eighteen of the 8-inch-gunned heavy cruisers in 1941 were postwar designs and construction, with nine of them completed in the 30s. Limited by the Washington Naval Treaty to 10,000 maximum standard displacement and 8-inch main batteries for cruiser types, all navies designed them to gain the heaviest armament, highest speed and greatest endurance within those limits. The heavy and light types which emerged often contrasted solely on the difference in main battery size rather than in their displacements.

The navy vested cruiser-type development in the hands of Bu C&R design section. Seven distinct heavy-cruiser classes evolved, the last two still under construction in December, 1941. First, in 1924 came authorization for eight cruisers: the two *Pensacolas*, four-turreted, flush-deckers in which New York Navy Yard and NYSB shared construction; the six sleek, triple-turreted broken-deck *Northamptons* of the same year had midships aircraft catapults and stowage as in the *Pensacolas*. These latter were split up among three private yards—Bethlehem Fore River, NYSB, and Newport News—and two navy yards for building. Two near-repeat *Pensacolas*, the 1929 *Indianapolis* class, went to Bethlehem Fore River, and NYSB. Eight "depression" heavies in two classes followed: the seven broken-deck *Astorias* of 1929–33, with the heavy aircraft equipment moved abaft the second stack from the earlier-favored midships position; and the one-ship *Wichita* class, a flush-deck *Brooklyn* class, light-cruiser type with 8-inch main battery and aircraft equipment on the fantail. She was the last heavy ordered until 1940. In these ships, private yards supplied their own propulsion-turbine products, while navy yards contracted generally with Westinghouse and, on one occasion each, with GE and NYSB. BW exercised a near-complete monopoly on the boilers. Four navy yards built five of these, and two private yards—Bethlehem Fore River and NYSB—the remaining three, resulting in a near equal division of construction between private and navy yards for the eighteen completed between the wars. This helped maintain some semblance of balance in the prime military-industrial complex for this category until 1940.

That year, however, the navy assigned the final prewar orders for fourteen more heavy cruisers in two main classes: eight of the *Baltimore-Oregon City*, based on enlarged *Wichita* hull lines. All of them went to Bethlehem Fore River for construction. This arrangement, of course, upset the neat balance between navy and private builders of the interwar period. Added to it were orders for six battle cruisers, misnamed "large cruisers" perhaps in an effort to avert foreign "reply" programs. These fast 27,500-ton ships were in themselves replies to German battleships of similar dimensions, slated for use in the Atlantic. These six *Alaskas* were ordered from NYSB in September, 1940. General Electric turbines and BW boilers went into all fourteen of these cruisers.

The production of navy-designed light cruisers after 1918 sought to replace with new vessels a host of pre-1910 light types, and provide a fast scout and screening force for the battle fleet. A total of nineteen were completed in the interwar period, and another eight ordered up in 1939 and 1940. It began with ten British-styled, 7,050-ton "fast scouts" of the

Omaha class, based on a 1916 Bu C&R design. After an incredibly long construction period at three private yards (Cramp, Todd at Tacoma, and Bethlehem Fore River), they were commissioned between 1923 and 1925. Foreign sources credited them as among the finest of their type in the world. Almost a decade then passed before the next order for seven 10,000-ton *Brooklyns* in 1933–34, followed by two near sisters of the *St. Louis* class in 1935. The unique feature about them was three triple 6-inch turrets forward (two turrets aft), following the Japanese heavy- and light-cruiser pattern of some years earlier. And suggesting the construction pattern which had evolved with the heavies, five went to private yards, NYSB and Newport News, and four to navy yards, a near balance. As in early heavy cruisers, the private yards supplied their own turbines, while New York Navy Yard, construction site for three of the government ships, built turbines for one Philadelphia Navy Yard ship and for its own vessels.

Then not until the great "Two Ocean Navy" bill of 1938 and supplements to it did the navy order further light types. Contracts for eight ships of the 40-knot *Atlanta* class antiaircraft cruisers, patterned by Bu C&R on the earlier British *Dido* class, went to three private constructors, Bethlehem Fore River, Bethlehem San Francisco and Federal of Kearny, in 1939 and 1940. Like the 32 *Cleveland* class of 1940, based essentially on the earlier *Brooklyn-St. Louis* design (minus number three turret), which were ordered from five East Coast private yards, none of the *Atlantas* were completed before the Pearl Harbor attack. All the *Atlantas* had Westinghouse turbines, and all the *Clevelands* GEs. BW exercised a total monopoly in the light-cruiser category. As with heavy-cruiser production, the navy, finding its own production facilities swamped by new ships on order, permitted a shift in the military-industrial complex which favored private builders at the expense of its own attempted monopoly.

If carriers and cruisers represented vital needs during the entire period, destroyers did not, at least until into the 30s. When the United States emerged from war in 1918, it had 349 DDs built or building, among them 250 very successful 1,100-ton flush-deck four-pipers. The numbers alone adequately met the needs of the Fleet and precluded any chance of additions until these began to reach over-age classification, twelve years after commissioning; hence, in the Depression period. The navy was much taken with the British wartime destroyer leader type, and during the 1920s attempted several times, always unsuccessfully, to get congressional approval for a few based upon Bu C&R designs. It had had no luck either for flight-deck aft cruisers or for numerous auxiliaries.

With some 90 DDs scrapped, converted, or lost in the first decade after the war, the United States following the London Naval Treaty of 1930, at last began an extensive replacement program with the eight *Farraguts* of

1931-32. The Bu C&R design closely resembled broken-deck British DDs of recent vintage. That was the pattern until 1940. Double stacks were in vogue into 1934, then single stacks through 1936, returning to two stacks thereafter. Armament was fixed at four or five single-purpose Bu Ord 5-inch 38-cal. guns for main battery, and eight to sixteen torpedo tubes. Six of the *Farraguts* saw construction in four navy yards. Bath Iron of Maine and Bethlehem Fore River were each allotted single ships, again suggestive that the navy intended to dominate this area of the military-industrial complex. The navy yards supplied their own type turbines and boilers in this order, while Fore River provided those for its own vessels and for those at Bath.

With the onset of President Roosevelt's assault on the Depression in 1933, orders followed for additional naval ships, including destroyers in ever-growing multiples. Sixteen *Mahans* of a new design were put under contract in 1933, followed by two sister repeats of the *Fanning* class in 1934. Pairs went to five navy yards; and the remaining six, again in pairs, contracted out to three private yards, Bath, Federal of Kearny, and United of New York. GE turbines and BW boilers went into all eighteen ships, but only BW would maintain its near monopoly for some time.

At the same time, 1933 through 1935, the navy placed orders for thirteen 1,800-ton destroyer leaders (DLs) with the eight *Porters* of 1933 and five *Somers* in two programs in 1934-35. The first group, on a navy design, were shared by NYSB and Bethlehem Fore River, while the *Somers* single-stackers evolved from a successful private design by Gibbs and Cox of New York with Bath Iron and Federal of Kearny, receiving the builders' contracts.

This shift to private design and construction, however, did not mean the end of navy participation in destroyer development. Rather a new mix resulted with private industry making further inroads into the large military part of the complex. The ten *Craven*-class single-stackers of 1934 epitomized that kind of arrangement for a time. Two were designed and built at Bethlehem Fore River with the others going to four navy yards using a Bu C&R design. Still they were the heralds of a further transitional shift to private designing for DDs for years to come. Bethlehem provided its own main propulsion components, with GE and BW supplying the others. The design trend, set in the *Somers* class DLs, continued thereafter. The designs for the twelve *McCall*-class DDs of 1936, fast, 1,700-ton single-stackers, were done by Gibbs and Cox for the seven distributed to five navy yards and the three to Federal of Kearny. The remaining two, the class name ship and sister ship *Maury* (DD 400, 401) were Bethlehem design products, constructed at Bethlehem San Francisco. Westinghouse and BW gained most of the contracts for turbines and boilers respectively. A closely allied variant design from Gibbs and Cox was adopted for the twelve *Sims* class, last of thirty-nine single-stackers built in these years. Three private yards—Bath Iron, Federal of Kearny, and Bethlehem San Francisco—shared the construction mandates with four navy yards on a 6-6 ratio and again Westinghouse and BW supplied the main propulsion components.

The year 1937 was a watershed in destroyer evolution for the navy. In preparing the FY 1937 budget, the navy initially planned to build a single class of twenty-four in order to complete the ninety-seven-vessel replacement program permitted under the London Naval Treaty of 1930. With the lifting of all international construction restrictions in the wake of the unsuccessful London Naval Conference of 1936, the navy instead rapidly increased its projections to an additional ninety-six and then to almost three hundred before the onset of the war. There followed first an increment of thirty-two *Benson*-class ships, thirty constructed on a Bethlehem design, and two on the basis of a pilot Gibbs and Cox design (DD 423, 424), thereafter adopted for the sixty-four ships of the *Livermore* class of 1938. Differing but slightly in dimensions and displacement, and notably distinctive for flat stacks in the Bethlehem type and round ones in the Gibbs and Cox design, the vessels, the last of two-stack, broken-deck types for the navy, were virtually a single class, including propulsion and power components (usually 650 psi Babcock and Wilcox boilers, and generally GE or Westinghouse turbines, generators, and switchgear). The navy had at last approached standardized construction programs. Finally evidence of the significant shift in the military-industrial complex mix for destroyers came with the award of seventy of the contracts to private constructors and but twenty-six to navy yards.

The configuration of the military-industrial complex for destroyers was confirmed with the authorization and ordering of the 119 ships of the flush-deck *Fletcher* class in 1940, and the 56 repeat *Fletchers* of 1941–42. Based upon a private Gibbs and Cox design, as were the 175 ships of the sister wartime *Sumner* and *Gearing* classes, only 32 of the *Fletchers* went to three navy yards (Boston, Charleston, Puget Sound). The remaining contracts and all those for the two wartime classes were awarded to more than a dozen private builders. As in the *Bensons* and *Livermores* a small number of contractors—generally GE, Westinghouse, and BW—shared prime machinery contracts and literally a myriad of others those for smaller parts. The navy gradually withdrew from the destroyer design and construction field.

One cannot leave the destroyer category without mention of the authorization for fifty destroyer escorts from Lend Lease funds in November, 1941. They were destined for Britain, but the navy later retained forty-four of them for bolstering its own antisubmarine warfare (ASW) capability for the Battle of the Atlantic. Gibbs and Cox prepared the plans, based on an Admiralty preliminary design and statistics for a 19-knot, 1,150-ton ASW type. Construction took place at five navy yards. Private yards participated heavily in later programs.

In turning to the last major type of combat-vessel development, the submarine, the composition of the military-industrial complex for it has long been clouded. The study here breaks into three fairly neat time periods. The first dates from 1918 to 1924; the second, from 1924 to 1932; and the last through the war period.

In the first, a mixed conglomerate was composed of the navy, Electric Boat Company of Groton, Connecticut, and the Lake Submarine Company of Bridgeport, Connecticut, in the design field; Lake, Bethlehem Steel, and the Navy shared the construction contracts; Busch-Sulzer of St. Louis and Electric Boat subsidiary, Nelseco of New London, the diesel engines; Electric Dynamics (another Electric Boat subsidiary) had nearly monopolized the generator and motor market (over Ridgeway Dynamo and Diehl Mfg. Co.); Electric Storage Battery (Diehl Storage Battery for Lake Boats only), the battery component; Sperry, the gyro compass; and the navy all ordnance. The period marked the completion of extensive wartime construction programs of the sixteen "O" class boats, the twenty-seven in the "R" class and the extensive 51-boat "S" class, all based on designs dating 1916 or earlier. Additionally, the first three of the postwar "V" class, designed in 1919, completed at the very end of this first period.

A parsimonious Congress was to appropriate funds for only six more submarines, the remainder of the "V" class, through 1932. It is a sad commentary that on the scale of the world standard for submarine technology and development, the United States ranked close to the bottom rung among the world submarine powers. All the "O," "R," and "S" class were obsolete on the basis of that world standard, when commissioned, if not when designed; this despite the attempt by the navy to backfit some advanced German technological excellence into eight of the "S" class boats just after the war.

Without doubt the most striking feature of the military-industrial complex in these years was the navy goal to rid the submarines of many of the substandard components which had crippled the submarine force in earlier years. That meant divesting itself of the sources of the problem: the private contractors like Electric Boat, Lake, Bethlehem Steel, and the diesel manufacturers, in the belief that the navy itself could master all of these fields. It tried. By taking over all torpedo development, it put the veteran E. W. Bliss Torpedo Company out of business by 1921. By 1924 the Lake Company of Bridgeport, Connecticut, had collapsed, and Simon Lake, possibly the most inventive genius in the pioneering days of submarining in this country, had to liquidate, as the navy took over all submarine designing and construction. Bethlehem Steel completed its last submarine in the mid-20s, and Electric Boat barely kept itself in business building bridges, printing presses, and a few antiquated submarines for Peru during the 1920s. Busch-Sulzer, a pioneer in two-cycle diesel development, turned to the commercial field exclusively after 1922, and Electric Boat mercifully liquidated its Nelseco subsidiary with its line of substandard submarine diesels at the end of the decade. In the process of invading these fields, the navy also broke some of the old, exclusive monopolies held by subcontractors, inviting, for example, Westinghouse, Elliott, Ridgeway, and General Electric to compete with Electro-Dynamics in the electrical field, and Arma to compete with Sperry for gyros. These were areas beyond its own competence.

The second period, from 1924 to 1932, was one without an industrial side to a military-industrial complex, save in parts subcontracting. Technically, then, a military-industrial complex did not exist. the navy held a clear monopoly. In those years, it designed and constructed five submarines in four classes (at Portsmouth and Mare Island Navy Yards): a minelayer, two classes of long-range cruisers, and the first of two coastal submarines, the latter conceived originally as a unified coastal and cruiser type. These projects attempted to produce successful prototypes, based upon a blending of German and American technology, required for the missions in War Plan *Orange* against Japan. In spite of the many technological improvements in these classes, none were ever repeated, and each vessel and type had a number of serious deficiencies.

In 1932 the navy, perhaps realizing its own limitations, re-created a true military-industrial complex. By sharing design and construction work with Electric Boat Company and leaving the diesel and air-compressor fields to private firms, it set a goal to evolve a successful fleet-type submarine, capable of fulfilling all the missions in the war plans. Out of the variety of experiences from the past and that clear goal, supported by adequate funding, the navy and nation built a force of some 200 standardized fleet submarines before the war started. It was a success story. Perhaps it would not have been one of the navy had not controlled the military-industrial complex through its inspectorate system and the Submarine Officers' Conference group, the real arbiter for quality control. The measure of success will be found in the historical record. The United States Submarine Force contributed mightily to the victory over Japan.

This kind of pattern is less clear in the programs which developed other naval vessels. Over eight hundred motor torpedo boats, for example, heavily influenced by the British *Vosper* type, were developed and constructed by private manufacturers like Elco and Higgins. Many auxiliary craft, including vessels for the Amphibious Force, evolved through conversions of naval or commercial vessels, private design and construction ventures, or navy prototypes, copied and produced by private firms.

Material procurement was vitally important in the naval military-industrial complex, as well. The carriers had to have aircraft and there was ordnance and communications equipment, among a vast number of other things. Initially the United States depended heavily on existing military aircraft for its carrier air groups. Most of these were converted to meet carrier requirements by the Naval Aircraft Factory. In the fifteen years following 1927, however, no less than seventy private design and manufacturing firms participated in the naval aircraft procurement program. Curtiss and Chance-Vought figured prominently in the military-industrial complex throughout the period. Boeing and Martin were replaced by such firms as Grumman, Douglas, and Convair for combat aircraft types in that same period.

The Naval Aircraft Factory, prodigy of the Navy's Bureau of Aeronautics, gradually faded in importance. Wright and Pratt-Whitney emerged as the most successful engine producers after 1935. It was these firms which produced the successful fighter, torpedo, and dive bomber, observation and patrol bomber types of the Second World War. In another area, Goodyear monopolized the production of lighter-than-air blimps. although by the end of the period private industry had successfully monopolized airframe and engine design and production, the navy exerted considerable control over the entire procurement program. The Bureau of Aeronautics still defined aircraft and parts specifications and managed an extensive naval inspectorate organization and aircraft-testing and evaluation program.

Paralleling this disposition within the military-industrial complex, the navy similarly exercised authoritarian controls over ordnance, communications, and electronics development until roughly 1939. In this vein the Bureau of Ordnance utilized its own prerogatives for the purchase abroad of weapons prototypes (e. g., the Swiss 20 mm. Oerlikon and Swedish 40 mm. Bofors antiaircraft guns), and its own facilities at the Naval Ordnance Laboratory at White Oak, Maryland, and the Washington Navy Yard Gun Factory to produce prototypes and limited production of numerous other gunnery, fire-control, and ballistics components. The Newport, Rhode Island, Torpedo Station served in a like capacity for torpedo production. The Naval Research Laboratory performed yeoman service in research and development phases of radar, radio, underwater sound, and other areas, ultimately contracted out for production to a myriad of private manufacturers. Despite the heavy press of work, only after 1938 did the navy secure government fiscal and legal support to open the floodgates for civilian participation in research, development, design, construction, and material production in large measure.

In an overview of the naval military-industrial complex a clear, overriding pattern is not discernible. Impermanence of a set pattern of relationships was rather the predominate variable. Each of the prime areas of ship-type and component development apparently had its own pattern. If anything, there was a gradual erosion of navy domination as it relinquished exclusive or shared design and construction chores to private industry. In some areas of development the Navy was clearly not even up to the tasks, and had often turned to foreign models. Yet in the main it was design, construction, and supply demands beyond Navy capabilities which caused it to turn over to private industry large sectors of the military-industrial complex which it had invaded during the interwar years. That trend rapidly accelerated after 1938 under impact of successive bills for the "Two-ocean Navy." New legislation permitted extensive funding of private industry to "tool up" for naval production. Directly negotiated cost-plus contracts became the usual method of procurement, and only then did a vast expansion of private participation in production on a nationwide scale ensue. Still the navy never abandoned its definitive role in definition of specifications and quality control. Even during the Second World War Navy Yards undertook construction of nine of the thirteen repeat *Lexington*-class aircraft carriers which reversed the old pattern of private construction monopoly for carriers in prewar years. Despite the fluid quality of the military-industrial complex, the products were generally creditable ones when put to the acid test of war. No military-industrial complex could have hoped for more than that. The lessons remain: the bottlenecks were broken and a viable MIC reestablished only when the threat of war was perilously imminent.

QUANTUM INCREASE: THE MIC IN THE SECOND WORLD WAR

The Second World War massively strengthened the old linkages between American business and the military. The effect was not only one of scale but qualitative as well, for profound changes were under way in science and technology from 1938 to 1945. There are, of course, dangers in generalizing about the fluctuating and confused economic planning, policy, and control, and the almost gossamer aspects of science and psychological warfare and publicity that effected the massive growth of the American industrial and military systems. And it should be kept in mind that there was much error and confusion, that it was human beings, often in a state of stress and fatigue, who shaped the output of the "arsenal of democracy."

This tapestry of activity intensified in richness of hue in the late 1930s with the placing of war-materiel orders in increasing volume by the British and French after Munich and increased defense funds voted by the United States Congress. Prior to Pearl Harbor, for example, America's aviation industry received a billion dollars in development capital from the British. The main problem for the Roosevelt administration, after Munich in 1938, when Hitler's warlike intentions became transparent to all but the self-deceiving and the obtuse, was preparing for war while talking peace. Strong political resistance to involvement prevented formation of a formal, effective war-production regulation system until after Pearl Harbor. And Roosevelt was no readier than Churchill to allow a central supply "czar" to really monitor and control the war effort. But some moves toward rationalizing the fragmentation were possible in 1940 when France's collapse generated enough panic to allow extensive mobilization of industry and manpower. Before and during the war, Roosevelt developed great skill at inventing his own lines of control through and around the bureaucratic maze, which counted for much in moving stealthily against congressional hostility. A larger general staff, charged by statute to plan for mobilization, more sophisticated planning in some areas, and Roosevelt's interest in naval affairs and the development between the wars of such coordinative structures as the Industrial College of the Armed Forces, closed some gaps of the kind that had made American promises ring hollow in the First World War. But many lessons of 1914–18 were ignored or lost, and many mistakes repeated.

There was criticism of the "alphabet soup" of bureaucracies involved in military-procurement and expediting roles. The legion of agencies suggested to some the organizational proliferation of the National Industrial Recovery Act in the early New Deal, for the Reconstruction Finance Corporation, the Office of Price Administration, the Office of Defense Transportation, the Office of War Information, the Board of Economic Warfare, the Army-Navy Munition Board, the Offices of Scientific Research and Development, and so on, in addition to the regular military and civilian bureaucracy. These agencies attempted to resolve the massive tensions generated by essentially uncoordinated, parochial, and long-starved armed services competing for critical materials and manpower. The growing rapport of the American military command with the British led to a tightening of the United States approach to military planning, such as the Joint Chiefs of Staff and further bureaucratization of Washington military, naval, and air commands. The emerging power and independence of the air force within the army was manifested in several ways. The air barons learned much from the Mitchell controversy in 1926 and strong links with some aircraft producers were built during the 1930s, even when money was short. The Air Corps publicity mechanism—Hap Arnold and Ira Eaker, two of Mitchell's key aides and Air Corps leaders during the buildup and the war, both went to journalism school at night after the Mitchell court-martial—built links with oil companies, airframe and engine builders, and the publicity media. By the end of the Second World War, the Army Air Forces had control of a quarter of the army's budget. And, more significantly, the Air Corps got the top slice of manpower quality, not only for aircrew but for menial ground jobs as well until the 1944 infantry replacement crisis.

Since there was no central monitoring and control agency, overlapping and conflicting resource demands became critical at many points. The armed services and branches often played dog in the manger with facilities and stocks of material, just as industries resisted the creation of potential competition. The formal separation of the General Staff and the logistical function in the War Department reorganization did not help, nor did the parochial interests and inertia of the technical branches, an old problem. The intricacies and harsh realities of lead time, priorities, stockpiling, and phasing of production and resources continually put crimps in well-laid plans, and confounded the dreams and promises of those who could not visualize the orchestration of men, space, and materials in a web of interlocking activities to produce a given output. Computers and PERT charts, imperfect as they seem today, were not available and guesswork led to waste. The complexities of interaction did, however, lead to happy results on occasion. One case, the development of the P-51, illustrates the complexities of defense production and expansion in the Second World War.

Liquid-cooled engine development in the United States was subsidized on a limited basis by the Army Air Corps during the 1930s. Funds were short in all phases of American defense development. The one liquid-cooled United States engine available in 1940 was the Allison Engineering Company's V-1710, similar in concept to the Rolls-Royce *Merlin,* but much weaker in power output. While Allison began work in 1930 and Rolls-Royce in 1933, Allison (A General Motors subsidiary after 1929) built one prototype at a time, while the latter built several. The army insisted on several key modifications as development proceeded. Allison's engine went to test in seven years—ahead of two competitors—but the *Merlin* took less than three and a half.

The *Merlin* engine had been developed from the Rolls-Royce *Goshawk, Kestrel* and the Rolls-Royce engine of 1931, and was partially based on data gained by Britain in winning the Schneider Trophy seaplane races. As the Royal Air Force (RAF) pulled ahead in the Battle of Britain, it became apparent that the *Merlin* was the best liquid-cooled engine in service.

By the late summer of 1940, RAF inspectors began to make critical comments about American-built aircraft. It was not easy for some Americans to accept the idea that the Europeans could be ahead in matters mechanical. A furious debate, begun in the United States regarding American aircraft quality, reverberated to England. As it became apparant that available United States first-line fighters were undergunned and underpowered in the European theater, the British relegated most US models to less active theaters of operation. The revelation led to emotional pronouncements in American service journals and the technical press, such as James Peck's insistence in the December, 1940, *Scientific American* that:

America's warplanes. . .outperform by far any European World War II craft of any type or model and they are built to a higher specifications standard and of materials that are vastly superior. . . . We inherit certain imponderable qualities with which America alone seems blessed in these dark days. . .our industry and engineering genius afford [the American aviator] the finest of equipment..That is the American way.

The hard-pressed British decided otherwise. Of eighteen American combat-type aircraft models sent to Britain on purchase or Lend Lease before

Pearl Harbor, twelve were either kept out of combat altogether or away from the "Big League" in air war, the European theater. Some of the models used in combat, like the B-17 and the B-24, were extensively modified as the result of unhappy British experience. The only variance in judgment between the United States and British air forces after Pearl Harbor was the US Army Air Force's (USAAF) use of the P-38 over Northwestern Europe.

In spite of patriotic anguish, it became obvious that America needed a first-rate liquid-cooled engine. At the same time, Lord Beaverbrook, the British Minister of Aircraft Production, was seeking more production facilities with a view to potential disaster. If Britain was overrun or bombed out of production, alternate sources—"shadow factories," some planned before the war and already completed—would be essential. The supply of the *Merlin* engine—the standard power plant for several fighters and for the forthcoming Lancaster and Mosquito bombers, as well as tanks and torpedo boats—would be critical in either case. As a result, on June 13, 1940, just before the fall of France, President Roosevelt was given the specifications of the *Merlin* engine, with subsequent rights to be negotiated later.

William S. Knudsen, ex-president of General Motors and Commissioner for Industrial Production, was given the task of fitting American *Merlin* production into the tangle of priorities and projects that mushroomed in the summer of 1940. Since the Ford Company's plant in France and Britain produced the *Merlin*, and since Ford had capital and space, Knudsen negotiated in early June, 1940, with Edsel Ford, who agreed that Ford would build 9,000 engines, 6,000 earmarked for the RAF.

At this point, Henry Ford reacted violently to an announcement by Beaverbrook that Ford would build engines for Britain. He told a red-faced Knudsen, "We won't build the engines at all. Withdraw the whole order. Take it to somebody else." Growingly unstable, Ford saw the move as a Roosevelt-European high-finance conspiracy. He said he would build 1,000 planes a day—a truly impossible goal—as well as design his own aircraft and engine. The Ford Company accepted a contract to build Pratt and Whitney radial engines, but Ford attempts to build aircraft by automobile mass-production methods were less than dramatically successful. The Willow Run plant was dogged by production bugs and failed to run to capacity. Edsel received a barrage of furious letters condemning Henry's refusal. The Canadian Parliament heard demands for confiscation of the Ford plants there. While Henry cheerfully accepted the James Watt International Model of the British Institution of Mechanical Engineers, the city of San Antonio canceled an order for twenty-two Ford cars. British Ford, which built 34,000 *Merlins* by the end of the war, bought ads stressing its British defense work. Secretary of the Treasury, Henry Morgenthau, appealed vainly to Ford on the basis of "fairness and policy."

Knudsen found another taker. Max Gilman, president of the Packard Motor Car Company, announced that Packard would hire 14,000 workers and produce 840 *Merlin* engines a month in fifteen months. But Packard, a luxury-car builder with only 700 workers, needed space and capital to get things under way. In August, to overcome bankers' resistance, the Defense Plant Corporation, established by the Reconstruction Finance Corporation, moved in. Packard would rent necessay plant space while the title stayed with the Government. Packard was the first US automobile company into aviation-engine manufacturing and received the first cost-plus-fixed-fee contract.

In July, 1940, three Rolls-Royce engineers proceeded to Detroit from Derby to advise on design, installation, and production. Meanwhile, 20,000 drawings crossed the Atlantic on a battleship deck in a freight-car-sized crate. An apocryphal story suggests this was most unnerving to a civil servant who came to dockside to collect the plans with a suitcase.

The job facing J. G. Vincent, Packard vice president of engineering and *Merlin* project chief was staggering, even though Vincent had had experience in Packard's *Liberty* engine project in 1918. The task required filling a plant nearly a mile long with machinery while designing work flow and converting Rolls-Royce drawings to American usage. At first, the *Merlin* seemed so complex that the wisdom of the project was questioned. Doubt was expressed that the engine might no longer be needed when production began. Before signing the contract, Vincent formed a special engineering group, and met with Ford personnel regarding their preliminary work.

The RAF sent Packard a stock *Merlin* 28 engine to aid the conversion. Packard engineers had denied that close Rolls-Royce tolerances were feasible for volume production. But double-checking the stock engine indicated that they did exist. Then a financial cloud appeared on the already-turbulent horizon. Since two-thirds of the engines were for Britain, Reconstruction Finance Corporation support threatened to go aground on legal rocks. At this point, before Lend-Lease, the British Purchasing Commission advanced $20 million to Packard as capital assistance. Forty percent of United States pre-Pearl Harbor aircraft production was paid for by British and French capital. As it turned out, the first nine *Packard-Merlins*, symbolizing teething troubles, cost Packard $6,250,000. The profit was $6,206, a far cry from Packard's high cost-plus gains of *Liberty* engine manufacturing in the First World War.

Another problem of large proportions in World War I had been that of patents. Several British licensers who had placed contracts in the US were later awarded damages by the United States Government for patent infringement. In the case of the *Merlin,* the British Purchasing Commission indemnified the United States Government against patent action by Rolls-Royce.

The passage of the War Powers Act in 1941 allowed contract modification of the engine. The legal-technological confusion over contract redrafting was no small matter. By the end of the war, the contract, signed by the War Department, the British Purchasing Commission, and Packard, was modified 199 times and was a foot-thick document.

Vincent decided not to visit the Rolls-Royce works. Constrained by the principle of full interchangeability with British-made engines, Vincent nevertheless intended to design the operation, reduce handwork as much as possible, and stay close to his own methods. He soon found that British plans lacked details customary in American shop practice. The British passed on rather detailed information through verbal agreements between shop foreman and engineers.

Making a complex aircraft engine proved quite different from automobile manufacturing. Working drawings had to be converted from British first projection to American third projection, a reversal of the point of view from which each particular part was seen. In addition, data not on the British plans had to be added to the drawings to guide the American workmen, and conversions had to be made from the metric to the inch system. And, since there were three basic types of British threads involved with variations on each, a special chart had to be prepared for distribution to the American subcontractors describing each type in detail.

The next phase of conversion required setting manufacturing priorities in terms of complexity and securing of data not included in the British shop notes, some of which were ambiguous by American standards. Before construction began, parts had to be analyzed metallurgically to assure parallel chemical composition. And all the while new help was being recruited and trained, as new machines were procured and phased into the growing operation.

Due to shortage of skilled labor, use of automatic machines and accelerated training was essential. There were twice as many parts in the engine as there had been in the entire 1941 Packard Clipper automobile. A *Merlin* required seventy-seven times the Clipper's amount of assembly time, as well as assembly and reassembly during rigid testing and measuring of clearances of a ten-thousandth of an inch. By 1943 Packard had 39,000 employees—more than twice the original estimate.

But Packard achieved mass production by December, 1941. In spite of cramped conditions, labor problems, and changes in specifications from Rolls-Royce during setup, Packard eliminated two-thirds of the handwork. One variant in method which demonstrated the difference between American and British approaches was the use of spacing washers used in assembly to take up play caused by machining. While the British practice was to grind the washers to tolerance, Packard response made a variety of sizes, and filled in with combinations.

Volume is not always the main goal in manufacturing, and certainly was not in World War II. This was seen early in the war when the British recognized a seemingly conflicting requirement for high-quality, highly finished aircraft *and* mass-produced short-lived planes. This problem became accentuated in 1942–43 when German advances in fighter design made quick response vital. The mass-production lines of Packard at Detroit and Ford at Dagenham did not allow the rapid changeover on the *Merlin* which the Rolls-Royce home works at Derby with its large staff of men trained in the craft tradition could provide. Packard and Ford could build cheaper. But the *Merlin* went through fifty-two separate marks (model changes) during the war. Engine power was doubled and rated altitude nearly tripled by continual refinements, often under heavy combat pressure.

The Packard engines delivered to Britain went to Bomber Command. Various marks of the Packard-built *Merlin* powered the Lancaster Mark III, the Royal Air Force's principal heavy bomber in the Second World War. In addition to boosting the sluggish performance of the Kittyhawk P40F, the Packard *Merlin* was also the power plant of most Spitfire marks and in seventeen Mosquito marks. But fate had a hand in shaping the most spectacular use of the U. S. *Merlin.*

The US Army Air Force was slow to appreciate the *Merlin,* and initially those delivered to the Air Force were installed in the Curtiss P-40, which had been using the *Allison.* However, while Packard was tooling up, the British asked North American Aviation to design to their specifications a new fighter which became the A-26. Initially powered by the *Allison,* it proved upon delivery to be the best US-made fighter to date, but slow by British standards, particularly at higher altitudes. But the USAAF paid little attention and its own official historians labeled the apathy as "close to. . .the costliest mistake of the war." But what made the P-51 the best American fighter of the war (and a champion in postwar air races) was the marriage of the North American airframe with the *Merlin* 61 and later marks, most of which were Packard-made. This had been initially done by the RAF at Rolls-Royce at the suggestion of Major Thomas Hitchcock, United States air attaché in London. A better fit than the *Allison* two-stage liquid-cooled engine, the *Merlin* boosted the operational speed of the "Mustang" from 375 to 430 miles per hours, and later to 450. The P-51 became one of the best fighter escorts of the war, although exceeded by some Spitfire marks in speed and rate of climb. By 1945, Packard had turned out 55,523 of 166,000 *Merlins* built.

The *Merlin* story touches on another aspect of American aviation procurement: Howard Hughes. General Henry Arnold, head of the USAAF in World War II, tried to get *Merlin*-powered British Mosquito bombers for photo-reconnaissance. Frustrated in attempts to borrow or buy Mosquitos, he overrode Air Materiel Command cautions and ordered procurement of Hughes' F-11, which was not delivered until a year and a half after the war. The delay led to dramatic congressional hearings. Interestingly, the reason Arnold cited in *Global Mission* for not accepting a British offer of Mosquito drawings for United States construction was: "After our experience with the British *Merlin* engine (trying to change their metric drawings to standard measurements) that was out of the question." But the navy was stung as well in the case of the "Spruce Goose," Hughes' giant plywood flying boat. The behemoth was ordered early in the war for use across the Pacific in fear of Japanese interdiction of convoys. Like the F-11, it was not flown during hostilities.

There were other problems on land and at sea as well in terms of equipment quality. Fuses of US Navy submarine torpedos proved defective in early combat patrols, leading to a crash research and development project and eventual closing of the Newport Torpedo Factory. The M-1 Garand rifle, designed in the late 1930s, was finally in the hands of most army and marine forces by 1943. It had chronic problems with sand and dirt stoppage, however; and when it fired its last round, it ejected the clip with a loud telltale ring, signaling to the enemy a pause to reload. The only submachine gun in major production early in the war was the Thompson, favorite of Chicago gangsters and film makers, which had a high unit cost and low accuracy. Most of the two million made went to Allied nations. Later marks were followed by the M-3 "grease gun," but all fell short of the German MP 38 and 40. The Browning automatic rifle and the Browning .30-caliber machine gun, both standard with the army and marine infantry, were heavier, more prone to stoppage, and more difficult to maintain than corresponding weapons of the Allied and Axis powers. Yet the American passion for standardization did avoid the Japanese dilemma of having three different cartridge-rim types for rifles, light and heavy machine guns. The improvising skill of American ordnance personnel and troops took up much slack in the system, and American troops benefited from miniature field radios and medical support unknown to other combatant nations.

At sea, the shipping shortage saw the Henry J. Kaiser system of mass production of Liberty ships, unglamorous but essential 10-knot transports. Early production bugs led to an occasional ship loss when fledgling workers brazed over rods on joints rather than welding a full bond. But as production systems matured throughout American industry, the volume astounded the enemy and Allies alike. One Liberty ship was built in four days fifteen hours. The following representative figures suggest some of the overall American production feat:

Table 4.

U. S. WAR PRODUCTION 1941-1945

2,695 Liberty ships	22 million steel helmets
3,700 military posts	95,000 railway cars
295,959 aircraft (58,000 to Allies)	7,500 locomotives
88,410 tanks	8 battleships
2.7 million motor vehicles	48 cruisers
400,000 artillery pieces	349 destroyers
100,000 mortars	412 destroyer escorts
6.5 million rifles	203 submarines landing craft
6.1 million carbines	79,125 landing craft
2 million submachine guns	27 carriers
3 million other small arms	110 escort carriers

Of the $304 billion that the United States spent on military-related items in the Second World War, $49 billion went to Lend-Lease. Of the $30 billion which went to the United Kingdom, $6 billion was returned in the form of exchange services and goods.

In raw terms, the United States expended a significant portion of its vast oil reserves and the Mesabi iron range in a war of materiel. The defects in American armament already noted were offset by volume and quality in those areas most commensurate with American peacetime industry. The Churchillian aphorism about the war being won by the C-47 transport, a military version of the Douglas DC-3, and the bulldozer, was more than half truth. The scale and quality of American logistics staggered the poverty-stricken British and the Russians as well. The Seabee naval construction battalions performed engineering miracles, often in the middle of battle—and were formed on the expertise and "shop culture" skill of American industry. The Alcan Highway defied the predictions of experts, as did "Pick's Pike," the Ledo Road from Northern India into China. The air convoys across the Hump similarly confounded Japanese, and perhaps Chinese, expectations. The fantastic array of equipment and creature comforts attendant on American operations in the Pacific generated "cargo cults" among Pacific islanders who hoped to call back the great fleets and bases of 1942–45.

A major force monitoring the United States war effort was the Committee to Investigate the National Defense Effort, formed in the spring of 1941 as the result of a resolution by Senator Harry S. Truman of Missouri. The committee sat until 1948, eventually under three chairmen, its testimony running to tens of thousands of pages (almost six hundred feet of shelf space) as it delved into areas of potential inefficiency and abuse that its broad charge covered. Truman maintained a low posture, avoiding grandstanding publicity and using investigators and the committee counsel for close-in work. The committee served two basic purposes. It brought abuses and defects in the defense machinery to the attention of Congress and the public, and it created an atmosphere where corner-cutters faced the imminent threat of investigation and nonjudicial revelation of mis- or malfeasance and publicity.

There were, of course, organizational problems and abrasive personalities threaded through the machinery of defense procurement and expedition. General Brehon Somervell of the Army Service Forces was a pretty crusty character. Admiral King fought to wrench procurement away from Undersecretary James V. Forrestal. Labor leader Sidney Hillman, Associate Director of the Office of Production Management (OPM), suggested to many a Renaissance politician. The OPM, with command split between Hillman and former automobile executive William S. Knudsen, came under early scrutiny and was replaced in 1942 by the War Production Board under Donald M. Nelson.

One of Truman's motives in cutting into the vast and often impenetrable tangle of expediency, confusion, and greed, was his detestation of lobbyists as a symptom of big corporate power at the expense of the small businessman—which Truman himself had once been. From June 1, 1940, to April 30, 1941, Truman noted, $3 billion was awarded in government contracts to firms whose executives were in Washington in the bureaucracy as "dollar-a-year" men. They were still paid by their companies, and far more influential than lobbyists. Some found it difficult to sort out the war effort and the postwar interests of their firms. The armed services' relations with certain firms had been maintained during lean peacetime-budget years through personal, informal contracts. They often tended to be generous to old friends. Nine of thirteen companies on navy contracts in 1941 were awarded fees and possible bonuses in excess of their total corporate net worth in 1939. One such firm's profits increased eight-hundredfold. Yet the question that was frequently asked was: What price victory? Or, more pointedly: How cost-effective is defeat? In all areas of procurement, the tendency was, for purposes of ease, to award the big firms contracts. The Army Ordnance Corps, for example, fought Truman Committee efforts to have the government purchase direct from subcontractors rather than through the "Big Three" auto firms which would purchase spare parts and resell to the government. Ordnance argued that big corporations had the know-how and administrative network which the government would duplicate in dealing directly with the smaller manufacturers. There were counterparts to the "Big Three" syndrome in other areas of procurement, especially in aviation and shipbuilding.

The war was an opportunity for millions of workers as well as manufacturers. The use of inspectors with small salaries—the navy alone had 38,000—and low prospects of promotion to monitor wild growth was perhaps naive. But the fact that few excesses appeared even in postwar audits was a tribute to the sense of duty of most such government agents. But scandals there were, including blockage of plant construction in aluminum and steel, apparently to preempt postwar competition. Cheating on inspection standards led to the death of air trainees, and armor-plate tensile-strength tests were fudged. Glenn Martin insisted on pushing ahead with the B-26 Marauder bomber, even though its small wing area and poor glide characteristics made it known among flyers as the "Flying Prostitute—no visible means of support." Only a personal confrontation with Truman before the committee forced a redesign.

Nevertheless, in spite of such efforts to balance and diffuse procurement, small businessmen found opportunities hedged in by large firms' government subsidy to build space, by priority allocations in favor of large firms, and by high wages and advancement potential offered by big companies already under multiple government contracts. In some cases unions joined in and charged exorbitant rates for work permits.

Congress considered the problem of excess profits before America's entry into the war, and its debates on the subject in the summer of 1940 stopped most defense procurement for three months until legislation resolved questions of tax amortization and profit limits which subsequently led to excess profits taxes, the formulation of rent freezes, and wage and price controls—all in awareness of the profiteering in 1917–18, and the interwar hearings on the merchants of death.

In policing potential abuse of the windfall provided by war, a primary lesson of 1917–18 was applied in the avoidance of the use of "cost-plus-a-percentage-of-cost" contract, an incentive for waste. Limits were tightened in the Second World War, and ceilings set. The award of the Army-Navy "E" for efficiency was a tool of psychological warfare used to appeal to the patriotism and zeal of workers and management. From 1941 to 1943, the sense of urgency created forward motion. The use of consumer rationing channeled toward military use raw materials and food which were then apportioned through priority systems. (Some criminologists later argued that at least 25 percent of American businessmen, and perhaps more than half, were involved in black-market violations).

Dissent against the war was denied general publicity as was desertion and draft avoidance. Industrial absenteeism and labor problems appeared from time to time, but only rarely on a major scale. Labor crises did appear, particularly among the miners, under the leadership of the articulate and combative John L. Lewis, and in the railroads as well. Problems with civilian workers of the kind faced by Major Devereux on Wake Island and Admiral Dan Barbey in the Southwest Pacific were also generally out of the public view. But, after 1942, strikes were undoubtedly fanned by the soaring corporate profits and the lack of goods on which workers could spend money. War-bond drives were designed not to buy war materiel but to soak up surplus earnings which could generate inflation. And occasional abuse by management of the "essential industry" draft exemption generated tension as well. Nevertheless, labor benefited from the military-industrial system as the wage-freeze led to negotiation over "fringe benefits" like health insurance.

Branch and service rivalry within the military led to the need for continual and elaborate administrative adjudication. Batteries of judge advocate officers were arrayed close to manufacturing centers to cope with contract litigation. To strengthen administrative control in the military, direct commissions and general officer status were awarded to senior executives in expediter roles. William S. Knudsen, for example, was a four-star general.

There were, of course, subtler questions to be decided, such as the problem of cartels and international firms in every territory linked to American businesses. It seemed to some that the selection of bombing targets was edged around by the fact that destruction of key sites or processes might have postwar economic implications. Diplomacy also touched on the question of production. A windfall for the American airline industry was a British-American agreement early in the war regarding production priorities. Since Britain was under attack, it was decided that America would build Allied transport aircraft. When the war ended, United States airlines had access to stocks of two- and four-engined transports immediately useful as civil airlines vehicles, while the virtually bankrupt British made do with converted bombers.

The role of science and industry in the service of the war was fantastic by prewar standards. The allocation of $2 billion and a quarter of a million people to the Manhattan Project—the atomic bomb—was a prodigious gamble. The Truman Committee had to be steered away from its sacrosanct boundaries, and Ronald Clark, in *The Bomb That Failed,* speculated as to the impact of the boondoggle if the bomb had not worked. The Manhattan Project was paralleled by less spectacular, but crucial, efforts by hundreds of scientists applying techniques of "operations research" (OR) to military problems. OR had evolved in the late 1930s when British scientists used multi-disciplinary teams and scientific method to design an air-defense net based on radar, fighter aircraft, radio and telephone systems, antiaircraft guns, etcetera. The need for high-speed calculation in OR led to the construction of electronic vacuum-tube computers. The Allied elimination of U-boats in the Atlantic was greatly assisted by an OR approach. In the case of the development of Air Force battle armor, scientists, art curator armor experts, and metallurgists worked together to dramatically reduce aircrew casualties in Europe. OR was also applied to weapons development, and the analysis of problems in the field began to shape weapons systems, rather than the vendor developing and promoting weapons based on intuitive marketing.

Relations between the services and industry was sometimes closer than between military command levels. The gap between operational units and their headquarters and bases was overcome only partially and unevenly. General Curtis LeMay told in his memoirs of the vain struggle to get the effective mercury vapor bombsight to replace the highly touted but relatively inadequate Norden bombsight. The services were sluggish themselves in reading the needs of field units, and the focus of OR was necessarily selective and limited. Informal battle bulletins, service schools, and the popular military publications carried an uneven flow of lessons learned in battle, especially when, like S. L. A. Marshall's findings about low infantry effectiveness, they were embarrassing. Industry sometimes did more to close the gap than the formal military structure. Technical representatives ("tech. reps."), like Colonel Lindbergh, appeared in the field, carrying information back to the point of design and production, a trend which would grow dramatically in the next generation of weapons development, one which tended to blur the boundary between military and civilian.

A related area requiring delicate balance, similar to the problem facing General Ripley, the Chief of Ordnance in Lincoln's day, was the sifting of varieties of equipment on the basis of quality as well as cost. Hedges had to be built against potential failure. Only one very expensive prototype B-19 was delivered to the Air Corps. The Riesing submachine gun and Johnson automatic rifle eventually became collectors' items. The tank-destroyer concept was a hedge against losing the battle of tank production with Germany. The B-32 Dominator program was an expensive but vital alternative program paralleling the B-29. Such parallel programs were expensive, since development to prototype was often the most costly phase of production in money and man power. But cases like the Dominator dramatized the difficulty of balancing cost against combat effectiveness in wartime. Barracks and 'tween-decks jokes about equipment being bought on low bid were made only half in jest.

In spite of growing sophistication in scientific military problem solving, instability and economic overheating stemmed from the crudity or absence of effective measuring instruments. The United States was lucky in one respect, for it tooled up at a time when the Great Depression had cleared the decks for redesign of the economy, with millions of men and vast amounts of resources, expertise, and space available—and motivated for revenge by a surprise attack. The wild enthusiasm with which long-anxious manufacturers and out-of-work workers attacked the problem created a roller-coaster atmosphere. That and the administrative fragmentation leaves the viewer with hindsight amazed that there was not more waste and greed on the scale of the Credit Mobilier. From 1943 on, the phasing of the economy toward peacetime was as awesome a problem for administrators in government and private industrialists as was gearing up for war. The free-wheeling atmosphere of wartime production, with full tax write-off on equipment and plant in five years, and antitrust laws ignored, was matched in the hasty contract termination and conversion in 1944 and 1945. Statutory contract renegotiation in 1942–43 had paved the way slightly, but the Baruch-Hancock Report's suggestion of a sixty-day phase-out—"fair, firm and fast"—shocked many congressmen and administrators. Yet here too the integrity of most government negotiators staved off much potential abuse, although some argued that renegotiation strangled innovation along with excess profits. Some corporate executives were so eager to get into peacetime mode that they bypassed the chance for profits under the wartime system. With special provision for termination financing, the US economy went into a growingly liquid state from 1944 on in anticipation of full employment and a postwar boom. During all phases of World War II—in the prewar buildup, in the scurrying after Pearl Harbor, in the groping for stability in 1942-43, and in the phase-out—the government stood by with money to ease each point of stricture. The result was an economy stronger in the wake of war than any power in history. US industry emerged from the crucible of war shored up by an American gold monopoly, by new and undamaged facilities, with a vast array of new experiences and techniques, and habituated to a profitable symbiosis of military expediency and industrial power. The release of long-pent frustration and the needs of war generated a flash of energy which almost eclipsed the long night of the Great Depression.

The richness of American resources and the flush of victory obscured much waste and confusion. Much of the cost of the war was passed along to the future via the national debt. There had been no organizational genius like Albert Speer—and perhaps no need for one—to deftly orchestrate American resources. The extent of waste and scrappage can, perhaps, never be approximated. The competitive free-enterprise system implies wastage which economies based on weaker resource footings cannot always afford. But America could—or thought it could—and the results are still coming home to roost at the time this is written in 1975.

The extent to which the federal government was involved in massive social engineering was not fully sensed. If it had been, it seems unlikely that anyone would have had the time or inclination to do anything about it. But there were symptoms. One was the 1943 Detroit race riots in which the flow of rural blacks to northern industry was dramatized, as was the functional segregation in northern cities and formal segregation in the US armed forces. Racial troubles were endemic during the war in northern cities and around southern military camps where black troops were stationed. Perhaps the greatest failure of US military and political leadership in tne Second World War was their inability to involve blacks in the war effort more effectively than had been the case in World War I. The achievement of industry in this case was perhaps somewhat better than the military. But in both segments of the military-industrial system, most black workers and soldiers held the lowest and most marginal roles, in some cases because of deficient education and training but also due to stereotyping, which broke down only toward the war's end and then only partially.

Granted the war was, as Andrew Hacker noted in *The End of the American Era,* a "good thing" for many Americans and that it set precedents and built linkages between the military and its suppliers stronger than ever before. But there had been also massive changes in military technology, increased lead time, costs, hazards, and sophistication that made it impossible for a major industrial power to collapse its postwar military system in the classic Anglo-Saxon tradition of:

> In time of trouble, not before,
> God and the soldier we adore,
> But when trouble's past and all things righted,
> God's forgotten and the soldier slighted.

Too much had changed. Techniques of planning and projecting had been refined. The destructive power and range and speed of weapons had increased. The margin for error was shaved from years in 1940 to hours in 1945. America was faced with a collapse of its oceanic buffers, and an end to 150 years of hothouse isolation which protected it against the crude realities of unfortunate Europe and Asia. In spite of the spectacular successes, the American reflex against *res militariae* slumbered on during the Cold War. For the achievements of 1941-45 were so dazzling that the links between patriotism, self-interest, and production were not questioned seriously for almost two decades, when in the late 1960s, the shadows of Vietnam eclipsed the bright afterglow of the Great Crusade for Freedom.

THOMAS E. KELLY

THE CONCRETE ROAD TO MIC:
NATIONAL DEFENSE AND FEDERAL
HIGHWAYS

It was the dream of the Old General that a man could get into his car;
turn the ignition key; back out of the driveway; stop at the intersection;
make a right turn on to Interstate 490 and proceed south to Interstate 90
and then west to San Francisco, 2,900 miles away. In the year 1956, with
the price of gas at 23.9¢ per gallon, the dream of the General was good
and the people accepted his wisdom. He also dreamed that if a war came,
a big sign would go up on the highway and the road would be closed to all
except military traffic. For General—by 1956, President—Dwight D. Eisenhower remembered his first encounter with cross-country driving and also
the ease with which the German army, and later his own men, moved on
the *Autobahn*.

But in 1974 the General's dream came into question. With its forward
and backward linkages the automobile industry was the key industry in
the United States. Over 20 percent of all steel produced found its way into
the automobile industry; 66 percent of all the rubber manufactured in the
United States rolled on our highways, and 90 percent of America's gasoline
contributed to the smog pall over those highways. Because of the gas crisis
in the winter of 1973–74, concerned Americans began to wonder about
the wisdom of turnpike driving, especially the cross-country, non-traffic-
light variety. Calling the Old General's dream for an accounting, it seemed
easy to fix the blame on the military-industrial complex, especially since
the highway could close in the event of a national military emergency. But,
in doing so, the public overlooked the lobbies of automobile manufacturers,
oilmen, highway contractors, real-estate developers, politicians, and highway
officials who are beneficiaries of the national highway program.

In the Federalist Papers, Number 14, James Madison expounded his view of the Constitution's relation to the transportation problem. According to Madison, ". . .the intercourse throughout the Union will be daily facilitated by new improvements. Roads will everywhere be shortened and kept in better order; . . .and interior navigation on our eastern side will be opened throughout, or nearly throughout, the whole extent of the thirteen states."

Except for roads constructed by the army fighting Indians on the frontier and for the Lancaster-Philadelphia Turnpike, there was an absence of major road construction in the thirteen original states. The main reason for inactivity was the ongoing constitutional debate over internal improvements. On the issue of roads, the strict constructionists clearly were in a dilemma. The Constitution authorized the expenditure of funds to build and maintain post roads, but practically all roads could be construed as post roads. Even with this advantage the broad constructionists were only able to win one major victory in the drive for federal internal improvements: financing for the National Road which was authorized in 1806.

Albert Gallatin, Secretary of the Treasury under President Jefferson, issued in 1808 the now-famous *Report . . . on the Subject of Public Roads and Canals*. He presented a very detailed analysis of the nation's transportation network and its problems. He recommended that a communications network be established connecting the northern and southern states and also the trans-Appalachian West with both North and South. Money to finance this program would come, he proposed, from initial sales of the western lands. His ambitious proposals, however, became entangled in the constitutional debate. It is significant that Gallatin's proposals had the approval of the strict constructionist, Jefferson. Indeed, Jefferson in his Second Inaugural Address noted that the Treasury surplus should be, "applied to rivers, canals, roads. . . ."

In this early period of road building the role that the military—that is, the army—played is difficult to discern. Certainly the roads built during the early Indian campaigns were military roads, yet they also served the settler as well. No complete records exist concerning the exact nature of the military's involvement in road construction prior to the War of 1812. Quartermaster General Thomas S. Jessup wrote in 1831 that some roads had been built by the army before and during the war, but that no records existed. We do know that the army assisted in construction of the National Road and repaired the famous Natchez Trace, connecting Nashville, Tennessee, and Natchez, Mississippi, before 1812.

The military disasters of the war led to a change in thinking about federal assistance. The inability of Generals Hull, Harrison, Wilkinson, and Jackson to move supplies and troops quickly and efficiently within interior lines of communications led to embarrassing defeats and a high cost for the war. In fact, Wilkinson was later court-martialed for his failure against the British at La Colle Mill in Canada—a failure brought about in part by poor transportation. The change in policy was best exemplified in a letter to General Jackson from Secretary of War William Crewford:

The employment of troops in opening military roads. . .has been determined upon by the President, after due deliberation. It is believed to be no less necessary to the discipline, health, and preservation of the troops, than useful to the public interest.

In other words, Madison was saying that better roads are necessary for the defense of the nation and that the army, having nothing better to do, should help to build them.

Problems arose with building roads under the guise of internal improvements. Here Madison proved to be squarely in line with the strict constructionists in the debate over implied powers. As long as a road could be termed a military road, Madison and the Congress would approve its construction, as in the case of Jackson's Military Road which connected central Tennessee to New Orleans. When road construction was labeled an internal improvement as in the "Bonus Bill of 1816," Madison vetoed the measure even though Congress had passed it. The President believed there were not "sufficient precedents" to allow him to sign the measure—a position which deviated greatly from the position he had set forth in Federalist Paper Number 14.

That guardian of states rights, John C. Calhoun, espoused a far different position as Secretary of War in 1819 than he would later in his political career. Calhoun's 1819 report to the Congress stated, "A judicious system of roads and canals, constructed for the convenience of commerce and the transportation of the mail only, without any reference to the military operations is itself among the most efficient means for 'the more complete defence of the United States.'" Calhoun's reasoning for this position was that ". . .the roads and canals which such a system would require are precisely those which would be required for the operations of war. . . ." He thought that a good transportation network was indispensable to the United States because of the country's dependence on a militia and the relationship of its population to the size of the land. The doctrine which Calhoun ennunciated in 1819—that roads which promote commercial expansion are the same as those needed for national defense—recognized that strictly military roads were very few. President James Monroe, however, refused to accept Calhoun's position and approved only those roads which were described as strictly military.

The debate over federal assistance had changed its focus by 1822 when

Monroe vetoed the Cumberland Road Bill. Whereas in the early years of the republic the focus of the debate was the enumerated powers of the Constitution, Monroe in his lengthy veto message allowed that Congress could appropriate money only if it served the ends of common defense and the national welfare. He sidestepped the question of how Congress could determine whether a project would assist the common defense or national welfare. Two years later Monroe did sign the General Survey Act which gave the federal government—that is, the army—the power to conduct surveys for roads and canals which would serve postal, military, and commercial purposes.

The General Survey Bill marked a watershed in the military's role in road building. The bill committed the military to surveying and its inevitable follow-up: construction of roads themselves. On the frontier the army played a most important role in road building in Michigan, Arkansas, Florida, and even on the northeastern frontier in Maine. In 1836 Congress appropriated $100,000 to build the "Great Military Road" as a barrier against the Indians from Minnesota south to Louisiana. In the words of John Quincy Adams, "The Quartermaster General. . .is engaged not merely in erections and accommodations for the troops, but in the construction of roads and bridges for the citizens at large." Given the army's mission to protect emigrants on the frontier and the need to develop a communications system, road construction became a necessary part of the army's role on the frontier. In addition, until the founding of Rensselaer Polytechnic Institute in 1829, West Point was the only institution which educated engineers to perform these duties. So there were other reasons than purely military ones for looking to the military for assistance. Throughout this time frame the interrelationship between military and commercial roads can be best summed up in the words of Secretary Calhoun: "The road or canal can scarcely be designated which is highly useful for military operations, which is not equally required for the industry or political prosperity of the community."

The army entered a second stage in road building in 1838 with the creation of the Corps of Topographical Engineers. Congress had formed the Corps of Engineers in 1802 as a bureau within the US Army and eleven years later a few European-trained topographical engineers joined the Corps of Engineers. Under the energetic Colonel John J. Abert, the topographical engineers took over civil works construction from the already overburdened Corps of Engineers. Finally, in 1838, Secretary of War Joel R. Poinsett defined the duties of each organization, assigning the construction of defensive fortifications to the Corps of Engineers and of civil works construction to the new Corps of Topographical Engineers.

W. Turrentine Jackson in his seminal study, *Wagon Roads West,* notes that the Corps of Topographical Engineers had assistance from the settlers in the Trans-Mississippi West. Throughout the 1840s and 1850s the debate over the constitutionality issue continued, and internal improvements were still judged by the criteria offered by James Monroe. If the inhabitants might benefit directly from a road within their territory, there would be little chance of a bill passing. If, however, the road were described as a military road and would benefit the defense posture of the territory, federal assistance was usually forthcoming. The Corps of Topographical Engineers reached its apex of influence between the years 1853 and 1857 when over $1.3 million was appropriated for constructing wagon roads in the West. In 1856, however, President Franklin Pierce began assigning road construction to the Department of the Interior, thus bypassing the Topographical Engineers and assuring their eventual fall from power. With the advent of the Civil War, the Corps ceased to exist (1863), and its officers and duties were once again assigned to the Corps of Engineers.

But the defunct Topographical Engineers left an invaluable legacy of new roads and improvements in existing roads throughout the Trans-Mississippi West. The Topographical Engineers also made the first accurate maps of the West, and gave detailed geological and botanical descriptions of the land and its resources in their reports. The Corps conducted the Pacific Railroad Surveys and mapped the routes that the Southern Pacific, Central Pacific, and Northern Pacific would later follow in the post-Civil War railroad-building era. Their published observations of conditions in the West made the settlers' uncertain journeys much easier. As William Goetzmann has observed, the Corps, ". . .was a central institution of Manifest Destiny."

This picture differs from conventional images of the West. Both in its enlisted and officer ranks, the army led the Western Expansion. The first settlers, unprepared to meet the challenges and uncertainties of frontier life, asked the federal government for help. In this case it was building a communications network. The federal government responded by assigning the task to the military, perhaps the only institution organized and equipped to handle it in early America. It differs markedly from the usual portrait of nineteenth-century America as one embracing *laissez-faire*. Studies by Carter Goodrich and Harry Schriber note that the government extended the same kind of support during the canal-building boom. In the antebellum period the army certainly did act as the purveyor to Manifest Destiny. In analyzing the first seventy years of the republic the frontier virtues of independence and courage, which Frederick Jackson Turner and others ascribe to the settlers, are to some extent valid. But the historian searching for the antecedent to the modern military-industrial complex must seek to understand this early dependence upon the federal government.

The best example of the people manipulating the government is the army's change in status after the Civil War. The antebellum army had been actively involved with Western Expansion; the post-1865 army was relegated to guarding the settler and especially the new railroads from the hostile Indians. One military scholar, S. L. A. Marshall, has even intimated that the army's role on the frontier was to bring civilization to the Indians. Actually, it was to protect the economic investments in towns, railroads, and farms from the people who had original rights to the land. This interpretation is one which most scholars do not subscribe to in their reading of military history. So the role of the army had evolved from explorer and builder to protector—all without challenge.

Still, the real union was that of industry and government as the government catered to the railroad at the expense of the settler. The railroads received over 181,000,000 acres of land to induce them to build westward. Other evidences of a government-industry link were the passage of the Desert Land Act of 1877, the Timber and Stone Act of 1878, and the fraudulent practices of speculators under the Preemption Act and Homestead Act.

Because of the nation's fascination with the speed and power of the iron horse, the campaign for roads lagged. Indeed Martin Dodge, in the *League of American Wheelmen* magazine remarked in 1900 that people believed that the railroad would replace both horse and highway. Jeremiah Jenks, a proponent of road improvement, wrote: "A very large proportion of our people have never seen a really good road for building purposes, and have in consequence no clear idea of the gain that would come from good roads."

According to American mythology, it was the bicycle which brought the good-roads movement: the cyclist needed good roads to ride on and consequently lobbied for that purpose. The cyclists founded the League of American Wheelmen in 1880, ". . .to ascertain, defend, and protect the rights of wheelmen, to encourage and facilitate touring." The story was somewhat more than mythology, because some members of the US Army thought that the bicycle would replace the horse. In fact, the Army even drew up a draft manual for cycling and sponsored a tour from Fort Missoula, Montana, to St. Louis in 1897.

The reality of the good-roads movement differs from the myth. The cost of a bicycle in the 1880s—from $50 to $200—was prohibitive for most Americans. Also, a study of the membership in the League shows that about 60 percent of its members came from New York and New England. When one considers that the League was founded in the capital of the Gilded Age, Newport, Rhode Island, the tenuousness of the so-called bicycle boom becomes much more apparent. The bicycle was a plaything of the wealthy, not a cross-class utilitarian instrument. Only in the late 1890s, when the cost of owning a bicycle was reduced, did it gain a utilitarian rather than a recreational value. Thus the pressure for better roads was coming from a small, concentrated, vocal minority not a broad-based spectrum as commonly thought.

Pressures from varied interest groups—the bicycle lobby, farmer groups, railroad interests, and road builders—led to the establishment in 1893 of the Office of Road Inquiry in the Department of Agriculture. Under the leadership of Roy Stone the new agency collected data on roads and assisted states in developing road programs. Arguments for road improvements received a boost when two counties in New Jersey, Essex and Union, paved their roads, causing improvements in real-estate values. This was not the only argument offered. The old standby arguments were resurrected from the first half of the nineteenth century—when in doubt return to the Constitution. In the words of Stone:

The interest of the general government in common roads has been newly demonstrated by recent events: on the one hand a successful experiment in the rural free delivery of mails, and on the other, a failure of railway transportation for troops in an emergency. . . . It needs post roads and military roads all over the country.

Roy Stone was not alone in using military reasons to promote better roads. The Joint Committee of the 63rd Congress reported to the Congress.

Federal aid to good roads will accomplish several of the objects indicated by the framers of the Constitution—establish post roads, regulate commerce, provide for the common defense, and promote the general welfare.

Throughout the nineteenth century the two most overused reasons offered for federal intervention in the construction and improvement of existing roads were the need to build (1) post roads, and (2) military roads. Both reasons contradict the philosophy offered by Calhoun that the important military roads would be the same as those developed for commercial purposes. But instead of building the roads themselves, state and local authorities looked to the federal government in Washington, cited the importance of military roads and expected the national government to build and maintain them.

During the early 1900s federal legislation was introduced in every Congress, but no bills were passed, nor was any money appropriated. The arguments, which accepted the ability of the federal government to appropriate money, centered mainly upon what type of aid. But they frequently broke down on sectional lines. The real impetus for the first federal-aid-to-highways law came from mass production of the automobile, and to a lesser degree from World War I. By 1915, there were already two million cars on the antiquated wagon-road system, numbers which would increase to ten million by 1920. The logistics problems of moving large numbers of men and equipment during the war put such a strain on the railroad system that finally the government was forced to take over its operation. National leaders saw that the United States needed another transportation network to supplement the railroads.

In July, 1916, the first federal aid to highways was approved; its purpose was, ". . .to provide that the United States shall aid the States in the construction of rural post roads, and for other purposes." Public Law 156 implemented a change in budgetary procedures by appropriating monies for a number of fiscal years, thus binding other Congresses to the program. Decisions concerning which roads to build or improve were left to the Secretary of Agriculture. In terms of military planning, this was a major defect, since the military had no way to influence the choices. The needs of the war machine pointed this out and this feature was corrected through creation of the Council of National Defense. The Council consisted of the Secretaries of War, Navy, Commerce, Labor, Agriculture, and the Interior. One function was ". . .to supervise and direct investigations. . .as to the coordination of military, industrial, and commercial purposes in the location of extensive highways. . . ." Under the direction of the Highways Transport Committee of the Council, the Army's Motor Transport Corps drove trucks from Detroit to Baltimore in the winter over largely unimproved roads.

An event which served to dramatize the need for better roads took place during the summer of 1919. Secretary of War Newton D. Baker authorized the first transcontinental convoy to proceed from Washington, D. C., to San Francisco, California, a distance of 3,242 miles. The caravan consisted of seventy-five vehicles and was commanded by Lieutenant Colonel C. W. McClure. Included in the roster of officers was the junior Major Dwight D. Eisenhower. After a journey of sixty-two days, the caravan arrived in San Francisco on September 6. Natural delays such as sand and mud, combined with man-made delays such as construction and poor bridges, accentuated Secretary Baker's request for military highways in his send-off remarks to the convoy. The legislative programs continued with the passage of the Federal Aid Highway Act of 1921. Under this program states received assistance for up to 7 percent of the highways in the state with a maximum of 3 percent allotted for interstate highways. All powers and duties of the Council of National Defense relating to highways were transferred to the Bureau of Public Roads, Department of Agriculture.

The cooperation which the Federal Aid law ordered was already in practice. On July 24, 1919 the Secretary of War directed that

. . .the General Staff make a study of highways within the Continental limits of the United States and desirable from a military point of view. All the interested departments of the Government and sub-divisions should be consulted. . . . Types of roads, bridges, etc., necessary and priority in construction should be indicated.

In November the War Department and the Bureau of Public Roads agreed ostensibly to the Calhoun Formula: "The roads which must be constructed for commerce and national development will in general be identical with those required for military purposes." They also agreed to set standards of construction which would meet both commercial and military needs. That the War Department was not just paying lip service to the Bureau was emphasized in a letter to the department heads (later Corps Area Commanders) from the Director of the War Plans Division. The letter said that it was desirable to make "use of existing roads and local road projects. . .without impairing appreciably the military value of the system."

Finally in October, 1922, the report, WPD 484-16, was completed and forwarded to the Secretary of Agriculture for dissemination. The study took the form of a map, known as the Pershing Map. On it were drawn the major strategic highways which the War Department felt were necessary to connect "all our important depot, mobilization, and industrial centers, which, as thus connected will give us a transcontinental route." This plan was in contradistinction to a transcontinental road which the lobby groups favored in the same manner as a cross-country railroad. In the letter transmitting the map the then Secretary of War, John Weeks, said, "A transcontinental road which merely crosses the continent is of little military value." Weeks went on to say that he was "most heartily in sympathy with the arrangement now existing between the War Department and the Department of Agriculture." The marriage of the two government agencies would last throughout Thomas MacDonald's tenure as Chief of the Bureau of Public Roads.

In 1939 the two-way partnership of the Bureau of Public Roads and the War Department received a new member, the American Association of State Highway Officials (AASHO). AASHO had represented the interests of state and local highway officials since 1914 and MacDonald, upon becoming chief, had made the bureau a member. With the likelihood of war approaching, AASHO requested that the War Department appoint a committee to discuss construction standards and the selection of routes helpful to National Defense plans. The War Department agreed to send four representatives to the conference, with this comment by Secretary of War Harry Woodring: "In view of the importance of the. . .subject. . .the opportunity to cooperate with your committee is appreciated." Later, in 1939, Henry Wallace, Secretary of Agriculture, and Woodring wrote a letter to the

President saying that financing of highways through toll roads was not feasible and that the so-called Calhoun Formula ". . . was still the best means of having commercial and military highways."

Then, in June of 1940, Roosevelt requested a report on the highway system as it related to the National Defense. MacDonald's staff, in conjunction with military and state officials, drew up a report, "Highways for the National Defense" and sent it to the President in February, 1941. Because the war was at hand the difference in the philosophy of the military and the bureau's staff became much more apparent. MacDonald's philosophy was to build the best road system possible at the time because the initial investment would always be less than a later one. The report recommended the correction of weaknesses in the interstate system, the construction of access roads, and long-range planning. The War Department in an interoffice rebuttal to the report took a pragmatic position that access roads—that is, roads which connected defense installations and important industries with the interstate system—were most important. The report went on to request that, when members of the military appeared before Congress, they should stress those sections as opposed to the bureau's position. They should also emphasize that long-range planning and repairing of the interstate was ". . . not considered to be of sufficient importance to divert funds, energy, materials, and equipment from more pressing national defense requirements. . . .Further improvements of the strategic network is not an urgent need."

Congress, however, accepted MacDonald's recommendations almost in their entirety and passed the National Defense Highway Act in November, 1941. The Japanese interrupted the planned program and the position which the military argued in the congressional hearings was adopted during the course of the war. The emphasis on the construction of access roads led R. H. Baldock at the Thirtieth Annual Meeting of the Western Association of State Highway officials to say, "Unfortunately during World War II highways were considered by many of the national authorities as expendable." Given the immediate needs of the national defense effort, the army's program was the most rational in view of its wartime logistical needs.

The strategic or interregional highways were ignored during the war. In April, 1941, Roosevelt appointed the National Interregional Highway Committee to study the need for a system of national limited access highways and its relationship as an economic measure to combat postwar depression. Two years later the Congress requested that the Bureau of Public Roads make, ". . .a survey of the need for a system of express highways throughout the United States. . .together with such recommendations for legislation as is deemed advisable." The bureau answered the requests from the committee and the Congress with a single report, *Interregional Highways,* which called for the establishment of an interstate system of 34,000 miles. Both defense agencies and the state highway offices had contributed to the report. The study led to legislation in 1944, The Federal Aid Highway Act, and three years later the official designation of the National System of Interstate Highways. Even with its designation, the interstate was not funded until 1952. And that was only a token appropriation of $25 million against a total budget of $652 million. The following year Secretary of Defense Charles Wilson complained to Secretary of Commerce Sinclair Weeks about the low priority accorded highway construction. Of the fifty access roads the Defense Department had requested action on since 1950, only four projects had received attention.

It remained for the Old General, now President, to implement a dynamic federal-aid program for the interstate highways. In July, 1954, Eisenhower, speaking through Vice President Nixon, called the national highway system "obsolete." In September, he appointed General Lucius Clay head of the National Highway Advisory Committee, charged with exploring ways to modernize America's highways. After holding hearings in October, the committee made its report to the President in January, 1955. In section three of the report, "Why the System is Inadequate," national defense needs are not even mentioned and throughout the report only cursory notice is given to national-defense needs. In terms of civil defense the importance of the interstate system was in the evacuation of the civilian population from urban areas. The committee did not foresee the urban rush hours and massive traffic jams created by the suburban sprawl which the urban expressways encouraged.

The report spelled out in concise terms the financing of the interstate program. It called for a ten-year program costing $101 billion, which would be partly financed by a $20 billion bond issue for the interstate system. On February 22, 1955, Eisenhower sent the Clay report to Congress along with a report by the Bureau of Public Roads. While he did not specifically request that the Clay program be enacted, he did claim that the bond issue was the best method of financing the interstate system. But the bond issue proved to be the major obstacle to passage in 1955. Opposition in Congress crystallized around the establishment of a corporation to issue bonds to pay for the program.

The Senate passed a bill (S 1048) similar to past federal legislation, while at the same time it rejected the Administration proposal. The House failed to pass its own traditional highway bill and voted down the Administration version. Eisenhower was deeply distressed by Congress' failure to enact highway legislation and in his 1956 State of the Union Message he again requested highway legislation. He said that America needed a modern highway system for "personal safety, the general prosperity, the national security of the American people. . .and to solve our mounting traffic problem."

Eisenhower also realized that diligent planning and lobbying would have to precede the reintroduction of the measure in the next session of Congress. He formed a special cabinet committee under the chairmanship of Sinclair Weeks, who tried to alleviate differences among the various special interest groups. Included in the group were Albert Bradley of General Motors, John V. Lawrence of the American Trucking Association, and J. H. Bivins of the American Petroleum Industries. There were no military representatives on the committee, thus reinforcing the notion that the only fuction the military performs is to satisfy the scruples of those who see highways as a defense need. They act as a "window dressing," while the real power is vested in the economic interests.

Besides his 1956 State of the Union Message, and the cabinet-level lobbying, Eisenhower also was willing to accept any other sound financial plan in order to assure passage of the program. With the logs properly rolled, the Highway Act was passed out of conference by a voice vote in the House and an 89-1 vote in the Senate. Eisenhower signed the bill on June 26, 1956. The new law brought life to the National System of Interstate and Defense Highways by federal payment of 90 percent of the interstate costs through the Highway Trust Fund.

Thus thirty-four years after the first Pershing Map was developed, the defense highway system became a reality. Very little had changed during those thirty-four years. The new system was essentially the same one which the army and the bureau had agreed upon in the years immediately after World War I. The cooperation which MacDonald and the army had fostered between 1919 and 1953, when he retired, was lost under the new program. Evidence of this lack of communication which was the antithesis of Mac-Donald's program appeared in the "Great Bridge Conspiracy." Vertical clearance under the new program continued at 14 feet. The Secretary of Defense and the Commissioner of the Bureau of Public Roads had agreed upon this height in March, 1949, in compliance with the 1948 Highway Aid Act. At that time the maximum clearance required by the army's general purpose and combat vehicles was 12 feet, 6 inches. This figure corresponded with a 14-foot clearance which the two agencies thought was most appropriate for the national-defense needs.

Apparently the bureau felt that even with the new advances in technology, a 14-foot clearance was appropriate for the new defense-highway program. There was only a cursory consultation with the Department of Defense on this issue. As the special House Subcommittee which was formed to investigate the bridge question reported in 1961:

Shortly after the standard was adopted, the Defense Department began to entertain second thoughts. But, it took 3 years, 6 months and 10 days after the adoption of the 14-foot standard before the vertical clearance was raised to 16 feet. During this time, over 2,200 affected structures were built to a standard that was already obsolete.

The subcommittee found that the highway system which was supposedly planned for national defense floundered on budgetary constraints, not on defense needs. It seemed that very early in the program all sides agreed that there was a need to change the vertical clearance, but the Defense Department and the Commerce Department each thought the other agency should pay for the remodeling.

While the lack of communication was evident on one level between the two government agencies, the 1956 legislation, through its Highway Trust Fund, unleashed the building of highways anywhere, anyplace, anytime. Thus, the military-industrial complex has ceased to exist in military and highway planning, even though the military was deeply involved in road planning and construction in the nineteenth century and even though the military still has a real need for a developed system of roads to meet national-defense requirements.

While military influence on highway building has ebbed, except for the access-roads program, the highway lobby's influence has grown correspond ingly. Its power was demonstrated in 1966 when President Johnson tried to slow inflation caused by the Vietnam War by withholding $1.1 billion from the highway trust fund. Johnson chose the most appropriate time for the announcement: after the 1966 elections, with the actual order coming on the Wednesday before Thanksgiving. The highway lobby, arguing that the public welfare must be safeguarded and that Johnson's action was illegal, was able to mount a campaign to force Johnson to reconsider and release the monies.The mere act of pressuring Lyndon Baines Johnson into doing something against his will attests to the strength of the highway lobby.

Lewis Mumford, writing in the 1960s, echoed the power of the lobby by saying, "Highways are impressive, flashing things to build. No one is against highways." But, Nadarite groups in Seattle, San Francisco, and New York have effectively attacked the lobby's power and have stopped projects. The road builders continue to justify their desire to build with the rationale of national defense. And so the insanity goes on.

Can anyone truly justify the wide swath through our cities as important to our national defense? The lobby can: "They will enable us to evacuate the city in case of nuclear attack." Has the lobby ever attempted to leave the city during rush hour? It is not difficult to imagine both military and civilian vehicles trying to leave a city after a thirty-minute warning of attack has been given. The fallacy in the lobby's arguments is apparent, yet, instead of opting for mass-transit solutions to solve transportation problems in the cities and assist in ecological solution, the lobby panders to the American desire for individual freedom at the expense of the general welfare.

EDWARD C. EZELL

PATTERNS IN SMALL-ARMS PROCUREMENT
SINCE 1945: ORGANIZATION FOR
DEVELOPMENT

Since the end of World War II, the United States has been seeking better infantry weapons. The quest for a new rifle has been filled with frustration. Due to unrealistic military requirements, poor management, disputes within NATO and congressional tightfistedness, it took twelve years to develop a replacement for the M1 Rifle. Additional failings on the part of the commercial producers of the M14 Rifle delayed the delivery of that weapon for several more years. Secretary of Defense Robert S. McNamara, commenting in July, 1961, on this poor record, said, "I think that it is a disgrace the way the project was handled. I don't mean particularly by the Army, but I mean by the Nation." McNamara added that "it is a relatively simple job to build a rifle compared to building a satellite. . .or a missile system."

It is unclear whether these comments represented the personal feelings of the Defense Secretary or whether this was just a public utterance for the benefit of the Congress. Whatever their source, McNamara's words reflected a growing discontent with the manner in which the Army had conducted its search for a new lightweight rifle. In 1961, there was considerable casting about for a villain on which to place the blame. The convenient scapegoat was the Springfield Armory.

Springfield had served the nation for 167 years. While its performance record during that time had been mixed, there was no clear evidence that the armory alone was responsible for the problems encountered in the development of the M14. Still, some public critics felt that the armory had been assigned that project and had handled it badly. The Secretary of Defense noted that the rifle project had been permitted to languish for years and saw no excuse for allowing this state of affairs to continue. He warned that there was "no reason why we should expect it to be tolerated in the future."[1] Three years later, in a spirit of mounting criticism, McNamara announced his decision, based upon economic criteria, to close the armory.

This decision to "phase down" the armory raised many questions and caused bitter recriminations within the defense community. Had the Defense Department decided to close the armory because of its failure with the rifle program? What did the McNamara whiz kids really know about rifles, or for that matter about defense matters in general? More pertinent to the overall history of small-arms development and procurement in the United States was the basic question: Why had the nation found it so difficult to select and produce a new rifle? Equally important were the problems encountered in the Lightweight Rifle Program indicative of greater failings within the realm of defense research and procurement?

At first glance, the Springfield Armory might seem to have been at fault. Closer scrutiny brings this easy assumption into serious question. As criticism of the M14 grew, the military began to look for another rifle. The public controversy and the technical difficulties which surrounded the newer weapon, the M16, surpassed those encountered with the M14. Unlike its predecessor, the M16 was a private venture developed outside the army's research and development system. The M16 was rushed through the testing and evaluation stages so it could be placed in the hands of American troops in Vietnam. As a result of hurried development and hasty troop familiarization, serious difficulties followed this rifle's introduction into combat.

The subsequent experiences with the projected replacement for both the M14 and M16 were even more unhappy. The Special Purpose Individual Weapon Project (SPIW) grew out of the Project SALVO experiments which had earlier led to the development of the 5.56mm M16 Rifle cartridge. SPIW was to have been a quantum jump in the state-of-the-art, firing dart-like steel flechettes instead of conventional bullets. After more than a decade of research, four developmental contracts were awarded in 1963. The army projected a four-year completion time line for a prototype suitable for mass production. In the decade that followed, this project encountered numerous technical roadblocks and experienced costs unprecedented in infantry-weapon procurement.

Of the many problems that have plagued the army's rifle program, two factors have been especially important. Poor management of both development and production has been one source of trouble; failure to reconcile the needs of the men who would use the new weapon with the responsibilities of the technicians who would develop it, the other. The infantry could have told the Ordnance Corps what it needed, leaving the ordnance specialists to develop a suitable product. But this system never functioned properly; not only did the infantry and Ordnance Corps fail to pull together, often they worked at cross purposes. Both problems were ultimately related to the organizational structure of the US Army in general and the structure of the Ordnance Corps in particular. But the creation of the Army Materiel Command in 1962 eliminated the Ordnance Corps in name only. This organizational change did not solve the difficulties organic to the manner in which the army acquired its infantry weapons.

Organization for development and production has long plagued army ordnancemen. Many of the problems are related to the nature of the American arsenal system and its relationship to private industry. In the late eighteenth century, the small US Army needed a reliable source of arms and ammunition. The number of gunmakers and allied artisans being insufficient for the job, Congress, therefore, established two national armories to insure a steady supply of small arms and accessories for the Regular Army. From 1794, the role of the Springfield Armory was the fabrication of small arms, with American industry assisting in periods of national crisis.

The armory at Springfield, Massachusetts, was once regarded as a wellspring of "Yankee ingenuity." During the nineteenth century, its arms and manufacturing techniques were admired and emulated throughout the world. The manufacture of small arms has played an important part in the evolution of mass-production techniques which characterize modern industry. It must be noted, however, that the innovative spirit which existed at the Armory was channeled into the more efficient production of small arms rather than into research and design. A separate division dedicated to weapons design was not established until 1891. Even then the stress was placed on minor product improvement rather than on developing totally new designs.

The bias favoring manufacture over development continued throughout the life of the armory. The difficulty was an institutional one. By virtue of their role within the structure of the armory, the industrial engineers stressed efficient production and, therefore, traditionally insisted that changes in weapons be kept to a minimum. In addition, these production engineers always felt that changes which were absolutely necessary should conform with established fabrication techniques. Most suggestions for the adoption of new designs were looked upon as unwarranted interference from those who did not understand production problems.

Innovators, whether from within the armory or from the outside, were berated as dreamers who "upset the methods that had worked for many years."[2] Sometimes this attitude was justified, sometimes not. A good example of the latter was the belief held by the industrial personnel at the armory that the M1 Rifle could not be mass-produced because the breech mechanism was too complicated. They suggested that such a rifle had never been fabricated in large quantities. Ergo, the M1 could not be manufactured. Had the army listened to these Cassandras, the M1 Rifle might never have been manufactured. However, the opinion of the production people did not prevail. John Garand said that his rifle could be mass-produced, and to prove his point he designed and made much of the tooling with which the M1 was fabricated. Using that machinery, the Springfield Armory and Winchester successfully manufactured the M1 Rifle during World War II.

That same prejudice of production engineers against new designs was encountered early in the Lightweight Rifle Program. Earle M. Harvey designed a rifle, the T25, that could be produced with nonspecialized tooling, but the armory's production engineering branch rejected the weapon. Again they argued that the design was unacceptable because it could not be produced upon existing equipment. Instead of Harvey's new design, the armory engineers favored an updated version of the M1. For that updated weapon, which later became the M14, they had the tooling already designed by Garand. Innovation yielded to product improvement.

The story was much the same with the M16. When the prototypes of this rifle were presented to the Ordnance and Springfield personnel for evaluation, they rejected it too. "We were up against the NIH Factor—Not Invented Here," recalled George Strichman, president of Colt Industries. "The rifle's basic problem was that it hadn't been invented by Army arsenal personnel."[3] By comparison to the M14, the M16 in its experimental form was rather exotic, since it incorporated many new alloys and would require totally new production equipment wherever it was manufactured.

While the conflict between production and design engineers is an inevitable one, it has been minimized in both the public and private sectors by intelligent management. The apparent conservatism of the production engineer must be considered within the context of his responsibilities. From the standpoint of the production staff in any factory, new designs or technological innovations create disorder. Conversely, the development engineer is hired to foster new ideas. The two groups naturally look upon each other with a jaundiced eye. Each seems to be causing trouble or making life difficult for the other. Because these two groups differ in outlook and purpose and because both are important, management must mediate. The responsible individuals within the Ordnance Corps and the armory failed to resolve the clash between the two points of view.

Good management could have been acquired, however. The army and the Ordnance Corps had adequate opportunity to see the dangers of this conflict between design and production personnel. To paraphrase one writer's comments on World War II research and development, the Ordnance Department did not learn, as American industry had, that it is fatal to place a research organization under a production department. The very structure of the Ordnance Corps was one of its chief limitations to effective research management. An ordnance officer, from his first days in the corps, was taught that the basic mission of his service was production. This lesson was so deeply ingrained that concern for the development of new weapons was quite secondary.

It is a simple truth: research and production are incompatible. Vannevar Bush, the director of the wartime Office of Scientific Research and Development, stressed this point. "New developments," he argued, "are upsetting to procurement standards and production schedules." He went on to say that those people in charge of production are always under pressure to insure the steady flow of standardized materiel; this is especially the problem when time and money are short. The primary function of the Springfield Armory was the production of an adequate supply of reliable arms for use in the field. Springfield, therefore, was judged with the Ordnance Corps by its production performance. As Vannevar Bush indicated, research is the exploration of the unknown, "It is speculative, uncertain. It cannot be standardized." Morever, "it succeeds in virtual direct proportion to its freedom from performance controls, production pressures and traditional approaches." New weapons "must be the responsibility of a group of enthusiasts whose attentions are undiluted by other and conflicting responsibilities."[4]

There are several alternate types of organization that can provide an environment conducive to creative arms development. First, there is the establishment of independent research and development facilities, such as the Office of Scientific Research and Development, to eliminate the conflict between development and production interests. A second approach is the possibility of creating, within the existing agency, a semiautonomous research division, such as the recently created Army Armament Command at Rock Island Arsenal, Illinois. A third, but by no means final, alternative would be reliance upon contracting with commercial research organizations for research and development. There are precedents for all of these courses of action.

The independent research and development facility emerged in the latter decades of the nineteenth century. In its earliest phase, industrial research was merely an adjunct to manufacturing. That was the era of the plant chemist, who orginally had been hired to conduct tests for the engineers. Soon he became a valuable addition to the company, as he began to suggest methods for reducing costs and expediting work in the factory. Some useful discoveries were made in the mid-1800s, but there were no freewheeling, unfettered investigations. Research was definitely production-oriented.

By the early decades of the twentieth century, American industry was beginning to see the value of disassociating their research programs from the functions of the factory. In 1900, General Electric created the first industrial research laboratory in the United States dedicated to fundamental scientific research. In establishing the General Electric Research Laboratory, the company acknowledged that the electrical industry owed its existence to earlier scientific explorations.

The semiautonomous research-and-development approach is best suited to product areas where the amount of research is limited, but a continuing development capacity is desired. Such a semiautonomous organization can be an adjunct to or a branch of a production-oriented organization. For the development engineer the critical element in such an organization is an equal voice in decision making and freedom from external interference.

As a third alternative, the army could rely upon commercial contractors for research and development, following the pattern of the Air Force and the National Aeronautics and Space Administration. Throughout the 1940s and into the 50s, the Ordnance Corps called upon private industry for research assistance in the development of aircraft cannon. The Armour Research Foundation of the Illinois Institute of Technology, General Electric Company, Aircraft Armaments Inc., Winchester Division of Olin Corporation, Maremont Corporation, Colt Firearms, and a number of other firms were included in this effort. While many of these groups did excellent work, there was evidence that a coordinating agency such as Springfield was absolutely essential to the success of these projects.

The difficulties of managing development were great enough, but they were compounded by an archaic system for determining specifications. This process allowed the combat services to determine the specifications of a new weapon. The development of new military equipment always began with the establishment of requirements and specifications by the line agencies through the Ordnance Committee. Since the creation of that committee in 1919, the line officers serving on it have been selected for their field experience with weapons. Their opinions regarding the improvement of weapons have been based upon intuition rather than technical understanding. The specifications set by the Ordnance Committee for the most part limited rather than advanced creative development. These line officers saw new developments as a threat to the way of life to which they were accustomed. Therefore, novel designs were often shunned. Creative individuals within the armory and private inventors were discouraged when their ideas did not fit into the existing ways of doing things.

Resistance to new weapons is natural. The combat officers' oppositions come from the same source as the production personnel's reluctance to adopt new designs. As one author indicated:

Military organizations are societies built around and upon the prevailing weapons systems. Intuitively and quite correctly the military man feels that a change in weapon portends a change in the arrangements of his society.[5]

Since change was not favored, it was not encouraged. The requirements established by the Ordnance Committee were usually defined in terms of improving existing weapons. As a consequence, there was little room for major innovation.

The operation of the armory was indicative of 'the Ordnance Department as a whole. Most ordnancemen catered to the requests of the military consumer. The nature and definition of the Ordnance mission dictated this attitude. The Lightweight Rifle Program (1945–57) was not conceived in terms of new ideas; instead, the army operated within the traditionally limited framework of reducing weight and increasing firepower.

The Lightweight Rifle Program offered an opportunity to rethink small-arms use. Indeed, the Ordnance Corps began the program at an auspicious time. During the Second World War the German army had developed a new class of infantry weapons which offered much promise. Called *Sturmgewehr*, or assault rifles, these weapons provided an alternative to the standard rifle or submachine gun. While these new intermediate-range weapons did not have the great ranges of the rifle, they could be fired accurately during automatic fire. This latter capability was lacking in the underpowered submachine guns.

The American infantry wanted a light automatic rifle that fired a full-power rifle cartridge. These two characteristics were incompatible, because a weapon of the type demanded would be uncontrollable during automatic fire. The infantry, at the time unwilling to rethink its tactics, wanted to make this new weapon conform with old doctrines. The designers saw that this was unreasonable, but the infantry and not the design engineer set the requirements for the rifle.

The American design engineers were not alone in their appreciation of the *Sturmgewehr*. The British, Belgians, and Soviets set out to design assault rifles immediately after the war. Earle M. Harvey, John Garland, Cyril Moore, and other American engineers attempted to do likewise. In each country, the arms designers met opposition to the new type of weapon. Only in the Soviet Union was the conservatism of the military overcome.

The Soviets recognized early the futility of trying to fire a full-power cartridge in a light-automatic rifle. After the war, the Russians developed a family of small arms firing an intermediate-range cartridge. The first weapon in this family was the SKS-45 semiautomatic carbine. This weapon was supplemented and later replaced by the Kalashnikov group of automatic weapons (AK). The assault rifles, supplemented by light machine guns firing the same cartridge, provided the Soviet, Chinese, and Allied armies with a major increase in firepower.

Specifications and organization tell the tale. The Soviets were successful because their requirements were reasonable. They wanted an assault rifle, and they were willing to adapt their military structure to utilize the new weapon. To obtain such a weapon, they realized that they would have to sacrifice range and killing power. They felt that such a concession was acceptable if they could equip their infantrymen with automatic weapons. The Soviets intended to fight the enemy at short assault rifle ranges. Having made this decision based upon World War II experience, they set out to get a new weapon. They seemed justified in their decision and happy with the results.

The United States established impossible requirements and has been unsatisfied with the resulting weapons. Blame could not be placed on unreasonable requirements and specifications; a sick institution had to be at fault. That is, Springfield Armory had failed. The armory, therefore, was judged and found incapable of conducting first-rate research and development programs. When Springfield was studied in 1963 by the Army Weapons Command for the Pentagon, it was decided that the armory's research and development function could be carried out more satisfactorily and economically by the Rock Island Arsenal.

The army's post-World War II experiences with small-arms production had been equally unsatisfactory. Problems with the M14 in particular extended beyond the developmental stages, when further failures appeared during its manufacture. The first commercial producers, Winchester Repeating Arms Company and Harrington & Richardson, were not capable of manufacturing a reliable weapon at a reasonable cost. Secretary of Defense McNamara was aware of these problems. At one point, he even called the early production of Harrington & Richardson "miserable." These problems were the direct result of the Ordnance Department's inability to manage the contracts that were let for the M14. The problem was brought into line only after the Ordnance Department was merged with the other technical services to form the Army Materiel Command and after McNamara had established Project 110 to study small-arms procurement; also, the Office of the Project Manager for the M14 Rifle was delegated to oversee the rifle's production.

But the problems did not end when M14 production was terminated in 1963. The Colt M16 Rifle became the *cause célèbre* in 1966–67, when stories from Vietnam indicated that the weapon was seriously malfunctioning in the field. The subsequent series of congressional investigations traced these problems to improper testing of the rifle/ammunition system and to inadequate familiarization training for the troops who were using the weapon in the field. Close on the heels of these public troubles, the army's SPIW Program was, in 1969, scrutinized by the General Accounting Office because of cost overruns. By 1973, the army was still no closer to obtaining a satisfactory version of SPIW, although millions had been spent on the

XM19, a prototype being developed by AAI Corporation of Cockeysville, Maryland. Clearly, organizational improvements were needed. The key question was: Could satisfactory changes be found?

The decade 1963–73 was spent searching for an organizational framework that would alleviate the troubles experienced since the mid-1940s. As a first step toward providing a better organizational structure for the procurement of combat hardware, the US Army had created the Army Weapons Command at Rock Island in 1954. AWC, a subdivision of the Ordnance Corps, was charged with the overall supervision and coordination of the efforts of the army arsenals that were producing small arms and artillery. Ammunition and combat-vehicle procurement were overseen by two separate commands; the Munitions Command and the Automotive and Tank Command. The creation of the Weapons Command did not alter anything significantly. AWC continued the production orientation of ordnance procurement, and the same type of ordnance officers continued to fill the positions in the newly established bureaucracy. Further, the Weapons Command staff often bickered with the staffs of the subordinate arsenals, as AWC interposed itself between the armory and the headquarters of the Ordnance Corps. Structural changes were still demanded to correct deficiencies.

During the 1960s, several major alterations were attempted, but they produced few positive results. First, the US Army created the Army Material Command (1962) to replace all of the old technical services—Ordnance, Quartermaster, Signal, and Chemical Corps—with one agency responsible for research, development, production, distribution, and maintenance of all materiel. Then on November 19, 1964, McNamara announced the decision to close the Springfield Armory, together with a number of other installations. Springfield's Research and Development Mission was transferred to Rock Island Arsenal, which was also the home of the Weapons Command.

From that point in time, a relatively confused and divided structure was introduced into the rifle-acquisition process. A small-arms weapons laboratory was established at Rock Island under the direct control of the Weapons Command Headquarters. This laboratory was never satisfactorily staffed because only 20 of the 480 eligible Springfield research and development engineers and technicians agreed to transfer to Illinois. The Weapons Command found it very difficult to monitor research-and-production programs at East Coast factories or to provide the technical assistance and quality-control supervision that had once been the hallmark of Springfield Armory. As the problems with the M16 Rifle became public, the army created a special study group to search for a site on which a new small-arms research center could be established. The outcome of that study was the founding of the US Army Small Arms Systems Agency (USASASA) at Aberdeen

Proving Ground on August 15, 1968. Having barely padlocked the doors at the armory, the Army Materiel Command cut the opening ribbon on the new Small Arms Systems Agency.

Unlike the Springfield Armory, USASASA was not to have operational laboratories; instead, it was a systems analysis and research management group. While the small-arms laboratory at Rock Island Arsenal supervised production engineering and the Project Manager Rifles Office monitored rifle production, the Small Arms Systems Agency was to be responsible for the management of research-and-development projects conducted by contractors. All this could have been an ideal division of labor, but shortcomings soon appeared. As the war in Indochina drew to a close, the small-arms development budget was cut sharply. Production of the M16 Rifle was likewise scaled down dramatically. The army's first response was to close the Office of the Project Manager for Rifles. As it became clear that rifle designs are not plucked from the air by systems analysis or computer-aided design engineering, the army decided to "disestablish" the five-year-old Small Arms Systems Agency, effective July 16, 1973.

As a prelude to the disappearance of USASASA, the Army Materiel Command reorganized the Weapons and Munitions commands. In recognition that rifles and other weapons must be developed concurrently with the ammunition, the army decided that an Armament Command that concentrated on weapons/ammunition systems made more sense than the divided responsibilities that had characterized the previously separate and partially autonomous Weapons and Munitions commands. The new Armament Command came into existence on January 11, 1973, and it is far too early to tell if ARMCOM is the answer to the organizational difficulties that have been faced in the procurement of rifles since 1945. A study committee appointed by the Department of the Army has expressed some concern about the effectiveness of ARMCOM:

> The Armament Command is ably structured to perform product improvement and readiness. We observed several excellent examples of their ability to provide improvements to weapons systems through new components. Impressive also was their ability to quickly analyze user problems by teams in the field and by laboratory simulation. Available are examples of excellent operations which demonstrate close working relationships among laboratory technicians, engineers, and ARMCOM field technicians. ARMCOM is attempting to place some emphasis on better planning in the basic research and exploratory development area. *However, the production, product improvement, in-house maintenance and materiel management functions seem to absorb the major efforts to the detriment of new item development.* [italics added] [6]

As an official acknowledgement of the problems existing in the development and procurement of its weapons, the army had established at the end of 1973, a blue-ribbon committee "to conduct an independent review of the Army's total materiel acquisition process."[7] The Army Materiel Acquisition Review Committee (AMARC), headed by Wendell B. Sell, was far more critical and insightful than might at first have been expected of a group established by the Army to study its own track record. Starting with basic facts, the committee concluded that "the Army has had in its history an undue number of materiel acquisition failures."

Looking for the source of these failures, AMARC suggested that the central problem was the vocational culture of the army. Explaining this more fully, the committee pointed out that the organization that trained officers and men for combat was not suited for developing personnel to manage the development of science and technology.

. . .this "tight" culture has intersected negatively any free-wheeling, truly imaginative, and flexibly controlled approach to new weapon inventions and even new weapon development.[8]

AMARC produced a bookful of recommendations, many of which called for further reorganization within the Army Materiel Command.

The major change suggested was the creation of a new Armaments Development Center at a single location. Although AMARC suggested that this could best be accomplished in an evolutionary fashion—by consolidating selected research-and-development elements from Frankford, Picatinny, Rock Island, and Watervliet, together with other organizations such as the Ballistic Research Laboratory—the effect has been revolutionary. The decision has been made to close down Frankford Arsenal, and similar moves are anticipated following the submission of the report of the Army Materiel Command, Committee-Armament. That ad hoc committee, created by the commander of the Materiel Command, presented in December, 1974, alternative proposals for the establishment and location of an Armament Development Center, but action on those suggestions was still pending in June, 1975.[9]

Other AMARC recommendations included the following concern about building a professional cadre for the armament research-and-development system:

1. Train career specialists in research and development, instead of relying upon combat officers or technical officers on short tours of duty to fill such positions.

2. Assign combat officers with appropriate experience to act as consultants on user aspects of development programs, while maintaining considerable freedom of action for the Armaments Development Center staff.

3. Rely more heavily on contracted research, after the example of the Air Force and the National Aeronautics and Space Administration (NASA),

thus eliminating some of the personnel constraints imposed by the Civil Service. With these changes AMARC thought it would be possible for the army to create a group of bright young men who could initiate new programs and see them through to their completion.

As with the creation of the Armament Command, it is still too early to tell what effect AMARC's recommendations will have on American small-arms procurement. The M16 Rifle remains the standard shoulder weapon, while prototypes of the prime candidate for its replacement—the 6.0mm Squad Automatic Weapon—are being developed by Ford at Newport Beach, California, and by Maremont at Saco, Maine. The outcome of that contest, too, is unclear. But one point is certain; the AMARC study is a healthy step forward. Without this official recognition of the management problems in this field, there would have been very limited hope for the elimination of its difficulties.

NOTES

1. U. S. Congress, Senate, *Report by Preparedness Investigating Subcommittee on Armed Services, United States Senate under Authority of S. Res. 43 on M14 Rifle,* 87th Cong., 1st sess. (Washington, 1961), p. 1.
2. Howard R. Bartlett, "The Development of Industrial Research in the United States," in *Industrial Research* by the National Resources-Planning Board (Washington, 1941), p. 24.
3. Trevor Armbrister, "The M16 Rifle Controversy" (unpublished typescript of article prepared for *Saturday Evening Post*), 1968, p. 9. The NIH Factor had been present before. The Army had rejected the Belgian Fabrique Nationale Light Auto Rifle and the British E. M. 2 Rifle in the mid-1950s because of "political" rather than technical shortcomings.
4. J. P. Baxter, *Scientists Against Time* (Boston, Little, Brown, 1946), p. 12.
5. E. E. Morison, *Men, Machines and Modern Times* (Cambridge, Mass., M. I. T. Press, 1966), p. 36.
6. "Report of the Army Materiel Acquisition Review Committee" Vol II, (1 April, 1974), p. II-6.
7. Memorandum, General Fred C. Weyand and Herman R. Standt to Wendell B. Sell, "Army Materiel Acquisition Review Committee (AMARC)," 6 December 1973, as reproduced in "Report of the Army Materiel Acquisition Review Committee" Vol. II, p. A-1.
8. Ibid., p. VII-2.
9. Ibid., Vol 1, 1 April 1974, pp. 27-28; and Army Materiel Command, Committee-Armament, "Final Report AMC Committee-Armament," 4 vols. (December, 1974).

ALVIN R. SUNSERI

THE MILITARY-INDUSTRIAL COMPLEX
IN IOWA

The term military-industrial complex was coined by Malcolm Moos and
popularized by President Eisenhower in his farewell address. It suggests
that a conspiracy exists between military leaders and industrialists; one that
is designed to protect their vested interests. Actually, rare indeed is the
individual who is not benefiting in some way from his or her involvement
with the great American smorgasbord that is the military-industrial complex.
Therefore, in order to more accurately measure the extent of American
dependency on Pentagon dollars, I found it necessary to originate the
MITLAMP (military-industrial-technological-labor-academic-managerial-
political complex) concept in my research activities.[1]

The military sector of the complex consists of the men and women on
active duty whose current allowances make up 30.79 percent of the defense
budget. Also included in the military segment are retirees and veterans receiving checks that amounted to close to $12,500,000,000 (fiscal year
1974). Consideration must also be given to the political-economic clout
possessed by veterans' organizations such as the American Legion, Amvets,
and the Veterans of Foreign Wars. These are the organizations that exercise
such political pressures that the Veterans Administration budget amounted
to over $14,000,000,000 this past year.

The industrial category consists of over one hundred defense contractors
whose economic base is the budget provided by the Federal Government
for defense purposes. Retired officers on the payrolls of these companies
numbered 3,233 in 1973. And one of the more troubling policies in this
sector is that 57 percent of the contracts were still awarded on a non-
competitive basis as late as 1973. Consequently, with continued interest
in new weapons, it is no wonder that industry is looking forward to even

more lucrative contracts now that the Vietnam War is ended. A further disturbing consequence of the military-industrial relationship is the fact that over 275 former defense-industry managers are now holding ranks of GS 13 or higher in the Department of Defense.

Important in the technological sector of the MITLAMP are those individuals engaged in occupations requiring experience in computer management. Also included in this category are those working with firms engaged in off-campus research projects. An example of this activity is the Air Force System Analysis Program that was introduced by Robert McNamara and his whiz kids. Also, there are the numerous firms, small and large, engaged in the continuing search for a share of the billions of dollars spent on research-and-development activities since World War II. I define them as the representatives of the *qualitative* side of the arms race.

The labor segment consists of the 5 percent of the work force directly involved and 16 percent indirectly dependent on Pentagon dollars for employment. It is no secret that the most powerful labor leader, George Meany, stands consistently in support of a high defense budget.

The academic division is founded on defense-related expenditures taking place on various campuses in the United States. Indeed, $2,015,000,000 of the $8,676,000,000 earmarked for research-and-development projects was targeted for expenditures on selected larger college campuses in fiscal year 1974.

The managerial grouping consists of the men who "oil the wheels of administrative machinery"—the 7.8 percent who are engaged in the managerial functions designed to mobilize and organize the intellectual, scientific, technological, and manpower resources in support of MITLAMP objectives. In addition, another 9 percent are indirectly involved in the operation of the MITLAMP. Excellent examples of this activity are the hard- and soft-sell methods formulated by Madison Avenue types to recruit an all-volunteer army. Not to be overlooked, of course, are the numerous maneuvers of the Pentagon lobby on Capitol Hill.

The political segment includes the politicians in Congress who are in harmony with the objectives of the MITLAMP, such as F. Edward Hebert of Louisiana, John Stennis of Mississippi, and Henry Jackson of Washington. It should be noted that these men represent states benefiting greatly from MITLAMP expenditures. Congressional doves, however, are also wary of losing defense contracts in their states. As Congressman Les Aspen recently admitted, at a meeting of the Organization of American Historians, the best way for the military-industrial complex to stifle him would be to grant his constituency a large number of defense contracts.

All of which means the financial power of the MITLAMP is massive, intertwined among various sectors, and deeply embedded in the economy. Indeed, because of the complexities of defense spending, it is impossible, under present standards of measurement (percentage of GNP devoted to defense), to determine the full impact of defense expenditures on the economy. More than one scholar has stated the difficulty of determining fully how much is really spent on the military. Harold Hughes, former senator from Iowa, in response to a recent inquiry, confirmed the difficulty of penetrating the Pentagon veil. Therefore, in the opinion of this writer, the only way that one can arrive at a more valid truth is to apply the MITLAMP concept in microcosmic fashion to a restricted region—such as the state of Iowa.

Why Iowa? This state was chosen because so many people accept the idea that Iowa's economy is basically agrarian and thus cannot be too involved in MITLAMP operations. In fact, when the Iowa Director of Development was once asked for his estimate of defense expenditures in the state, he described them as being inconsequential—forming less than 1 percent of Iowa's economy. Consequently, if a greater dependence on Pentagon dollars could be discovered, I reasoned that individuals in other states might be concerned enough to discover the extent of their economic dependencies on defense contracts.

THE MILITARY SECTOR

In Iowa, the military sector of the MITLAMP is comprised of several distinctly different and yet interrelated groups. These divisions are: (1) the active military; (2) the National Guard and Reserve components; (3) and veterans and veteran organizations such as the American Legion, Veterans of Foreign Wars, and the Amvets; finally, also included are various governmental agencies designed to assist the active military as well as veterans. The impact of the military segment of the MITLAMP is as diverse as the groups which comprise it. Therefore, in order to determine the impact of the military upon the lives of Iowans, each group must be examined separately.

The number of men on active duty in Iowa has seldom exceeded 400 to 500 in recent years. They are, for the most part, the recruiters stationed in urban centers and advisers to National Guard and Reserve units located throughout the Hawkeye state. In fiscal 1974, the total active payroll in Iowa was $5,348,000 or approximately $10,000 per man. In most instances, fiscal 1974 figures are employed in this article. On the state and local levels, however, fiscal 1974 figures were not available. Consequently, it was necessary to use fiscal 1973 data. All final tabulations are based on fiscal 1974 figures. This amount is relatively small, but when added to other small amounts the figure becomes significant. In addition, $16,746,000 was spent

on civilian pay and "business needs" (rentals, supplies, utilities), as well
as advertising and other methods designed to recruit individuals into the
armed forces.

Federal funds totaling $22,111,000 were furnished to the National
Guard and Reserves during the fiscal year 1974 with over $30,000,000
allocated to equip the Guard. Moreover, the state of Iowa's expenditures
on the Guard for fiscal 1974 was $1,689,607. These figures do not include
the funds allocated for the construction of armories in Iowa, which is financed both by the state (25 percent) and Federal (75 percent) funds. Due
to legal technicalities, however, the funding averages 35 percent for the
state and 65 percent for the federal government. The 64th General Assembly appropriated $480,000 for army construction and rehabilitation. During
the years 1974–78, five armories costing a total of $4,197,000 are slated
for construction in the state. Unfortunately, there are no total dollar-value
figures available for the present army and Air National Guard installations.
One officer, who is a realtor, suggested a conservative value of $125,000,000.

The financial impact of the National Guard upon Sioux City and Des
Moines is significant, for the total Army and Air Force National Guard
payrolls were over $1,623,000 and $4,175,140 in fiscal 1973. In addition,
the state of Iowa includes fifty-two communities with eighty-three one-
hundred-men units on the federal payroll. Most of the payroll money is
channeled into the economies of these communities. The pay allowance
for the Reserve units must also be added before employing the multiplier
effect.

The multiplier refers to the fact that a permanent increase in government
expenditures will permanently increase the annual income stream by some
multiple of the government increase. For example, in the case of the Iowa
military sector, the $44,215,000 allowed to float in the state must be
multiplied by 1.56 in order to discover the real impact of the outpouring
of Pentagon dollars in the state. For, in employing the Charles T. Kindle-
berger technique, which deals with inter-economy transactions of the
multiplier effect, I reached the conclusion that each dollar coming into
the state results in $1.56 being generated into the state economy. This
figure, according to the economists consulted, is a *conservative* multiplier.

The veterans of Iowa number over 386,000 men. As an organized group,
these individuals represent a great political and economic power. For example, Selective Service now depends in part on the American Legion to
assist in ensuring that young men are registering for the draft at age eighteen. More closely related to this paper is the fact that veterans in Iowa
receive a total of $133,286,000. Moreover, these compensations, pensions,
readjustment payments, and loan dollars pumped into Iowa by the VA are
prime dollars that are not taxable. In applying the multiplier effect,

$133,286,000 minus $13,328,600 (money saved by recipients) plus deduction of $56,643,000 spent on imports, results in $63,314,400 added to the economy. One then must add the $51,193,000 spent on construction and hospital administration to arrive at a total sum of $114,507,400 that must be multiplied by the 1.56 multiplier. Also, because the $133,286,000 are prime dollars, they too must be added to the total sum. In the end, $311,917,544 is added to the Iowa economy. Add to that sum the $68,959,800 spent on the National Guard/Reserves and regular units after applying the multiplier effect, and the figure totals of $380,877,344, exclusive of state appropriations and the value of defense installations. Finally, the $20,845,000 annually paid to professional retirees must be included in the total spent by the Pentagon on the military in Iowa. Multiplied, this figure reads $32,518,200. When added to the VA and other Department of Defense expenditures, the sum equals $413,395,544 which is 3 percent of the Gross State Product (GSP) of Iowa.

THE INDUSTRIAL SECTOR

Four methods were employed to determine the extent of Iowa industry's dependence on Pentagon dollars: oral history, correspondence, qualitative evaluation, and quantitative analysis. Interviews were held with industrialists and later sent to firms that were recipients of defense contracts in recent years. After continued effort, 52 percent of the firms contacted responded by completing questionnaires or answering questions put to them orally. One drawback is that only firms with contracts amounting to more than $10,000 were listed by the Department of Defense. For this reason, the framework within which the inquiry was conducted includes only the responding larger firms. Moreover, the responses were varied, and ranged from an attitude of cooperation to a notable reluctance to tell the truth. Most of the companies, however, were cooperative.

Several of the larger companies belong to associations that are representative of their desire to obtain defense contracts. Included are the National Manufacturers Association, Bidders Mailing List, and the National Chamber of Commerce. Only one firm, Kramer Brothers of Des Moines, was unaware of the lobbying activities by these or other organizations for the purpose of obtaining defense contracts.

Through the cooperation of several of my students, it was discovered that normally none of the contracts are awarded to the lowest bidder. Rather, in order to enter into competition for contracts a firm must contact an official involved with negotiations as the government does not do the shopping. Moreover, introduction is expedited only if the company is recommended by another firm already performing contract work. Even then, contract decisions remain uncertain because of constant proposals for renegotiation between civilian government personnel and company representatives.

The bidding procedure is less involved when a firm is established exclusively for the purpose of defense contracting or works directly with government agencies. For example, the Iowa Army Ammunition Plant of Burlington and Stanley Consultants of Muscatine are directly associated with the Atomic Energy Commission (AEC) and the Army Corps of Engineers. In such cases, output specifications are merely a sign the contract will be on a cost-plus-fixed-fee basis. The bidding process is bypassed for subcontractors who work with the primary firm, as is the case with Fisher Controls of Marshalltown. Virtually all the firms receive contracts for manufacture of their primary products. One company official made the disturbing observation that recent government contracts consistently involve greater expenditures for defense-related goods in Iowa.

In the aftermath of the completion of the investigation, the research team found that 10.2 percent of the revenues of the responding firms were based on Pentagon dollars. Indeed, all indicated some percentage of revenue from defense contracts with the lowest being ¼ of 1 percent and the highest 85 percent of total income. All the large industries indicated an increased degree of dependence on Pentagon dollars.

In order to determine some type of common ground for accumulation of all this information, a multiple regression analysis was implemented by the students. This process consists of plotting selected variables against a dependent variable. The group conducting the investigation chose the size of a firm's contract as a dependent variable against which were plotted the following: the selection of the state in which the plant is located; the size of the city in which the firm's headquarters is located; the type of priority product; and the continuity of the appearance of the firm as a defense contractor in 1971 or 1972 or both years. These variables were chosen as a means to compare the relationship between the selected variables and the size of the firm's contract. The information was then coded and sent to the computer. An equation evolved which indicated the overall significance of each variable that proved to be valid. As a result, we came to the conclusion that there is a direct relation between the selected variables and the size of the contract. This conclusion prompted development of the following hypotheses: (1) There exists direct relation between the size of the contract and the location of the firm. The companies in the southeastern section of Iowa are the more fortunate beneficiaries of defense contracts. (2) There exists a direct relation between the size of the contract and a tendency of the contracting firm to be located in a city with a population between 20,000 and 50,000. (3) There exists a direct relation between the size of the contract and the types of products to be designed for construction work, petroleum-related products, or heavy machinery in specific areas where there exist the following conditions: (a) firms selected specifically for defense work; or (b) firms selected to supply only food and personnel consumer products. (4) There exists a direct relation between the size of the contract and a tendency on the part of the government to approve new contracts to firms that were included on the 1971 and 1972 defense-contract list. The researchers then discovered evidence to support these hypotheses geometrically, giving each even greater validity.

Therefore, a firm which manufactures heavy machinery in a city of 35,000 in Southeastern Iowa has a fairly reliable chance of becoming a regular recipient of Pentagon contracts. Naturally, there are exceptions to this conclusion, but the general implication is certainly significant when one takes into account the vast amount of information collected. It should also be noted that these statements are made only with respect to those firms in the study—the companies that comprise a greater number of the larger industries in Iowa.

When the multiplier effect is employed, it becomes obvious that the economic impact of defense contracts varies from town to town. In this sense, however, there are always beneficial consequences of the contracts. For example, the total income generated by the multiplier effect is of such magnitude that its absence would cause economic stagnation and depression in the city in which the firm is located temporarily. This negative effect would then spread and the impact would be felt even at the state or regional levels. One cannot expect industry to lose over 10 percent of its revenue and the community not experience some type of repercussion. Thus, Iowa industry is significantly dependent upon defense contracts. But how important is its dependence? The following suggestion was made by the team, based on their study: Industries in Iowa which receive defense contracts over a period of time develop a reliance on those contracts as an additional source of revenue. Once established, this source becomes an integral part of the total revenue and its loss would cause economic hardship. Such a process is not conspiratorial, not is it deliberate. Rather, it is a national tendency toward a realization of a rational economic goal: the accumulation of profits and economic security.

Burlington, for example, located in Southeastern Iowa, is a community most dependent on defense expenditures. The average payroll for recent years was over $34,000,000 for the Iowa Army Ammunition Plant, which served as a direct flow into the city's economy. The 4,000 employees also contributed to the community welfare projects, and the maintenance of the plant involved even more personnel. Without these contracts there would be no plant in Burlington, meaning there would be 4,000 fewer jobs. Consequently, when one applies the 1.56 multiplier effect one discovers $53,040,000 generated into the Burlington economy.

The cities of Waterloo and Cedar Rapids are also highly dependent upon defense expenditures. The Chamberlain Manufacturing Corporation of Waterloo received $17,725,000 in defense contracts in fiscal year 1973, while Collins Radio of Cedar Rapids was the recipient of $49,070,000. If multiplied by 1.56, the sum channeled into the local economies of these cities equals $104,200,200.

THE TECHNOLOGICAL SECTOR

In investigating the impact of Pentagon dollars on the industrial sector in Iowa it was also possible to discover the significance of the technological sector on the economy of the state. For example, in Iowa the research-and-development breakdown reveals that 4,466,000 research and development dollars were expended by the Defense Department. Such expenditures illustrate the standard operating procedure of quantitative production at plants in times of war and qualitative production in times of peace. Collins Radio in Cedar Rapids and the Chamberlain Manufacturing Corporation in Waterloo were two of the major recipients of these contracts. In the end, after applying a 1.56 multiplier effect, a total of $6,935,760 was spent in Iowa in fiscal 1974 by the Pentagon in contracts with the firms that responded to the questionnaires.

THE LABOR SECTOR

Equally relevant to the military-industrial complex project in Iowa are the results of the inquiry made into the relations between the MITLAMP and labor. As a prerequisite to this examination, an attempt was made to establish some framework for an appraisal of the defense work force. A totally accurate examination of dependence of labor on Pentagon expenditures is not possible—but fairly reliable estimates were developed.

At least 1 percent of the Iowa work force is *directly* involved with production of defense-contracted products. Among the respondents, those involved in subcontracting number approximately 2 percent. Therefore, at least 3 percent of Iowa labor is specifically employed in defense-related work. This revelation is significant because the figure is based only on information gathered from half the firms in Iowa that responded to the questionnaires. Moreover, only those companies with contracts valued at more than $10,000 were even available for analysis. The dependence of Iowa labor on defense contracts at the community level looms even larger when one considers that only a rambling sample has been taken.

Many individual communities were analyzed in an attempt to determine the specifics of the dependence of workers upon the Pentagon. In this sector, the multiplier effect was also utilized. Of primary value was an article from the monthly *Labor Review,* July, 1968, by Robert Roger Refler and Paul Downing, entitled, "Regional Effect of the Defense Effort on Employment." In this essay, the indirect effects of each one hundred dollars of defense-contract pay on the labor force are examined. The size of the paycheck, the market area, level of consumption, and the consumer buying patterns all determine the seepage and diffusion of this process. As an in-depth format, the firms are categorized according to major and minor defense contracts.

When applied to Iowa, this then shows that an oligopolistic market structure exists in our defense industry, as the top ten firms in the state account for 88 percent of the contracts. Some of these firms employ 100 percent of their workers in the fabrication of defense-related products. Such is the case with the Burlington Iowa Army Ammunition Plant (IAPP) that is managed by the Silas-Mason Hanger Company, Inc. Using the multiplier of 1.56 drawn from the industry study, and applied to this area only, it is estimated that the closing of IAAP would result in 4,000 jobs in Burlington being eliminated. Moreover, with a small base population such as Iowa possesses, the relative aspects of the dependence of the community on defense-related contracts is as important as absolute figures. Unfortunately, this category is difficult to estimate for a variety of reasons. For example, Fisher Controls of Marshalltown subcontracts for items designed for both civil and military use. The contractors, however, seldom reveal the intended disposal of the products. Consequently, it is suspected a considerable number of the 2,700 employees are dependent on the Pentagon dollars.

Another facet deserving consideration is the fact that the history of some companies shows the military defense contracts may have had such a great influence on production in the past as to form the foundation for the larger labor force of the present in certain areas. This concept is best exemplified by the Firestone Rubber Company of Des Moines. It evolved from the original 100 percent defense-oriented employment to less than 2 percent today. Because of the original orientation, there was constructed the economic base for 2,500 jobs in Des Moines in 1971. Thus, the indirect process is a reality in Iowa today. The most extensive data was revealed in the studies of the dairy and meat-packing labor forces in Iowa. This information is pertinent, particularly when considered in the context as a major portion of the workers employed in the state. For example, defense contractor Wells Blue Bunny Dairy in Le Mars has a market area of two hundred miles radius from that town because of the necessity for processing, transporting, and distributing their goods. An indeterminate number of jobs are affected by the amount, type, and terms of defense contracts with the dairy.

Denison, Iowa, is even more dependent on defense contracts. Of the 200 workers employed by World Wide Meats in processing and packing meat in 1972, 104 were involved in defense-contract work. Since 22 percent of the manufacturing work in Denison is performed by this company, over 11 percent of the employees in Denison are dependent on defense contracts. When one relates this plant activity to the feeding, raising, slaughtering, processing, packing, transportation, grading, distributing, and sales management, one only begins to realize the immense negative impact on the regional economy that would result if the World Wide meat-packing plant were closed.

The conclusions to be drawn from this sector of MITLAMP activity would certainly be more lucid if a greater number of firms had responded to the questionnaires. The results of the work of the labor-study group, however, clearly show that a substantial segment of Iowa labor in various communities is dependent upon defense contracts. Finally, the spin-offs in employment resulting from those contracts are so extensive as to make the state as a whole sufficiently dependent on defense contracts to experience repressive economic consequences if those contracts are canceled.

THE ACADEMIC SECTOR

Ironically, the most uncooperative institutions encountered by the research team were the two major state universities—State University of Iowa and Iowa State University. Neither readily responded to the questionnaires and the Reserve Officers Training Corps (ROTC) Commandants were hostile in their reactions. The private institutions and the University of Northern Iowa, however, were more responsive.

The University of Iowa, the University of Northern Iowa, Drake University, Iowa State University, and the twenty-five other private colleges and universities in Iowa receive a variety of funds from the Federal Government and thus are directly and indirectly involved in the military-industrial complex. Two questionnaires were sent to the business offices of these institutions. The first dealt with the National Aeronautics and Space Administration and the Atomic Energy Commission. The second was related to the ROTC program and the Veterans Assistance projects. Officials at the two largest schools were surveyed on an oral-history basis when possible.

Information obtained revealed that Federal money is channeled through the following agencies: Atomic Energy Commission, Department of Defense, National Aeronautics and Space Administration, Reserve Officer Training programs, and the Veterans Administration.

The Reserve Officer Training Corps has programs at Iowa State University, Drake University, University of Iowa, and Coe College, with military budgets totaling $755,837 in fiscal 1973. These programs are important to hundreds of students as they provide scholarships that cover tuition and room and board, as well as books and fees. In addition, these activities employ a significant number of personnel whose collective salaries range from $78,000 at the University of Iowa to $50,000 at Coe College.

The Veterans Administration makes an important contribution to the Veterans Educational Assistance Program and War Orphans and Widows Educational Assistance Program. This sum, $220 per month for a single full-time student, does not go directly to the institution but is paid to the veteran. The total amount varies in proportion to the number of qualified veterans at each school. The University of Iowa veterans received $4,300,000, while most of the small schools averaged $10,000 in veteran payments, which are too closely related to the Pentagon to be ignored.

The Atomic Energy Commission—closely related to defense interests— also is a major source of funds for Iowa State University. The Ames Laboratory received $7,500,000, the Institute for Atomic Research, $232,000, while other grants and contracts totaled $335,000. The University of Iowa received $68,000 in funds, while no significant amount was allocated to the small schools. The National Aeronautics and Space Administration (NASA), which is also related to the Department of Defense, spent $5,300,000 at the University of Iowa, including an unusual contract for the study of the necessity of gravity for the normal growth of turtles. NASA also allocated $785,000 for research and development. Iowa State University received $87,000 in grants and contracts, while the private schools received too little to consider.

In addition, the Department of Defense recently allocated a large amount of money to Iowa State University, the University of Iowa, Drake University, and Coe College in direct payments for grants and services. These expenditures include: University of Iowa—general contracts including one establishing a commission on malaria by the Armed Forces Epidemicological Board, $975,483; US Air Force—$33,616; US Army Corps of Engineers—$133,384; US Navy—$140,466. Drake University and Coe College received $60,000 and $54,000 respectively in funds from the Department of Defense, while Iowa State University was allocated $1,396,000 by the Pentagon as follows: US Air Force—$225,000; US Army Civil Engineering—$90,800; US Navy Electrical Engineering—$118,000; Department of Civil Defense—

$111,000; Defense Department Water Resources Institute—$58,000. Another important program linked to national security is the National Defense Student Loan Program, which affords many students the opportunity to go to school and forms an important part of the school's economic base, as body count is the name of the game on so many campuses. And although the larger percent of the money allocated is spent at the two large universities, the small schools do feel the impact. One president said he might be forced to close the doors of his college tomorrow if National Defense loans and veteran's benefits were no longer available.

The military-industrial-complex white-collar managerial class in Iowa, based on figures supplied by 60 percent of the firms and offices queried, amounts to approximately 8 percent of the total managerial force. Many are employed in government agencies such as the research and development sector of the Small Business Administration. Also, there are those engaged in a variety of activities, i.e., the advisory group seeking to develop a more efficient recruiting program for the armed services.

In examining the political sector, one fact was made obvious. Except for Harold Hughes, all of the responding political figures, while they differed on some points—for instance, the importance of foreign aid—did agree that defense expenditures should be continued as long as they were not wasted and were conducive to the development of adequate defenses. As Congressman Les Aspen has noted, it is political suicide to do otherwise. Even Senator Dick Clark, a professed liberal from Iowa, was proud to announce a new defense contract for Collins Radio shortly after his election in 1972. Implications of the situation are obvious: each sector of the MITLAMP indicates an interdependence on other sectors in which a substantial amount of research has been conducted.

Obviously, from the evidence presented in this essay, it is impossible to discover the full extent of Iowa's dependence on defense dollars without years of research and use of the most sophisticated equipment. Even by conservative estimates, however, the sum arrived at is awesome and indicative that Iowa is much more reliant on Pentagon dollars than is commonly assumed. Let the figures speak for themselves. Included below are amounts arrived at after employing the 1.56 multiplier effect. The managerial and labor benefits are included in the sectors of the MITLAMP that are listed.

Military-includes VA and Retirees benefits		$413,395,544
Industrial		262,474,680
Technological-includes Atomic Energy		
and	Commission expenditures on	
Academic	weapons and nuclear space systems	27,044,160
Total		$702,914,384

It must be remembered that this figure is only a conservative estimate based on incomplete evidence.

It is my estimate that 8 percent of Iowa's Gross State Product is based on Pentagon dollars. It is interesting to note that the percentage of GSP remains approximately the same as in fiscal 1973, despite a reduction of $32,744,000 in military active-duty pay. This situation is not healthy when one considers all of the ramifications (including inflation) of such an economic abnormality. The picture becomes much more disturbing when one realizes Iowa is thirty-fourth as a recipient of defense expenditures. One can only ponder the extent of the reliance of the entire nation on the MITLAMP.

In order to arrive at a more valid understanding of this problem, scholars must cease looking to the percentage of GNP as the source of all truth. Instead they should seek to discover the *dependency* of the nation on Pentagon dollars as I have sought to do in Iowa. Only in this quantitative manner will we arrive at a closer truth and better understanding of the complexities of the unique phenomenon of the twentieth century that is the MITLAMP.

NOTES

1. This essay is based upon research and assistance from individuals, students and faculty, including: Kenneth L. Allers, Karl E. Anderson, Willard L. Brandt, Rickey L. Briggle, James M. Clark, Terry B. Coghlan, John J. Copic, Paul T. Cusmano, Darrell D. Druvenga, Lonnie Franks, Paul M. French, Thomas R. Frost, John A. Gjerde, Michael E. Hanson, Frederick E. Hartz, Robert L. Huber, Kent S. Kane, Steven R. Kohn, Leonard V. Larsen, Major John P. McAnaw, Dennis L. Miller, Alben T. Myren, Linda Petersen, Michael J. Petersen, Michael T. Prahl, Bruce W. Quegg, Jeffrey S. Schlei, Ruth E. Schlesinger who acted as chairman for the project, Frank E. Sump, and Daniel Thompson. Professors Wylie E. Anderson and Fred Abraham also contributed valuable advice in the use of the multiplier effect. Also, without the cooperation of many industrialists, labor leaders, and armed services personnel, it would have been impossible to complete the project. Finally, some of the passages in this article were included in an earlier essay entitled, "The Army and the Economy: Iowa as a Case Study," in *The United States Army in Peacetime,* Robin Higham and Carol Brandt, eds.(Manhattan, Kansas, Military Affairs and Aerospace Publishing, 1975).

EARL A. MOLANDER

HISTORICAL ANTECEDENTS OF
MILITARY-INDUSTRIAL CRITICISM

The public outcry which rose against the military-industrial complex
and most specifically against the aerospace/defense industry in the 1960s
was in some respects a distinctive phenomenon of the period. It grew out
of the public concern for dramatic increase in the size of the peacetime
defense budget in the late 1950s, was catalyzed by Eisenhower's warning
against "the acquisition of unwarranted influence...by the military industrial complex" in his 1961 farewell address, and came to full bloom as a
part of public reaction to American involvement in the Vietnam War and
the movement to make American business more "socially responsible." To
a lesser extent, it derived from frustration growing out of the realization
we had created a weapons arsenal that could potentially annihilate civilization; the awareness, and then seeming insolubility, of problems in the
American social fabric; and the end of the American Dream—affluence had
not brought the expected happiness to many Americans, and they sought
a convenient scapegoat. This environment proved receptive to the same
liberal and radical critique of the American industrial and defense establishment which had existed in this country for the previous half century, but
which with the exception of a brief period in the 1930s, had been largely
ignored by the bulk of the American public.

The separate distrust of the military establishment and of American business is a long-standing and well-documented fact in American social and
intellectual history. What is in many respects unique in military-industrial
criticism is the simultaneous attack on the military and industry as a unified
body, an attack which integrates the criticism previously directed at the
two as separate institutions. This essay will endeavor to show that this
unified attack on the military and industry also has some strong antecedents

in modern American and European history. Particularly, it will show that those aspects of military-industrial complex criticism which focus on the aerospace/defense industry are part of a number of historical movements which have concerned themselves specifically with military-industrial integration in the arms business. Because of its deep roots in American culture and Western culture generally, this historical criticism of the arms business was in many respects as important in bringing the military-industrial complex attack to popularity as the unique conditions which prevailed in America in the 1960s.

HISTORICAL CRITICISM OF THE ARMS BUSINESS

One need not go back very far in American history to find a precedent for military-industrial criticism. In the 1930s there was a visceral attack both in Europe and America on armaments manufacturers. In this country, the merchants-of-death scandal, culminating in a congressional investigation headed by Senator Nye of North Dakota, had a dramatic impact on American attitudes towards the arms industry. Even more recently, at the end of World War II, it was a popularly held view that there had been a Japanese military-industrial complex—a "Gumbatsu-Zaibatsu complex," as one contemporary Russian writer has called it—behind Japanese military expansion, and an equally sinister German military-industrial complex behind the Nazi movement. Like the contemporary attack on the military-industrial complex, these movements perpetuated a historical distrust of military-industrial relationships which had long existed in American society.

Economic Motives in Warfare

To fully understand the origins of the military-industrial-complex criticism, one must begin with the long-standing distrust of businessmen and their unbridled pursuit of profits, dating at least to classical times, and the equally long-standing concern over economic motives in warfare. Throughout history, politicians, merchants, and generals have found successful warfare to their liking, whether fought for colonies, for markets, or for plunder, a fact which has rarely gone unnoticed by their contemporaries. However, Richard Lewinsohn, in his book, *The Profits of War Through the Ages,* has emphasized that, while bankers, shipbuilders, and other classes of businessmen have long been associated with war making, the arms merchant, and especially the arms manufacturer, is actually a relative latecomer to the profits of war, and, as we shall presently discuss, to the roster of professions attacked by promoters of peace:

In history, the first to make profit from war were those who carried arms; next were those who financed armaments, and only much later those who made them. This sequence does not seem altogether natural. The armorer's is one of the most ancient of trades and one might suppose that wealth and power were from an early date derived from it. But this was far from being the case. From occasional allusions in literature, we know that in the ancient world some armorers were well-to-do. We are told, for instance, that Sophocles was the son of Sophillus, a rich Athenian armorer. But neither in Greece nor Rome were great fortunes made in armaments. And in the Middle Ages the armorers were respectable artisans without any great ambitions. In some towns highly skilled specialists arose, Seville, Toledo, Milan, Nuremberg and Liege achieving a reputation for exceptional workmanship. But even here, the master forgers attained a comfortable *bourgeois* station, but no more.[1]

The distrust of businessmen and the broad concern with economic motives in warfare are established historical facts and might in themselves be enough to have laid the foundations for military-industrial criticism. But there are three other historical movements which also are important. They are: (1) the movement to establish a permanent peace through disarmament; (2) the legal debate over the rights and obligations of neutrals regarding the sale of arms to belligerents in wartime; and (3) the public concern with the price, quality, and delivery of military supplies sold to the government. The first two of these concerns date to the seventeenth century, the third to the American Revolution. In the following pages we will give a brief review of these movements up to the beginning of the twentieth century when, in the shadow of the ominous cloud of World War I, they coalesced and came to focus on the armaments industries of Europe and America.

Disarmament

As J. F. C. Fuller so amply demonstrated in *Armament and History,* munitions have played a pivotal role in warfare from its very origins when the man armed with the better physiological weaponry—hands, feet, and teeth—could claw, kick, and bite his way to victory. This awareness of the value of weapons in warfare has created through history a slow but exorable arms race in which nations have devoted considerable time and resources to the development and production of new and better armaments. Although the resultant flow of weapons has usually been matched by efforts to avoid or at least limit warfare, it was not until the seventeenth century that these efforts focused on the armaments themselves and a genuine disarmament movement began.

From its earliest beginnings, the movement for disarmament has been three-pronged in its attack. First and foremost, disarmament has had an economic dimension, focusing on the costs of standing armies, their equipment, and warfare itself. Second, disarmament has had a political dimension; armaments are seen as a threat to liberty, whether as standing armies or as "military-industrial complexes." Finally, disarmament has focused on preventing war: critics observed that nations with a large store of armaments are inclined to use them, but more importantly, these armaments engender enmity with neighboring nations, leading to arms races and the increased likelihood of a preventive first strike being undertaken by one nation against another.

Early European Efforts at Disarmament

The first major disarmament writers were Europeans. The duc de Sully in *The Great Design of Henry IV* (1625), and Abbe C. I. Costel de Saint-Pierre in *Memoires pour rendre La Paix Perpetuelle en Europe* (1632) stressed what was to become for the next two hundred years the principle argument in favor of disarmament—the economic costs of war and the preparation for war. Unfortunately, the ceilings on armies and armaments which both suggested were widely noted, but never implemented. A century later, Emmerich de Vattel in *The Law of Nations* (1758) again raised the economic argument against armies and armaments, and also noted the threat to liberty they represented. In 1795, Immanuel Kant in his famous essay on *Perpetual Peace* warned of the danger of war created by the availability of armaments. But again, these admonitions fell on deaf ears among European heads of state.

The Disarmament Movement in America

Resistance to armaments had an early beginning on the American continent, and not surprisingly, it is to the Quakers that Americans owe their disarmament heritage. As early as the seventeenth century, American Quakers were preaching nonviolence and, in the eighteenth century, voting against military expenditures for the French and Indian War. While governor of Pennsylvania, William Penn not only preached Quaker pacifism but also put his theories of disarmament into practice by placing totally disarmed colonies in western Pennsylvania among hostile Indian tribes. But those in opposition to armaments and force in early America were clearly a minority. As Merle Curti has noted:

> The American colonies were planted and grew to full stature in an age when few questioned the glory of physical prowess, the effectiveness of force, and the inevitability of war. With some notable exceptions, the

English-speaking colonists who settled on the Atlantic seaboard brought
with them the dominant attitude toward war and force. . . . Occasionally, as
in the wars against France, colonists hesitated to vote military supplies and
to engage in the hostilities vigorously, but their hesitation was based on self-
interest. They did not question the wisdom or the justice of the conflict. . . .
Although many Americans hated the idea of war in theory, all but a minority nourished the belief that in the last analysis, when peaceful efforts to
redress wrongs had clearly failed, a resort to the sword was justifiable in
the eyes of man and God.[2]

There is no clearer view of the stance of most eighteenth-century Americans toward disarmament than their position on the Revolution. "The
natural right of man to resist tyrannical authority" dominated any pacifist
sentiment: "The Revolution was a military struggle for independence and
the open appeal to the sword was questioned on pacifist grounds by few
indeed. . . . The plain fact [is] that our national independence was won on
the field of battle, not in the council chamber. . . . "[3] Benjamin Franklin's
views on armaments were probably typical of those of most of the leaders
of the Revolution. Although an ardent supporter of the revolt, Franklin
lamented the cost of armament and war, noting the loot labor, the lost
habits of industry, and the diminished quality of the citizenry because
soldiers rarely marry.[4] It remained, however, for Washington, in his farewell
address, to make the most enduring statement against armaments from
eighteenth-century American leaders. Washington's admonition against
standing armies was based on political, not economic grounds: "Overgrown
military establishments are, under any form of government, inauspicious to
liberty, and are to be regarded as particularly hostile to republican liberty."[5]
   The nascent United States did, in fact, try to practice a measure of disarmament in 1794 when Secretary of the Treasury Alexander Hamilton
encouraged Washington to seek a mutual limitation of armaments on the
Great Lakes. The proposal was eventually accepted by Great Britain, but
not until the Rush-Bagot Convention of 1817, the first successful disarmament agreement in modern history.
   Following the Rush-Bagot Convention, the American government, the
the American people, and the American peace movement turned its attention away from disarmament. It was not to be an American issue again until
the twentieth century, and not until then would it be widely recognized
that the arms merchant stood across the path to disarmament.

The Traffic in Arms

   It was arms trade, not arms manufacturing, which first raised public
awareness of the arms business. In the early seventeenth century in Europe
and in the late eighteenth century in America, the concern which brought

it into focus was the dispute over the rights of neutrals to sell military goods to belligerents in wartime. Hugo Grotius, the Dutch publicist, statesman, and jurist, in his great work, *The Rights of War and Peace* (1625), made the first contribution in this long-standing debate. Grotius first divided all goods into three groups: "Objects which are of use in war alone, as arms; others which are useless in war, and which serve only for purposes of luxury; and others which can be employed both in war and peace, as money, provisions, ships, and articles of naval equipment." He then expressed the view that neutrals were free to sell any articles of the first class to belligerents, but they were entitled to no recourse should such goods be captured by the enemy of the purchaser. Grotius thus made the control of traffic in arms a belligerent right and not a neutral duty, a position which was to prevail for the next three centuries.[6]

Over a century later, in *The Law of Nations,* Vattel reaffirmed this view with some refinement, arguing that neutrals could furnish arms and other war supplies to one belligerent as long as they were willing to furnish like supplies to the other. Whereas at one time states could maintain "neutrality" while shipping arms to one belligerent as long as the two had entered a treaty prior to the outset of hostilities, beginning in Vattel's time, neutrality required the adherence to the principles of "impartiality"—the neutral state was obliged to treat both belligerents alike—and "abstention"—neutral states were obliged not to give active aid to either belligerent. The distinction being drawn between the rights and obligations of neutral states and individuals in those states during this period deserves special mention. Vattel again emphasized that neutral governments bore no responsibility for the safety of "contraband goods" (as such arms came to be called) sold and/or carried by their own merchants.

The American Experience

The first formal American statement on the arms trade came in the United States Neutrality Act of 1793. Within a month of this neutrality proclamation, the British Ambassador called to the attention of then Secretary of State Thomas Jefferson the sale of arms by American merchants to France, with whom England was then at war. This brought forth Jefferson's oft-quoted interpretation of American neutrality (and defense of the American defense industry):

> Our citizens have been always free to make, vend, and export arms. It is the constant occupation and livelihood of some of them. To suppress their callings, the only means perhaps of their subsistence, because a war exists in foreign and distant countries, in which we have no concern, would scarcely be expected. It would be hard in principle and impossible in practice.

The law of nations, therefore, respecting the rights of those at peace, does not require from them such an internal disarrangement in their occupations. It is satisfied with the external penalty pronounced in the President's proclamation, that of confiscation of such portion of these arms as shall fall into the hands of any of the belligerent powers on their way to the ports of their enemies. To this penalty our citizens are warned that they will be abandoned, and that even private contraventions may work no inequality between the parties at war, the benefit of them will be left equally free and open to all.[7]

Atwater argues that such a policy was rooted more in economic than philosophical ground:

The United States, in 1793 and 1794, not only accepted the principles of impartiality and non-participation as applied by the European neutrals in the preceding years, but also enlarged upon them, clarified them and gave considerable impetus to their general recognition as obligations under the international law of neutrality. The American Government did not go so far, however, as had the European neutrals in prohibiting its nationals from supplying or carrying arms or contraband to the belligerents. This, it was felt, would impose too heavy a financial and economic sacrifice upon American industry. Therefore the United States made a careful distinction between government assistance or participation, which it promised not to engage in, and the acts of private citizens in aiding one or the other belligerent through the supplying or carrying of contraband, which it announced could take place freely subject to the risk of penalties at the hands of the belligerents. Thus, instead of following the complete standards of the Armed Neutrality, the United States, while accepting and enlarging upon the principles of governmental impartiality and non-participation, chose to retain for its private citizens the right to engage at their own risk in the profitable arms and contraband trade.[8]

For the next hundred years, the continuing challenge by foreign governments to the American policy of freedom of trade in arms was resisted. The policy was actually set aside on four occasions, but only to conserve arms for national use. This occurred twice in the late nineteenth century when war first with Great Britain and then with France appeared possible, in the Civil War, and again in the Spanish-American War. The American arms industry has operated in the international arms market with the full support of the American government throughout our history, just as it does today.

Government Contracting

Public concern with the price, quality, and delivery of military supplies sold to the government dates at least to the American Revolution. There were numerous efforts to control profiteering during the war, including legislation in Maryland and Virginia prohibiting merchants from representing the states in Congress, wage and price controls in New England, and a series of investigations into profiteering by government officials (including Robert Morris, chairman of the congressional finance committees) at the war's end, but they were largely unsuccessful. The period between the Revolution and the Civil War saw little public attention given to government contracting. However, the Civil War again brought forth unscrupulous contractors in all areas of government procurement, including weapons, prompting a congressional investigation whose final report was highly critical of the weapons industry:

> The government has been the victim of more than one conspiracy, and remarkable combinations have been formed to rob the treasury. The profits from the sale of arms to the government have been enormous, and realized, too, in many instances, even by our own citizens through a system of brokerage as unprincipled and dishonest, as unfriendly to the success and welfare of the nation, as the plottings of actual treason. [9]

The government had in part brought these abuses on itself by authorizing the several states and the generals commanding the several divisions of the army to procure their own arms at the expense of the federal government, thereby creating severe competition and a sellers' market for those limited numbers of arms available for sale. The result was arms of poor quality, some even unusable, being bought at prices up to ten times their prewar levels.

For thirty years after the Civil War, there was relative quiet for the arms merchants, again because there were only limited sales of weapons to the government during that time. Burdened with considerable excess capacity from the war period, the arms industry urged the Congress in 1878 to expand their weapons procurement from private sources, arguing they were far more innovative and efficient than government arsenals. However, arguments of the industry were successfully rebutted by the Army Chief of Ordnance, and the industry remained in a depressed state.[10]

In the early 1890s European nations and the United States began a race to build heavy naval armor which saw such exorbitant prices being paid by the US Navy for the heavy armor plate that it caused a congressional investigation. The Senate Committee on Naval Affairs was charged:

> . . .to inquire whether the prices paid or agreed to be paid for armor for vessels of the Navy have been fair and reasonable; also, whether any prices paid have been increased on account of patent processes used for the introduction of nickel, or for cementation by the Harvey process; and if so, whether the increases in price are fair and reasonable; whether the issuance of any of the patents was expedited at the request of the Navy Department; whether such patents were properly issued and were for inventions not previously known or used, and who were and are the owners of such patents; whether any officers of the Government were interested therein, or at the

time when any contracts were made were, or have since been interested in the patents or employed by the owners thereof, and whether any legislation is necessary to further promote the manufacture and cheapen the price of armor for vessels of the Navy.[11]

The committee found considerable evidence to substantiate claims against price-fixing by Bethlehem and Carnegie Steel companies, participation of naval officers in royalties on patents used by naval contractors, and the practice of naval officers taking temporary leave from their duties to work for these same contractors. The government responded with legislation to fix prices and prohibit the employment of retired or furloughed military officers by government contractors, but because of contractor resistance it was never effectively enforced.

THE ARMAMENTS MAKER IN THE TWENTIETH CENTURY

The early twentieth century brought together these three concurrent streams of thought—the peace and disarmament movement, the desire to control the arms traffic, and the scrutiny of government contracting practices. The interrelationship between these concerns was dramatized first in Europe and then in this country by what had come to be, in the foreshadowing of World War I, an international peace movement.

The international peace movement enjoyed spectacular growth in the period between the Spanish-American War and 1914. The movement was instrumental in giving broad publicity to the Second Hague Conference of 1907, which again considered the international traffic in arms, although its only action was to reaffirm the rights of neutrals to export arms to belligerents. The movement also focused its attention for virtually the first time on the manufacturers of armaments, especially the large European firms— Schneider-Creusot in France, Krupp in Germany, Vickers and Armstrong in England, and Skoda in Czechoslovakia.

One of the best-known and enduring attacks on armaments manufacturers came in 1905 in George Bernard Shaw's satirical play, *Major Barbara.* Shaw put these words in the mouth of Undershaft, the armaments maker:

The government of your country! *I* am the government of your country: I, and Lazarus. Do you suppose that you and half a dozen amateurs like you, sitting in a row in that foolish gabble shop, can govern Undershaft and Lazarus? No, my friend: you will do what pays us. You will make war when it suits us, and keep peace when it doesn't. You will find out that trade requires certain measures when we have decided on those measures. When I want anything to keep my dividends up, you will discover that my want is a national need. When other people want something to keep my dividends down, you will call out the police and the military. And in return you shall have the support and applause of my newspapers, and the delight of imagining that you are a great statesman. Government of your country! Be off with you, my boy, and play with your caucuses and leading articles and historic parties and great leaders and burning questions and the rest of your toys. I am going back to my counting-house to pay the piper and call the tune.[12]

In the United States, the peace movement found itself in conflict with the newly formed (1902) Navy League whose dedication to expansion of the Navy appeared to peace advocates to be less an outgrowth of patriotism than of the vested interests of some of its officers and supporters in the manufacture of war materials. This conflict reached its peak in 1914 when Representative Clyde H. Tavenner denounced the League on the House floor, accused its membership of profiteering, fraud, and false patriotism, and called for the nationalization of the arms industry.[13]

The attention given to armaments in the early 1900s was an outgrowth not only of the activities of the peace movement, but also of a series of armament scandals which rocked the major European powers. In England, there had been a number of minor scares and "scraps" (drives to scrap existing armaments and build new and better ones) which received some publicity, but none so much as the "Naval Scare of 1909," in which it was revealed that H. H. Mulliner, managing director of the Coventry Ordnance Company, had for three years been anonymously circulating a false rumor that the Krupp Steel Works was greatly expanding its capacity to enable it to outfit an enormously increasing German navy. The famous "Putiloff Affair" drew equally wide publicity in France. The Putiloff factory was a Russian munitions factory in St. Petersburg, jointly financed by Schneider-Creusot of France and Skoda of Czechoslovakia, then a Krupp subsidiary, and using Schneider patents. The firm was competing for Russian armament contracts against an alliance of British armaments firms and a French bank, Societé Générale. When a rumor began circulating in France that Schneider intended to sell its interest in the Putiloff factory to Krupp, Frenchmen became enraged at the possibility of French armament secrets being funneled to Germany through Krupp's access to Schneider patents.

The attack on the armaments industry during this prewar period had all the elements of the merchants-of-death scandal twenty years later, including charges of industry participation in war scares, international armaments cartels, and manipulation of the news media, as well as charges of conflict of interest on the part of government officials who awarded armament contracts. Some good examples of this genre include the National Labor Press' "The War Trust Exposed," the Union of Democratic Control's "The International Industry of War," the National Peace Council's

"The War Traders," the World Peace Foundation's "Syndicates for War," and "Dreadnoughts and Dividends."[14] The beginning of hostilities in Europe in the summer of 1914 stemmed the growing tide of armament criticism in Europe. But in the United States, criticism of the arms business continued through 1915 and 1916, largely because of the continuing debate in Congress and the press as to the legality, morality, and good sense of preferential arms sales by American firms to the Allies but not to Germany. The principle arguments on each side of this question were summarized in *The Independent:*

The argument that the exportation of munitions to the Allies should be stopped may be reduced to the following propositions:
1. It makes our country a workshop of death.
2. It is for profits, not patriotism.
3. It compromizes us in the eyes of humanity.
4. It makes us an ally of the Allies.
5. It fosters an industry whose interest will be to extend militarism in the United States.
6. It theoretically enables a small state to buy arms when attacked, but practically this right is of little value, as the small state is likely to be completely invested by its greater and more warlike antagonist.
The official justification by the Secretary of State of the exportation of arms can be epitomized as follows:
1. It is the accepted rule of international law, which no nation should break.
2. It is and has been the universal practise of nations -Germany and Austria included.
3. It is unneutral in that it would deprive England of her superiority on sea and not Germany of her superiority on land.
4. It enables the United States to keep a small military establishment in time of peace.
5. It enables all nations to go without storing up vast reservoirs of military supplies.
6. It thus tends to the peaceful method of settling international disputes.[15]

Almost unnoticed in this period was an article by Shailer Matthews in the *Journal of Political Economy* which went far deeper than any other writings in exploring the possibility that expanded American arms manufacturing capability could lead to a militarized economy and society. In warning of the dangers inherent in the private manufacture of armaments, Matthews noted that ". . .the propaganda for preparedness become[s] a means of perpetuating the . . . private business in war materials. . . ." and warned of ". . . the tendency of business like that of Krupp and Armstrong to fasten war upon civilization in the interests of industrialism."[16] American entry into the war in 1917 aborted arms criticism in this country, just as it had in Europe three years before. There were some, like

Senator George W. Norris of Nebraska, who believed that munitions makers and Wall Street financiers were pushing us into the war to guarantee their profits, but they were a minority. Most Americans were supportive of the munitions makers' contribution to the war effort, even when it became apparent near the end of the war that many were profiting immensely from it.

Following the war, the League of Nations made numerous attempts to secure international agreement on limiting the manufacture and trade in armaments. The Covenant of the League of Nations even included provisions which stated:

> The Members of the League agree that the manufacture by private enterprise of munitions and implements of war is open to *grave objections* [emphasis added] . . .
> . . .The League [is entrusted] with general supervision of the trade in arms and ammunition with the countries in which control of this traffic is necessary to the common interest.[17]

Within two months of the Treaty of Versailles, the Convention for the Control of the Trade in Arms and Ammunition was signed by twenty-eight powers at St. Germain-en-Laye, prohibiting the export to certain territories of arms and munitions used in war—except for the use of the signatory governments. But the Convention was never ratified by the major arms producers, including the United States, and never went into effect. There followed a series of meetings in Geneva throughout the early 1920s to secure international support for the principle of arms-trade control, spurred on by wars in China, Mexico, and Morocco fought with arms manufactured in Europe, Japan, and the United States. These efforts also met with failure in the large arms-exporting nations. The United States eventually sent to Geneva a delegation which signed the Arms Traffic Convention of 1925, but the Convention languished in the Senate Committee on Foreign Relations until 1934.

Criticism of the arms business among the general public was present but not widespread in the United States in the 1920s. Revelation of the extensive profits made by many American firms brought some criticism immediately after the war but were then largely forgotten. A number of writers picked up the theme of the League of Nation's Temporary Mixed Commission on Armaments whose 1921 report argued that armament firms had:

1. Been active in fomenting war scares and in persuading their own countries to adopt warlike policies and to increase their armaments;
2. Attempted to bribe government officials both at home and abroad;
3. Disseminated false reports concerning the military and naval expenditures of various countries in order to stimulate armament expenditures ;
4. Sought to influence public opinion through the control of newspapers in their own and foreign countries;

5. Organized international armament rings through which the armaments race has been accentuated by playing off one country against the other;
6. Organized international armament trusts which have increased the price of armaments to governments.[18]

These were the "grave objections" to which the Covenant of the League had alluded.

Americans were as apathetic to setting limitations on their arms industry as they were to joining the League of Nations. In fact, in early 1928 the political climate was so favorable to American munitions firms that Secretary of War Davis proposed that these firms be given contracts for "educational munitions making," to develop the advanced technology and production equipment that would be necessary should there be another war.[19]

The rapid turnabout in American sentiment which saw virtually the entire country join the hysterical attack on armaments manufacturers, culminating in the Nye Committee Investigation in 1934, began in the late 1920s. As Americans again began to look abroad, they saw that in the decade since the end of the World War the League had been largely unsuccessful in its efforts to institute international organization and outlaw war and armaments traffic. In Congress, the Burton Resolution in 1928 and the Capper and Porter resolutions in 1929 were introduced to "prohibit the exportation of arms, munitions, or implements of war to any nation which is engaged in war with another."[20] Although each failed to secure congressional approval, their debate renewed public interest in arms control. Then, in August of 1929, it was revealed that three large American shipbuilding firms had employed one William Shearer to sabotage the Geneva Naval Conference of 1927. A halfhearted Senate investigation resulted after considerable press coverage and, although it did nothing, the public's interest in the arms business was further aroused. The signing of the Kellogg-Briand Pact that same month, renouncing war as an instrument of national policy, was the first official indication of the end to American isolationist thinking.

In the early 1930s war clouds again appeared on the horizon. Japan invaded Manchuria, Italy conquered Ethiopia, and the Chaco War broke out in South America. More importantly, Hitler came to power and, in defiance of the Versailles Treaty, Germany began to rearm. The fear of war again took hold of the minds of many Americans and they began to search for ways to avoid another world conflict. In 1931 Congress established the War Policies Commission to study proposals for removing profit from war and the commission's star witness, Bernard Baruch, published his own treatise, *Taking the Profits out of War*. In 1932, the United States sent to the General Disarmament Conference at Geneva a delegation which for the first time had broad public support for American participation in international control of private (and state) arms manufacture. At home, the popular press again turned its attention to the role of the armaments industry in warfare. In the fall of 1931, *The Living Age* and *The World Tomorrow* carried articles attacking the European armaments firms for their false patriotism and indiscriminate trafficking in arms. In 1932, taking their lead from the British and French press, *The Literary Digest, The Nation,* and *The New Republic* joined the fray, accusing the international armaments industry of sabotaging the latest Geneva Disarmament Conference. A series of three articles in *The New Republic* by historian Charles A. Beard attacking the Navy League was perhaps the most important work in this early period, not only because of Beard's notoriety, but because the articles focused exclusively on the abuses of American, not European, armaments firms. These journals continued their attack on the munitions industry through 1933, and then, in the spring of 1934, two books, Engelbrecht and Hanighen's *Merchants of Death* and Seldes' *Iron, Blood and Profits,* and an article in the much-respected business magazine *Fortune* (reprinted with wide distribution in *The Reader's Digest*) brought the American munitions makers into the view of most American citizens. These works so aroused the American public and Congress to the supposed evils of private arms manufacture that when Senator Nye's proposal for an investigation of the munitions industry was finally brought to a vote on April 12, 1934, two months after it had first been introduced, there was not a single dissenting voice.

The day-to-day proceedings of Senator Nye's Munitions Committee hearings were given generous coverage in newspapers and magazines for the next two years. Yet when the committee had finished its hearings and prepared its report, the members were almost unanimous in their view that the evidence did not support the merchants-of-death charge. When the committee finally closed its doors in 1936, the possibility of a new war in Europe was becoming clearer, and by 1939 the merchants-of-death had once again become the "Arsenal of Democracy."

Critics of the Nye Committee have been legion, including President Truman, who called it ". . .pure demagoguery in the guise of a Congressional Investigating Committee." The committee was accused of having mistreated witnesses, excessively pursued newspaper publicity, and in their attack having given aid and comfort to enemies of the American system. The aspect of the committee most criticized was its alleged contribution to the passage of the neutrality laws of 1935–37. The laws were felt by many to have delayed the buildup of American military strength for World War II by as much as two years, a charge hotly denied by former committee members.

Although the armaments industry shared the criticism of excessive business influence on the Office of Production Management during World War II, which arose out of the Truman Committee hearings, the industry was largely free of criticism from 1936 until the military-industrial complex debate in the 1960s. It is ironic that it was in this period that critics asserted the armaments firms made their most significant inroads into American economic and political life.

SUMMATION

The combined attack on the military and industry derives, as we have endeavored to show, from historical movements to control armaments, the arms trade, and arms profiteering. Although varying in origin and content, by the start of the twentieth century they were all focused on the arms industry and its relation to the military establishment. The concept of a *unified* "military-industrial complex" dates to the start of the century as well, particularly in the attack on the joint military-industrial promotion of war scares in Europe and the conflict of interest and profiteering charges against military officers and their sometime industrial employers in this country. These early attacks did not charge the military-industrial *domination* of society as did the attacks of the 1960s. However, it is clear they had laid a solid ideological groundwork on which such a charge eventually would be constructed.

NOTES

1. Richard Lewinsohn, *The Profits of War Through the Ages* (New York, Garland Publishing, Inc., 1972; originally published by Dutton, 1937). J. C. Fuller, *Armament and History* (New York, Charles Scribner's Sons, 1945), p. 2. The proposed ceilings were so small in comparison to the prevailing forces that, had the plan been implemented, it would have constituted, in effect, a disarmament. Other early peace writers who favored disarmament on economic grounds include Abbot Charles-Irenee de Saint-Pierre in his *Projet* (1713) and John Ballers, *Some Reasons for a European State* (1710). Merle Curti, *Peace or War: The American Struggle, 1636-1936* (New York, W. W. Norton & Co., 1936), p. 18. Merze Tate, *The Disarmament Illusion* (New York, Macmillan, 1942), p. 3. See William Penn, *Essay Toward the Present and Future of Peace* (1692).
2. Merle Curti, op. cit., pp. 16-17, 21.
3. Ibid., pp. 22, 23

4. John Bigelow, ed., *The Works of Benjamin Franklin,* as quoted in Tate, op. cit., pp. 6-7.
5. Edwin D. Mead, *Washington, Jefferson and Franklin on War* (Boston, World Peace Foundation, 1913), p. 10. Curti, op. cit., p. 33. The author expresses the view that the motivations of both parties were principally economic in signing the treaty. Certain Chinese states made a disarmament treaty in the sixth century B. C. according to Mr. Liang-Chi-Chao in a pamphlet, *China and the League of Nations.* cf. Tate, op. cit. Quoted in Elisabeth M. Garber, *Control of the Sales of Munition of War* (Washington, Government Printing Office, 1941). 77th Congress, 1st Session, Document 19, p.2.
6. William C. Morey, "The Sale of Munitions of War," *The American Journal of International Law,* Vol. 10 (1916), p. 468. These principles were later to be embodied in the Hague Convention of 1907. Emmerich de Vattel, *The Law of Nations,* Book III, Cr. VII, nos. 105 and 111.
7. Elton Atwater, *American Regulation of Arms Export* (Washington, Carnegie Endowment for International Peace, 1941).
8. Ibid., p. 10. This occurred when American firms supplied arms to Texas in its war with Mexico (1842); to France, Great Britain, and Russia in the Crimean War (1854); to France in its war with Mexico (1862); during the Franco-Prussian War (1870); during the Haitian War (1888); to Chilean insurgents in the Chilean revolt (1891); and to England in its war with the Orange Free State (1899). See Morey, op. cit., pp. 475-480. Richard Kaufman, *The War Profiteers* (Indianapolis, Bobbs-Merrill, 1970), pp. 5-8. Although Robert Morris, Chairman of the congressional committees with authority over finances and government finances, has drawn considerable attention from historians for his exploitation of the public purse during the war, his activities, although criticized at the time, went unprosecuted. A Senate resolution to investigate his activities was never acted upon. See *Senate Journal,* 1st Congress (February 8, 1790), pp. 22-24.
9. Select Committee, US House of Representatives, "Government Contracts," House Report no. 2, 37th Congress, 2d Session, (December 17, 1861), pp. 34, 37-43.
10. See the memorandum from the Association of Manufacturers of Arms, Ammunition, and Equipment to the Secretary of War, in US Senate, Executive Document no. 17, 45th Congress, 3d Session, (December 20, 1878), pp. 2-5.
11. Committee on Naval Affairs, US Senate, "Prices of Armor for Vessels of the Navy," Senate Report no. 1453, 54th Congress, 2d Session, 1895, p. 1. Kaufman, op. cit., p. 10. Curti, op. cit., p. 196. Charles Noble Gregory, "Neutrality and the Sale of Arms," *The American Journal of International Law,* Vol. 10 (1916), p. 547.
12. George Bernard Shaw, *Major Barbara* (Baltimore, Penguin, 1971 edition),p. 124.
13. Clyde H. Tavenner, "Why Congress Should Take the Profit out of War and the Preparation for War." Extension of remarks in the House. *Congressional Record,* v. 51, pt. 17, appendix, May 12, 1914, pp. 551-560. The full particulars of the rather complex background to this affair are described in H. C. Engelbrècht and F. C. Hanighen, *Merchants of Death,* (New York, Dodd, Mead, 1934), pp. 128-139. In this same period in Germany Dr. Karl Liebknecht was denouncing the political influence of Krupp and other German armament firms in securing government contracts.
14. J. T. Walton Newbold, "The War Trust Exposed," The National Labour Press, 1916; Union of Democratic Control, "The International Industry of War," Pamphlet no. 7, London, 1915; George Herbert Perris, "The War Traders," (London National Peace Council, 1914), pp. 27-31; Francis McCullough, "Syndicates for War," *World Peace Foundation Pamphlet Series,* July, 1911, no. 2,part III; Phillip Snowden, "Dreadnoughts and Dividends," *World Peace Foundation Pamphlets Series,* 1914. See also Gilson Gardner, "Feeding the

War Ring," *Harper's Weekly* Vol. 60 (March 13, 1915), for an attack exclusively against American arms makers.

15. "Selling Death," *The Independent*, Vol. 83 (September 6, 1915), pp. 312-313.
16. Shailer Matthews, "Some Larger Aspects of the Trade in War Materials," *Journal of Political Economy*, Vol. 24 (January, 1916), pp. 17-19. A Federal Trade Commission investigation in 1918 concluded that profiteering did indeed exist and that "much of it is due to advantages taken of the necessities of the times as evidenced in the war pressure for heavy production [but] some of it is attributable to inordinate greed and barefaced fraud." Federal Trade Commission, "Profiteering," US Congress, 2d Session, Document no. 248 (June 27, 1918), p. 5.
17. Article 8, section 5, and Article 23.
18. As quoted in John Gunther, "Slaughter for Sale, "*Harper's*, Vol. 168 (May, 1934), p. 659.
19. See "'Education' Munitions Making as 'Peace Insurance,'" *The Literary Digest*, Vol. 98 (January 14, 1928), for the Secretary's recommendations and the response they drew in the press.
20. In 1922 a similar resolution had been introduced in the Congress, but was never reported out of committee. For a discussion of the differences among these resolutions see L. H. Woolsey, "The Porter and Capper Resolutions against Traffic in Arms," *American Journal of International Law*, Vol. 23 (April, 1929), pp. 379-383. Engelbrecht and Hanighen, op. cit., p. 205-217. Francis Delaisi, "Corruption in Armaments," *The Living Age*, Vol. 341 (September, 1931), pp. 50-56; and H. C. Engelbrecht, "The Bloody International," *The World Tomorrow*, Vol. 14 (October, 1931), pp. 317-320. "Munitions Makers Balk Disarmament," *The Literary Digest*, Vol. 113 (April 23, 1932), p. 14, and "Villains of the Disarmament Drama," *The Literary Digest*, Vol. 114 (July 9, 1932), p. 10. Robert Dell, "Sabotage at Geneva," *The Nation*, Vol. 135 (September 7, 1932), pp. 209-210; and Charles Beard, "Big Navy Boys," *The New Republic*, Vol. 69 (January 20, 1932), pp. 258-262; (January 27, 1932), pp. 287-291; (February 3, 1932), pp. 314-318. George Seldes, *Iron, Blood, and Profits* (New York, Harper's 1934), and "Arms and the Man," *Fortune*, Vol. 9 (March, 1934), pp. 52-57. John Wiltz, *In Search of Peace*, (Baton Rouge, Louisiana State University Press, 1963) pp. 36, 165-220, 227-231. *Investigation of the National Defense Program, Additional Report*, US Senate, Special Committee to Investigate the National Defense Program, 77th Congress, 2d Session, Report 480, especially Part 5 (January 15, 1942). Harold Lasswell's 1941 article, "The Garrison State," often cited as a forerunner of military-industrial criticism, actually focused exclusively on the growing influence of the military, a related but differentiable concern. *American Journal of Sociology*, Vol. 46 (January, 1941), pp. 455-468.

SUGGESTIONS FOR FURTHER RESEARCH

The contemporary orientation of most writing on the military-industrial complex suggests a need for greater investigation of the historical antecedents. The semantics of modern social science, as applied to the twentieth-century phenomenon, may provide a takeoff point for plumbing the wellsprings of nineteenth-century experience with industry, government, and national defense. But how can we synthesize the social, cultural, and political, as well as the technological and economic interrelationships of military-industrial linkages? Are we correct in artificially separating such topics as civil-military relations, war and peace, technology and man from the broader sweep of historical events? Can we really isolate whatever comprises the MIC for a given country or a given time-frame, or is it part of the overall national fabric in the period since the industrial revolution?

Does it have to do with something first discerned by the Stanford historian, Peter Paret, when he suggested that America the Beautiful has also always been America the Bellicose? Is the MIC a myth or an abberation, or is peace-loving America the ideal but not the reality? Coincidentally, then, what has been the relationship between growth of the military-industrial complex and military-industrial criticism? Does the latter lag in time, reliability, et cetera, or does it lead in democracies such as our own? Are MIC growth and criticism simply a part of larger social, economic, and political phenomena? Has the reemergence of a merchants-of-death notion in the 1960s given us any lessons with which to return to an earlier era for understanding the normality rather than the abnormality of military-industrial links in the name of national self-preservation?

The chronological order of the essays in this volume suggest their own internal problem areas warranting further research. Do we truly comprehend the trans-national implications of the European experience with the MIC? Can scholarship on "complexes" in Great Britain, Germany, France, Russia, Italy, Austria-Hungary, Spain, or Japan yield useful information about our own historical development of industrial-defense ties? Are national experiences dissimilar because of socio-economic-political differences?

There are numerous specific needs and opportunities for research in the area of nineteenth- and twentieth-century American military-industrial relations. The Army and Navy ordnance establishments have been curiously neglected by most historians. Organization and administration, as well as the entrepreneurial, scientific, and technical work of those departments demand further exploration. Individual ordnance officers such as the Army's Decius Wadsworth, George Bomford, James W. Ripley,

Alexander B. Dyer, Stephen V. Benet, or William Crozier, to name but a few, would add a much-neglected human dimension to the usually sterile accounts of techno-military-business activity.

Like that of the ordnance departments, much of the history of arms making lies fallow in archives and little-used manuscript collections. No general studies exist on the ongoing relationship between private contractors and government procurement agencies. While books and articles detailing the exploits of Eli Whitney, Samuel Colt, and other famous inventor-entrepreneurs are plentiful, they are generally uncritical and episodic. They tend to isolate their subjects from the mainstream of American industry. For a great majority of arms makers the only available information may be found in gun-collecting publications. The fact remains that the historical profession has yet to integrate satisfactorily antiquarian and professional material in order to analyze the business, military, and technological dimensions of arms making.

While the biographical approach would undoubtedly help answer many of the hows, wheres, and whens of arms making, broader investigations of communities of gunsmiths, munitions manufacturers, powder and accouterment makers, etc. based on regional economic models are even more promising for the insights they would reveal. Cursory research indicates, for example, that armorers from the Middle Atlantic states differed considerably from their peers in New England in the early days of the republic. Many revealing contrasts and comparisons can be made between the cultural background, training, technical tastes, and outlook on national and international matters of such figures as Nathan Starr of Middletown, Connecticut; Andrew Carnegie of Pittsburgh, Pennsylvania; or, say, the modern mangers of Lockheed, General Dynamics, or Northrup. To what extent such differences existed from one region to another or even within industries of the same region remains unclear. Such knowledge would shed much light on the character of the arms and armaments industry and the process of industrial development, not only in the nineteenth but also in the present century.

Historians have given scant attention to many other military-industrial-related subjects. As yet, no major study of cannon manufacture and foundry work in the United States has been published. Despite the fact that Ames, Columbia, Fort Pitt, South Boston, and West Point foundries were among the largest in the country, no one has investigated their business activities or assessed their contributions to metalworking in nineteenth-century America. Excepting the Springfield and Harpers Ferry armories, and a very inadequate work on the Naval Gun Factory in Washington, D. C., the same observation applies to major Government Arsenals at Frankford (Philadelphia), Allegheny (Pittsburgh), Rock Island, Watertown (Massachusetts), and Watervliet (New York). Similarly, the Navy yards—from Boston, New York, Philadelphia, Norfolk, and Mare Island, to smaller facilities at Charleston, Pensacola, and Pearl Harbor—have been inadequately treated from the standpoint of political, social, and economic impact on surrounding communities and regions. One can suggest similar ramifications for Air Force bases, Marine Corps installations, nay, all military bases and institutions from the Army War College to hospitals and supply depots. The implications of political generals and admirals and their congressional patrons precede the days of Mendell Rivers and Strom Thurmond. The records and correspondence of civilian managers, machinists, armorers, and other personnel in uniform and mufti constitute a rich resource for economic, labor, and technological historians. They also provide an indispensable data base for interpreters of the vast tentacles of the military-industrial interlock in this nation's history.

Admittedly, the history of the military-industrial sector suffers from the crudest conceptual foundations. Much of what has been written has been polemical or sensational. The inability of researchers to work in some corporate records has compounded the problem. United States Steel, Bethlehem, J. P. Morgan, International Nickel, and other concerns have often imposed restrictions which have mitigated against determined pursuit of the truth. Individually and collectively members of the historical profession must continue to press for access to corporate archives, with such facilities as the Eleutherian Mills Historical Library offering superb opportunities to avoid reversion to simplistic muckraking. In this manner, we may hope to gain better understanding of (1) a notion of the capitalistic executive drive toward market control; (2) the place and control that government must have in the "military-industrial complex," and (3) the way in which technological innovation operates out of economic gain on the one hand, and some felt need (i.e., a national need in both tactical *and* strategic senses) on the other.

Obviously one approach to in-depth examination of a specific part of the military-industrial complex might profitably come from study of the shipbuilding or aerospace industries. For example, the historical relationship between the industry and the military—beginning with the Wright Brothers' first Signal Corps contract and, including commercial aviation—needs elaboration. Similarly, the automotive industry and the Army might be illuminated by study of everything from armored vehicles through the ubiquitous jeep, and the naval side of the picture must surely encompass more than simply research on capital ships, whether they be battleships, carriers, or submarines. Perhaps study from the "micro" side of historical investigation will provide those vital answers to the "macro" questions posed earlier in this essay.

The military-industrial cake may even be sliced yet another way. First, we may safely ask whether or not we have fully explored all the dimensions of the World War II and postwar phenomena which spawned our concern with the problem in the first place. An approach to the vast amount of material in the period 1939–75 will undoubtedly suggest many possibilities to researchers in the years to come. Certainly more research needs to be done on the linkages between producers, the military, and academic researchers—a sort of addition of a fourth estate to the MIC. Thus we can add research "think-tanks" to military-industrial-political triads. How did wartime "real world" experience carry over into business, government, the military, and academe in terms of status and promotability after World War II? How did labor unions fit into the scheme from 1939–45, and beyond? What was the second effect of wartime procurement on lending institutions? Insurance? What about social clubs and groups in industry and the military, and their influence on contracts? Did it really pay in World War II to make top civilian executives commissioned officers? Or were they merely co-opted by the role and status of becoming "brass"?

The lode is vast. Yet the historians and policy makers of the future may spend much time tracing the footings of what became known as the military-industrial complex since they were inadvertently poured and hardened in the pressure of the Second World War. Or is this too deceptive? Like the New Deal and World War I, can the tracings for the MIC (given the above kinds of questions), be carried back further. We might ask the same questions as above for World War I, the Spanish-American War, and even the Civil War. The answers might be surprising. Indeed, reevaluation of such things as Federal highway programs, the military-industrial complex in so unlikely a spot as Iowa today, an updated study on Project Management in DOD today, or comparative analyses between the old Ordnance Corps and the modern Army Materiel Command, may give us the kinds of questions we need for finding the spring from which the MIC emerged in the nineteenth century. Until some of these gaps are filled in, historical understanding of the military-industrial complex will remain fragmentary, tentative, and incomplete. MIC promises to continue as the United States enters its third century of existence. It may be time to replace some of the hoary myths concerning War, Business, and American Society.

SELECTED BIBLIOGRAPHY

The following bibliography is not designed to be definitive. The editor and essayists in this volume merely suggest sources and areas for further inquiry into the labyrinth which forms the history of the military-industrial complex. This bibliography supplements those sources cited in the chapter notes of the text.

MILITARY-INDUSTRIAL COMPLEX - ORIGINAL SOURCES

Much of the preliminary spadework remains to be done for the historical dimensions of the American military-industrial complex. The rich resources of such diverse repositories as the various Presidential libraries administered by the National Archives; the Army's Center of Military History and US Army Military History Research Collection; Air Force, Navy, and Marine Corps historical agencies; the libraries of senior military institutions such as the Industrial College of the Armed Forces; Army, Air, Naval and National War colleges; and special historical operations conducted by US Army Communications, Electronics, Tank-Automotive, Materiel, Test and Evaluation, Combat Development and Experimental, Missile, Aviation Systems, and Ballistic Missile Defense System commands—all hold secrets of the historical dimensions of the problem. Even college and university libraries (Yale, Harvard, Clemson, to name but a few) have bodies of individual's papers helpful in this regard. Manuscript collections of the Connecticut Valley Historical Museum, Springfield, Massachusetts, and the Eleutherian Mills Historical Library, Greenville, Wilmington, Delaware, should also be consulted.

There are probably no substitutes, as usual, for the Manuscript Division of the Library of Congress, and the National Archives, both in Washington, D. C. The plethora of official government records should not daunt the dedicated student in his search of Army, Navy, Air Force, congressional, and other bureaucratic records in this regard.

GENERAL WORKS

Ambrose, Stephen E. and James A. Barber, Jr. *The Military and American Society* (New York, Free Press, 1972).

American Society of Naval Architects and Marine Engineers, *Historical Transactions, 1893-1943.*

Basiuk, Victor. "The Differential Impact of Technological Change on the Great Powers, 1870-1914: The Case of Steel," Unpublished doctoral dissertation, Columbia University, 1956.

Bruce, Robert V. *Lincoln and the Tools of War* (Indianapolis, Bobbs-Merrill, 1956).

Burns, Tom. "Research, Development and Production: Problems of Conflict and Cooperation," in Charles D. Orth, III, et. al., editors., *Administering Research and Development: The Behavior of Scientists and Engineers in Organizations* (Homewood, Ill., Irwin-Dorsey, 1961).

Cannon, Charles Alfred. "The Military-Industrial Complex in American Politics, 1953-1970," Unpublished doctoral dissertation, Stanford University, 1975.

Carey, Omar L., editor. *The Military-Industrial Complex and U.S. Foreign Policy* (Pullman, Washington State University Press, 1969).

Cypher, James Martin. "Military Expenditures and the Performance of the Postwar U. S. Economy: 1947-1971," Unpublished doctoral dissertation, University of California, Riverside, 1973.

De Pue, Leland. "The Influence of Silicon on Gun Metal Alloys," Unpublished doctoral dissertation, University of Maryland, 1961.

Gorgol, John Francis and Ira Kleinfeld. *The Military-Industrial Firm; A Practical Theory and Model* (New York, Praeger, 1972).

Hammond, Paul Y. *Organizing for Defense: The American Military Establishment in the Twentieth Century* (Princeton, N. J., Princeton University Press, 1961).

Harkavy, Robert E. *The Arms Trade and International Systems* (Cambridge, Mass., Ballinger, 1975).

Helmer, William J. *The Gun That Made the Twenties Roar* (New York, Macmillan, 1969).

Horton, Arthur G. "War Munitions and International Relations," Unpublished doctoral dissertation, University of North Dakota, 1937.

Huston, James A. *The Sinews of War: Army Logistics 1775-1953* [Army Historical Series] (Washington, D. C., Government Printing Office, 1966).

Hutner, Simeon. "Economic Maximation in Time of War: An Historical Survey," Unpublished doctoral dissertation, Princeton University, 1951.

"In Search of New Wars: Winding Down - After Appomattox," *Humanities,* 3, (1973), 1-2, 5.

Kaufmann, John H. "Estimation of Requirements for War; A Case Study in Steel," Unpublished doctoral dissertation, Harvard University, 1953.

Kaufman, Richard F. *The War Profiteers* (Indianapolis, Bobbs-Merrill, 1970).

Koistinen, Paul A. C. "The 'Industrial-Military Complex' in Historical Perspective: The Interwar Years," *The Journal of American History,* LVI, March 1970, 819-839.

Lens, Sidney. *The Military-Industrial Complex* (Philadelphia, Pa., Pilgrim Press and The National Catholic Reporter, 1970).

Lieberson, Stanley. "An Empirical Study of Military-Industrial Linkages," *The American Journal of Sociology,* 76, January 1971, 562-584.

Miller, John Perry. *Pricing of Military Procurements* (New Haven, Conn., Yale University Press, 1949).

Mooney, David J. "The Roles of the Military-Industrial Complex," Unpublished Masters thesis, George Washington University, 1973.

Morison, E. E. *Men, Machines and Modern Times* (Cambridge, MIT Press, 1966).

Pursell, Jr., Carroll, ed. *The Military-Industrial Complex* (New York, Harper and Row, 1972).

Rosen, Steven, editor. *Testing the Theory of the Military-Industrial Complex* (Lexington, Mass., D. C. Heath, 1973).

Smith, Gibson B. "Rubber for Americans: The Search for an Adequate Supply of Rubber and the Politics of Strategic Materials, 1934-1942, " Unpublished doctoral dissertation, Bryn Mawr College, 1972.

Stimson, Ralph H. "The Control of the Manufacture of Armament; A Study of the Alleged Influence of Armament Industries, Firms, and Interests Upon War-Scares, Competition in Armament, and the Outbreak of War," Unpublished doctoral dissertation, University of Illinois, 1931.

Winter, J. M. *War and Economic Development; Essays in Memory of David Joslin.* (Cambridge and London, Cambridge University Press, 1975).

Yoshpe, Harry. *Plans for Industrial Mobilization 1920-1939.* (Washington, Industrial College of the Armed Forces, 1945).

MILITARY-INDUSTRIAL CRITICISM

"Americans Made Rich and Powerful by the War," *American Magazine,* 81, February 1916, 17-20.

Angell, Norman. *The Great Illusion* (New York, G. P. Putnam's Sons, 1933).

"Armor, Trust Made or Home Made?" *Literary Digest,* 46, June 7, 1913, 1261-62.

Barnet, Richard J. and Ronald E. Muller. *Global Reach* (New York, Simon and Schuster, 1974).

Bisson, Theodore A. "Can We Trust a 'Zaibatsu' Japan," *America, 8,* October, 1944, 291-302.

Ekirch, Jr., Arthur A. *The Civilian and the Military* (New York, Oxford University Press, 1956).

Engelbrecht, H. C. and F. C. Hanighen, *Merchants of Death* (New York, Dodd, Mead, 1934).

Nichols, Neverly. *Cry Havoc* (London, J. Cape, 1933).

Noel-Baker, Philip. *The Private Manufacture of Armaments* (New York, Oxford University Press, 1937).

Trotter, Anne. "The Development of the Merchants of Death Theory of American Intervention in World War I (1914-1939)," Unpublished doctoral dissertation, Duke University, 1966.

U. S. Congress, 73d-74th, Senate. Special Committee to Investigate the Munitions Industry. *Munitions Industry* (Washington, D. C., Government Printing Office, 1934–36).

Wiltz, John E. *In Search of Peace* (Baton Rouge, Louisiana State University Press, 1963).

INDUSTRIAL CORPORATIONS AND MIC

American Iron and Steel Association. *The Bulletin of. . ., v 1-46; September 1866-December 1912.* (Philadelphia, American Iron and Steel Association, 1866–1912).

–––. *Statistics of the American and Foreign Iron Trade. . . Annual Statistical Report of the American Iron and Steel Association . . . 1868, 1871-1911.* (Philadelphia, American Iron and Steel Association, 1868–1911).

American Iron and Steel Institute, New York. *Annual Statistical Report of the. . . .* (Philadelphia, American Iron and Steel Institute, 1913–).

–––. *Bulletin of. . ., v. 1-4, v. 5, No. 1-5, January 1913-September/October 1917.* (New York, American Iron and Steel Institute, 1913–1917).

Bridge, James H. *The Carnegie Millions and the Men Who Made Them* (London, Limpus, Baker and Co, 1903).

Carnegie Steel Co. Ltd. *Ballistic Tests of Armor Plate* (Pittsburgh, Pa., Carnegie Steel Co. Ltd., 1898).

Cesari, Gene S. "American Arms-Making Machine Tool Development, 1798–1855," Unpublished doctoral dissertation, University of Pennsylvania, 1970.

Chandler, Alfred D. *Strategy and Structure: Chapters in the History of Industrial Enterprise* (Cambridge, MIT Press, 1962).

Cotter, Arundel. *The Authentic History of the United States Steel Corporation* (New York, Moody Magazine and Book Company, 1916).

–––. *The Story of Bethlehem Steel* (New York, Moody Magazine and Book Company, 1916).

Dunn, B. W. "Observations Made on the Manufacture of War Materials in the United States and Europe," *Journal of the Military Services Institution,* 32, 1903, 137-138.

Hughes, Rupert. "From Ore to Armor Plate," *Cosmopolitan,* 28, November 1899-April 1900, 405-413.

Jacques, W. H. "Description of the Works of the Bethlehem Iron Company," *Proceedings of the United States Naval Institute,* XV, 1889, 531-539.

Main, O. W. *The Canadian Nickel Industry* (Toronto, University of Toronto Press, 1955).

Richards W. and J. A. Potter. "The Homestead Steel Works," *Proceedings of the United States Naval Institute,* XV, 1889, 431-441.

Smith, Merritt R. "John Hall, Simeon North, and the Milling Machine; The Nature of Innovation among Antebellum Arms Makers," *Technology and Culture,* 14, 1973, 573-591.

Temin, Peter. *Iron and Steel in Nineteenth Century America* (Cambridge, MIT Press, 1964).

Thompson, John F. and Norman Beasley. *For Years to Come: A Story of International Nickel of Canada* (New York, G. P. Putnams, 1960).

"War Munitions Merger," *The Nation,* 102, February 1916, 204-205.

Woodbury, Robert S. "The Legend of Eli Whitney and Interchangeable Parts," *Technology and Culture,* 1, 1960, 235-253.

GOVERNMENT AND MUNITIONS

Aitkin, Hugh G. J. *Taylorism at Watertown Arsenal* (Cambridge, Harvard University Press, 1960).

Benet, Stephen V., compiler. *A Collection of Ordnance Reports and Other Important Papers Relating to the Ordnance Department.* 4 volumes. (Washington, Government Printing Office, 1878–1890).

Benton, James G. *The Fabrication of Small Arms for the United States Service* [Ordnance Memoranda 22]. (Washington, Government Printing Office, 1878).

Ezell, Edward C. "SPIW: A New Look," *The Rifle Magazine*, July-August 1969, 30-33, 54-56.

Hewes, James E. Jr. *From Root to McNamara: Army Organization and Administration, 1900-1963.* [Army Special Studies] (Washington, U. S. Army Center of Military History, 1975).

–––. "Management vs. Bureaus," *Marine Corps Gazette*, 51, February 1967, 39-41.

History of the Watervliet Arsenal, 1813-1963. (Watervliet, New York, Watervliet Arsenal, 1963).

Hurst, Richard M. "Managerial Controls in an Industrial-Type Military Installation," Unpublished doctoral dissertation, Northwestern University, 1959.

MacCarthy, D. E. and F. J. M. "The United States Armory at Springfield, Mass." *American Machinist*, 33, 1900, 265-273, 287-291, 311-314.

Mordecai, Alfred. *Report of Experiments on Gunpowder Made at Washington Arsenal, in 1843 and 1844* (Washington, T and G. S. Gideon, 1845).

–––. *Second Report of Experiments on Gunpowder Made at Washington Arsenal, in 1845, '47 and '48* (Washington, J. and G. S. Gideon, 1849).

Parkes, Oscar. *British Battleships; Warrior 1860 to Vanguard; 1950: A History of Design, Construction and Armament* (London, Seeley Service, 1957).

Ray, Thomas W. "The Bureaus Go On Forever. . ." *Proceedings of the United States Naval Institute*, 94, January 1968, 50-63.

Rodman, Thomas J. *Report on the Properties of Metals for Cannon, and the Qualities of Cannon Powder* (Boston, Charles H. Crosby, 1861).

Smith, T. Arthur and Ogden O. Allsbrook. *The Utilization of Military Resources* (Washington, Department of Army, 1967).

Snodgrass, Raymond J. *Concept of Project Management* (Washington, Historical Office, Army Materiel Command, 1964).

Trebilcock, Clive. "Legends of the British Armament Industry 1890-1914: A Revision," *Journal of Contemporary History*, 5, 1970, 3-20.

U. S. Congress, 87th, 1st Sess. Senate. *Report of the Preparedness Investigating Subcommittee on Armed Services, United States Senate Under Authority of S. Res. 43 on M-14 Rifle Program* (Washington, Government Printing Office, 1961).

U. S. Ordnance Department. *Report of Experiments on the Strength and Other Properties of Metals for Cannon* (Philadelphia, Henry Carey Baird, 1856).

Weimer, Clarence D. Jr. "Defense Acquisition Policies and Contractor Responses: A Comparative Analysis of Mangerial Response to Department of Defense Policies for Cost-Constrained Acquisition of Electronic Subsystems," Unpublished doctoral dissertation, George Washington University, 1975.

Whittlesey, Derwent S. "The Springfield Armory, A Study of Institutional Development," Unpublished doctoral dissertation, University of Chicago, 1920.

Yoshpe, Harry. *The Economics of National Security; Organization for National Security* (Washington, Industrial College for the Armed Forces, 1964).

NAVAL-INDUSTRIAL COMPLEX

Adams, John W. "The Influences Affecting Naval Shipbuilding Legislation 1910-1916," *Naval War College Review,* XXII, December 1969, 41-70.

Albion, Robert G. and Robert Howe Connery. *Forrestal and the Navy* (New York, Columbia University Press, 1962).

American Iron and Steel Association, compilers. *History of the Manufacture of Armor Plate for the United States Navy, December 1,1899* (Philadelphia, American Iron and Steel Association, 1899).

Bowen, Harold G. *Shops, Machinery and Mossbacks* (Princeton, Princeton University Press, 1951).

Brandt, Walter I. "Steel and the New Navy, 1882--1895," Unpublished doctoral dissertation, University of Wisconsin, 1920.

Brown, Louis E. "Millions for Naval Armor-The Remedy," *Scientific American,* 109, August, 9, 1913, 110.

Bunker, John Gorley. *Liberty Ships* (Annapolis, U. S. Naval Institute Press, 1972).

Durand, William. *Adventures in the Navy in Education, Science, Engineering and in War; A Life Story* (New York, McGraw Hill, 1953).

Eaton, J. G. "Domestic Steels for Naval Purposes," *Proceedings of the United States Naval Institute,* XVIII, 1892, 147-148.

Fassett, F. G., Jr., editor. *The Shipbuilding Business in the United States of America,* 2 vol (New York, Society of Naval Architects and Marine Engineers, 1948).

Hewlett, Richard G. and Francis Duncan. *Nuclear Navy, 1946-1962* (Chicago, University of Chicago Press, 1974).

Howeth, L. S. *History of Communications-Electronics in the United States Navy* (Washington, Government Printing Office, 1963).

Karsten, Peter. *The Naval Aristocracy* (New York, The Free Press, 1972).

Lane, Frederick C. *Ships for Victory* (Baltimore, Johns Hopkins Press, 1951).

AIRPOWER-INDUSTRIAL COMPLEX

Green, Constance McLaughlin and Milton Lomask. *Vanguard: A History* (Washington, National Aeronautics and Space Administration, 1970).

Higham, Robin. *Air Power: A Concise History* (New York, St. Martins, 1972).

McDaniel, William H. *The History of Beech* (Wichita, McCormick-Armstrong Co., 1971).

Miller, Ronald and David Sawers. *The Technical Development of Modern Aviation* (New York, Praeger, 1970).

Rubenstein, Murray and Richard M. Goldman. *To Join with the Eagles; Curtis-Wright Aircraft 1903-1965* (Garden City, Doubleday. 1974).

Schlaifer, Robert and S. D. Heron. *Development of Aircraft Engines-Development of Aircraft Fuels* (Boston, Division of Research, Graduate School of Business Administration, Harvard University, 1950).

Swenson, Lloyd S., James M. Grimwood, and Charles C. Alexander. *This New Ocean: A History of Project Mercury* (Washington, National Aeronautics and Space Administration, 1966).

Weinert, Richard P. *A History of Army Aviation, 1950-1962; Phase I: 1950-1954* (Fort Monroe, Va., Historical Office, US Continental Army Command, June, 1971).

THE POLITICAL PROCESS AND MIC

Clubb, Jerome M. and Howard W. Allen. "Party Loyalty in the Progressive Years: The Senate, 1909-1915," *Journal of Politics,* XXIX, August 1967, 575-577.

Davis, Vincent. *The Admirals Lobby* (Chapel Hill, University of North Carolina Press, 1967).

Kaufman, Burton Ira, "Virginia Politics and the Wilson Movement, 1910-1914," *Virginia Magazine of History and Biography,* LXXVII, January 1969, 3-21.

Riddick, Winston Wade, "The Politics of National Highway Policy," Unpublished doctoral dissertation, Columbia University, 1973.

Riddle, Donald H. *The Truman Committee* (New Brunswick, N. J., Rutgers University Press, 1964).

WORLD WAR I AND MIC

American Iron and Steel Institute, New York. *Maximum Prices on Iron and Steel Products,* . . .(New York, American Iron and Steel Institute, 1918).

Baruch, Bernard. *American Industry in the War: A Report of the War Industries Board* (New York, Prentice-Hall, 1921).

Beaver, Daniel R. *Newton D. Baker and the American War Effort 1917-1918* (Lincoln, University of Nebraska Press, 1966).

Clarkson, Grosvenor. *Industrial America in the World War* (New York, Houghton-Mifflin, 1923).

Cronon, G. David, ed. *The Cabinet Diaries of Josephus Daniels, 1913-1921* (Lincoln, University of Nebraska Press, 1963).

Crozier, William C. *Ordnance and the World War* (New York, Scribners, 1920).

Cuff, Robert D. *The War Industries Board; Business-Government Relations During World War I* (Baltimore, Johns Hopkins Press, 1973).

Daniels, Josephus. *The Wilson Era: Years of Peace, 1910-1917* (Chapel Hill, University of North Carolina Press, 1941).

———. *The Wilson Era: Years of War and After, 1917-1923* (Chapel Hill, University of North Carolina Press, 1946).

De Weerd, Harvey A. "Production Lag in the American Ordnance Program 1917-1918," Unpublished doctoral dissertation, Harvard University, 1940.

Holley, Irving Brinton, Jr. *Ideas and Weapons: Exploitation of the Aerial Weapon by the United States During World War I; A Study in the Relationship of Technological Advance, Military Doctrine, and the Development of Weapons* (New Haven, Yale University Press, 1953).

WORLD WAR II AND MIC

Ballantine, Duncan S. *U. S. Logistics in the Second World War* (Princeton, Princeton University Press, 1949).

Connery, Robert H. *The Navy and the Industrial Mobilization in World War II* (Princeton, Princeton University Press, 1951).

Craven, Wesley F. and James Lea Cate. *Men and Planes* [The Army Air Forces in World War II]. (Chicago, University of Chicago Press, 1958).

Fine, Lenore and Jesse A. Remington. *The Corps of Engineers: Construction in the United States* [US Army in World War II]. (Washington, Government Printing Office, 1972).

Furer, Julius. *Administration of the Navy Department in World War II* (Washington, Government Printing Office, 1959).

Goad, L. C. *A History of Eastern Aircraft Division General Motors Corporation* (Linden, N. J., Eastern Aircraft Division, General Motors Corporation, 1944).

Goldsmith, Raymond W. "The Power of Victory: Munitions Output in World War II," *Military Affairs,* X, Spring 1946, 68-81.

Green, Constance M., Thomson, Harry C., and Peter C. Roots. *The Ordnance Department: Planning Munitions for War* [US Army in World War II: The Technical Services] (Washington, Government Printing Office, 1955).

Holley, Irving Brinton, Jr. *Buying Aircraft: Materiel Procurement for the Army Air Forces* [Army in World War II] (Washington, Government Printing Office, 1964).

Millett, John D. *The Organization and Role of the Army Service Forces* [US Army in World War II] (Washington, Government Printing Office, 1954).

Nelson, Donald M. *Arsenal of Democracy: The Story of American War Production* (New York, Harcourt, Brace, 1946).

Rowland, Buford and William Boyd. *U. S. Navy Bureau of Ordnance in World War II* (Washington, Department of the Navy, 1953).

Smith, R. Elberton. *The Army and Economic Mobilization* [US Army in World War II] (Washington, Government Printing Office, 1959).

Thomson, Harry C. *The Ordnance Department: Procurement and Supply* [US Army in World War II] (Washington, Government Printing Office, 1959).

Yoshpe, Harry B. *Organization for Production Control in World War II; A Study of Follow-Up and Expediting Function of the War Department, 1939-1945* (Washington, Industrial College of the Armed Forces, 1946).

MIC AT THE LOCAL LEVEL

Allen, G. C. *The Industrial Development of Birmingham* [England] *and the Black Country, 1860-1927* (London, George Allen and Unwin Ltd., 1929).

Davis, Arthur K., editor. *Virginia Communities in War Time,* First, Second Series (Richmond, War History Commission, 1926-1927).

Deyrup, Felicia J. *Arms Makers of the Connecticut Valley: A Regional Study of the Economic Development of the Small Arms Industry 1798-1870* Vol. XXXIII, Studies in History (Northampton, Mass., Smith College, 1948).

Husing, John E. "The Relative Impact of Civilian versus Military Defense Payrolls on a Small Region, 1964-1968," Unpublished doctoral dissertation, Claremont Graduate School, 1971.

Le Bourdais, D. M. *Sudbury Basin: The Story of Nickel* (Toronto, Ryerson, 1953).

Lott, Arnold S. *A Long Line of Ships: Mare Island's Century of Naval Activity in California* (Annapolis, United States Naval Institute, 1949).

Peck, Taylor. *Round Shot to Rockets: A History of the Washington Navy Yard and U. S. Naval Gun Factory* (Annapolis, United States Naval Institute, 1949).

Schlegal, Morris W., editor. *Norfolk: Historic Southern Port* (Durham, Duke University Press, 1962).

Smith, Merritt R. "George Washington and the Establishment of the Harpers Ferry Arsenal," *The Virginia Magazine of History and Biography,* 81, 1973, 415-436.

U. S. Department of the Navy. *Activities of the Bureau of Yards and Docks.* (Washington, Government Printing Office, 1921).

Young, Lucien. *A Brief History of the United States Navy Yard and Station; Pensacola, Florida, and Its Possibilities* (Pensacola, Naval Station Press, 1964).

BIOGRAPHY

Allen, Frederick Lewis. *The Great Pierpont Morgan* (New York, Harper, 1949).

"American Krupp: Charles M. Schwab," *Forum*, 56, August 1916, 201–208.

Beasley, Norman. *Knudsen: A Biography* (New York, McGraw-Hill, 1947).

Cooling, B. Franklin. *Benjamin Franklin Tracy: Father of the Modern American Fighting Navy* (Hamden, Ct., Archon, 1973).

Hessen, Robert Allen. "A Biography of Charles M. Schwab, Steel Industrialist," Unpublished doctoral dissertation, Columbia University, 1969.

Nevins, Allan, and Frank Ernest Hill. *Ford: Decline and Rebirth, 1933–62* (New York, Scribners, 1962).

North, S. N. D. and Ralph H. North. *Simeon North, First Official Pistol Maker of the United States* (Concord, N. H., Rumford Press, 1913).

Reed, Wingate C. "Decius Wadsworth, First Chief of Ordnance, 1812–1821," *Army Ordnance* 24, 1943, 527-530 and 25, 1943, 113-116.

Simpkins, Francis Butler. *Pitchfork Ben Tillman; South Carolinian* (Baton Rouge, Louisiana State University Press, 1944).

Strauss, Lewis L. *Men and Decisions* (Garden City, Doubleday, 1962).

Vandiver, Frank E. *Ploughshares into Swords: Josiah Gorgas and Confederate Ordnance* (Austin, University of Texas Press, 1952).

Von Karman, Theodore with Lee Edson. *The Wind and Beyond; Theodore Von Karman; Pioneer in Aviation and Pathfinder in Space* (Boston, Little, Brown, 1967).

Wall, James Frazer. *Andrew Carnegie* (New York, Oxford, 1970).

INDEX

CONTRIBUTORS

Roger A. Beaumont is Associate Professor of History at Texas A & M University.

Daniel R. Beaver is Professor of History at the University of Cincinnati.

Benjamin Franklin Cooling is Assistant Director for Historical Services, US Army Military History Research Collection, Carlisle Barracks, Pa.

Edward C. Ezell is associated with the National Aeronautics and Space Administration.

Henry C. Ferrell, Jr. is Professor of History at East Carolina University.

Thomas F. Kelly, formerly on the staff of the US Army Military History Research Collection, is currently completing doctoral work at the University of Missouri, Columbia.

Johannes R. Lischka is Assistant Dean for Continuing Education, Francis Marion College.

Earl A. Molander is Assistant Professor of Management, Portland State University.

Theodore Ropp is Professor of History at Duke University.

Allison W. Saville is Curator, Philadelphia Maritime Museum.

Merritt Roe Smith is Assistant Professor of History at Ohio State University.

Alvin R. Sunseri is Associate Professor of History at the University of Northern Iowa.

Anne Trotter is Associate Professor of History at Memphis State University.